Low-Cholesterol Cuisine

ALSO BY ANNE LINDSAY

The American Cancer Society Cookbook

Low-Cholesterol Cuisine

ANNE LINDSAY

HEARST BOOKS
New York

First published as *The Lighthearted Cookbook* by Key Porter Books, Limited, Toronto, Canada, in 1988

Library of Congress Cataloging-in-Publication Data

Lindsay, Anne.
  Low-cholesterol cuisine.

  Includes index.
  1. Low-cholesterol diet—Recipes.   I. Title.
RM237.75.L56   1989   641.5′63   88-30145
ISBN 0-688-08712-4

Printed in the United States of America

First U.S. Edition

1 2 3 4 5 6 7 8 9 10

BOOK DESIGN BY HELENE BERINSKY

Acknowledgments

I'm very grateful for all the help and enthusiastic encouragement I've received during the writing of this book. A special thanks to Dr. Anthony Graham, chief, Cardiology Division, Wellsley Hospital. Thanks to Carol Dombrow, Sharon Joliat, and all the dieticians and nutritionists who gave their time. Thanks to Elizabeth Baird, food editor, *Canadian Living* magazine, for her help.

A very special thanks to dietician and good friend Shannon Graham, who works with me testing recipes. Thanks to Maggie MacDonald for her expert editorial skills.

Most of all, thanks to my best and most critical tasters and supporters, my husband, Bob, and children, Jeff, John, and Susie, for their understanding and patience while I was totally consumed with writing this book.

Contents

Introduction

Most people want to live as well as possible, as long as possible. This cookbook has been designed to help you do just that.

Recent research into the cause of cardiovascular disease (heart-related ailments and stroke) shows that the health of your heart may be more in your control than you've realized. There appears to be a direct connection between what you eat and your chances of developing a heart condition or stroke.

The dietary changes recommended to give your heart its best chance are not drastic. If you follow the dietary recommendations* as suggested by the American Heart Association, you'll be enjoying a wide variety of delicious foods, perhaps an even greater variety than you've enjoyed before.

Low-Cholesterol Cuisine contains everything you need to know to put your healthy heart plan into action—menus, recipes, lifestyle tips for various age groups, and some basic heart and nutrition information.

But before you start cooking, let's look at the scientific backdrop to this cookbook and the background for the recommendations.

Your Heart and You

CARDIOVASCULAR DISEASE—AMERICA'S NUMBER 1 KILLER

In 1989 alone, roughly one million Americans will die of heart- and blood vessel-related ailments. Many more will suffer non-fatal heart

*"Dietary Guidelines for Healthy American Adults: A Statement for Physicians and Health Professionals (American Heart Association, 1988).

attacks or strokes. Currently, sixty-five million Americans suffer from some form of heart or blood vessel disease, many of them middle-aged or younger.

While these statistics are frightening, the picture is not as bad as it once was. From 1976 to 1986, there was a 24.4 percent reduction in the heart-related death rate of people under sixty-five. Increased public education, life-style changes, and breakthroughs resulting from medical research all contributed to the decline. But more and more, the role of the individual to change those habits that lead to cardiovascular disease is becoming increasingly important.

DEFINING A COMPLEX DISEASE

The term "cardiovascular disease" includes all diseases of the heart and of the blood vessels that lead to various parts of the body. Two of the most common conditions, heart attack and stroke, are usually caused by narrowed blood vessels.

A heart attack occurs when there is an inadequate flow of blood to the heart muscle, while a stroke is usually caused by a lack of blood flow to the brain. The narrowing of the blood vessels leading to both the heart and brain, commonly referred to as hardening of the arteries, is caused by atherosclerosis.

How the arteries become narrowed over the years is that cholesterol, fat, and calcium are deposited in the artery walls. It's like the accumulation of plaque on teeth, only the results are more serious. The arterial build-up makes it harder for the blood to pass through, and should a blockage occur, as a result of a blood clot or of fatty deposits breaking off from the arterial wall, a heart attack or stroke results.

CONTROLLING THE RISK

Over the years, scientists have identified a number of factors that increase your chances of developing heart disease. Some, like heredity, you can do nothing about. But many of the major risk factors can be controlled, as you can see from these lists:

UNCONTROLLABLE RISK FACTORS

Family history of heart disease	Sex
	Increasing age

POTENTIALLY CONTROLLABLE FACTORS

Smoking	Diabetes
High blood pressure	Excess alcohol
Elevated blood cholesterol	Stress
Poor eating habits	Lack of exercise
Excess weight or obesity	

As you can see, the factors that are within your control far outnumber the ones that aren't. In this book, the focus is on those you can change, with particular emphasis on those factors that involve diet. But to start with, here's a short list of changes you should consider.

EIGHT WAYS TO A HEALTHIER HEART

1. Avoid smoking.
2. Have your blood pressure checked regularly and have it treated if it is elevated.
3. Have your blood fats, especially cholesterol, medically checked regularly.
4. Exercise at least three times a week, for a half hour each time. Consult your doctor if you are just starting to exercise.
5. Keep your stress level at a minimum.
6. Maintain a healthy body weight.
7. Limit your alcohol intake.
8. Eat a healthy diet based on the Guide to Good Eating (page 249).

The Food Factors

Food plays a large part in the enjoyment of life and, as the previous list indicates, a large part in minimizing your risk of heart disease. Blood pressure, weight control, healthy arteries, and blood cholesterol levels are all tied to diet.

If you've paid little attention to what you ate in the past, now is the time to take a hard look at your eating habits and make those changes that will help your heart. What are they? Here's the list of recommendations that encompasses the guidelines established by the American Heart Association.

GUIDE TO BETTER EATING FOR HEALTHY ADULTS

1. Eat a wide variety of foods and maintain a healthy body weight.
2. Limit your fat intake to 30 percent or less of total calories.
3. Limit saturated fats to no more than 10 percent of total calories.
4. Restrict cholesterol intake to 300 milligrams or less per day.
5. Protein intake should be about 15 percent of calorie intake.
6. Include more complex carbohydrates, such as fruits, vegetables, and cereal grains for their fiber and nutrient content.
7. Limit sodium intake in all forms to 3,000 milligrams or less per day.
8. Consume only one alcoholic drink or less per day.

Figuring Out the Numbers

Recommendations are all very well, but what does 3,000 milligrams of sodium look like? Am I now eating more than 30 percent of my calories from fat? In the following pages, each of the recommendations is explored in more depth. *Low-Cholesterol Cuisine* gives you examples of the amounts of fat, sodium, cholesterol, and so on, found in food. The recipes include that kind of information, too, and follow the American Heart Association's recommendations. Basically, what you should remember is:

- *LESS* total fat, less saturated fat, and salt
- *MORE* fruit, vegetables, fish, and whole grain breads and cereals.

If you're a typical American, here's what you're currently consuming compared to what you should be eating.

	Current Typical Consumption	*Recommended Consumption*
Carbohydrates	46% of calories	55% of calories
Fats	37% of calories	30% of calories
Proteins	16% of calories	15% of calories
Sodium	5,000 milligrams	3,000 milligrams
Cholesterol	400 milligrams	300 milligrams

The following sections go through the dietary recommendations to explain why they are necessary and what you can do to bring your eating habits in line with healthy living.

FAT—THE MAJOR FACTOR

In a typical day, Americans consume 37 percent or more of their calories in the form of fats. That's one third above the level considered to minimize the risk of cardiovascular disease.

Of course, a certain amount of fat in the diet is needed. An extremely low-fat diet is considered dangerous since fat performs many important functions in the body, like the transportation of some vitamins and the provision of essential fatty acids and energy. But most people go overboard. Here's where fat is found in the average American diet:

Common Sources of Fat

Fats and oils (including cream and bacon)	33%
Meat, fish, and poultry	26%
Dairy products	17%
Grains	9%
Fruit, sweets, and eggs	9%
Vegetables	6%

The Three Faces of Fat

All fats are not equal in their effect on blood cholesterol. Foods containing fats are made up of a variety of different kinds of fat. They are listed on page 14 under the kind of fat they are highest in.

Separating the "Good" from the "Bad" Cholesterol

All fats, including cholesterol, are transported through the body in the form of lipoproteins, which are a combination of fat and protein and can be considered "good" or "bad."

High-Density Lipoproteins—the "Good"

HDL's are relatively durable fat-carrying protein compounds that

Fat Type	Form	Sources
Saturated	Usually solid at room temperature	Butter, lard, vegetable shortening, coconut oil, palm oil, highly hydrogenated margarines, meat, poultry, cheese, dairy products, egg yolks, chocolate, coconut
Monounsaturated	Liquid at room temperature	Canola oil, olive oil, peanut oil, peanuts, peanut butter, cashews, avocado
Polyunsaturated	Liquid at room temperature	Safflower oil, sunflower oil, corn oil, soybean oil, cottonseed oil, sesame oil, some margarines, mayonnaise (depending on oil used in making it), fish, almonds, hazelnuts, pecans

actually carry excess cholesterol to the liver for processing and elimination from the body.

Low-Density Lipoproteins—the "Bad"

LDL's are less stable and more likely to break apart and to deposit cholesterol in the blood vessels, which can lead to atherosclerosis. Most people with high blood cholesterol levels also have elevated LDL levels.

Accentuate the Positive

A simple blood test will determine your HDL to LDL ratio. The higher the HDL, the better your chances of arterial health. There are a number of steps you can take to raise your level of HDL's.

- Increase your exercise.
- Keep your weight at a healthy level (overweight people are more likely to have higher levels of LDL's).
- Don't smoke.
- Reduce your intake of saturated fat.

The most effective dietary measure in reducing blood cholesterol is to reduce saturated fat. In everyday living the best way to do this is to reduce your total fat intake.

It is recommended that you divide your daily fat intake evenly among the three types of fat. This means 10 percent of your caloric intake from each of the fats—saturated, polyunsaturated, and monounsaturated—to make up not more than 30 percent of daily calories.

Good News About Polyunsaturated Fats

Polyunsaturated fats, such as safflower oil, help to decrease blood cholesterol levels, and some recent research indicates that some monounsaturated fats, such as olive oil, may do the same thing.

Recent developments in heart research show that one type of polyunsaturated fat, the omega-3 fatty acid from fish oils may help to prevent atherosclerosis. Omega-3 fatty acids are found in fish such as salmon, sardines, mackerel, and herring. These omega-3 fatty acids are also believed to lower blood pressure and blood fat in the form of triglycerides. This makes the blood less sticky, thereby less susceptible to the risk of blood clots.

It isn't recommended that you take fish oil supplements, but eating fish two or three times a week is considered a healthy investment in the future.

Cutting Out Cholesterol

An issue related to fat is cholesterol, a fatty substance the body needs in small amounts. The problem with cholesterol is that your liver will produce it, even if you eat no cholesterol in your food. A high level of blood cholesterol has been identified as a major risk factor in heart disease. You can do very little about the amount of cholesterol your body produces, but most people can lower blood cholesterol by limiting the amount of fat, particularly saturated fat, in their diet.

Limit your cholesterol intake to no more than 300 milligrams per day. Cutting down on foods high in cholesterol, such as egg yolks, organ meats, and shrimp will have the effect of lowering blood cholesterol in many people. A complete list of high-cholesterol foods is on page 251.

Just as it's important to have your blood pressure checked, you should have your doctor check your blood cholesterol level regu-

larly, starting at age twenty and rechecking at least every five years. Atherosclerosis can start at an early age.

Butter Versus Margarine

Both butter and margarine are fats, but butter is high in saturated fat and cholesterol, and should be avoided. Instead use a margarine from the recommended list on page 253. Margarine can be high in saturated fat, but has no cholesterol. For cooking, try an oil that is low in saturated fat.

Hydrogenation is a process used to turn a liquid oil into a solid fat. It is used in the production of most margarines so that the oil-based product can be spread at room temperature. But as a result of the hydrogenation process, a polyunsaturated vegetable oil becomes more saturated.

Not all margarines have the same degree of hydrogenation. In most cases, the harder the margarine, the more hydrogenated and more saturated it will be. Use those margarines subjected to the least degree of hydrogenation, so that they are lower in saturated fat and higher in polyunsaturated or monounsaturated fat.

To sort out margarines for yourself, read the labels. Avoid those that don't give the amount of polyunsaturates on the label and look for those that have at least 40 percent polyunsaturates. Some margarines declare as much as 55 percent polyunsaturates. (See page 253 for Recommended Margarines.)

	Milligrams Cholesterol per Tablespoon	Grams Saturated Fat per Tablespoon
Butter	30	7
Soft or hard margarine	0	1.5–3

Estimating Fat

The suggested menus and recipes in this book are all relatively low in fat and give the grams of fat per serving.

Calorie Intake/Day	Grams Fat/Day to Equal 30% of Calories
1,200	40
1,800	60
2,200	73
2,500	83
3,000	100
3,200	107

For this to be meaningful, look at the chart on page 18 to see how many grams of fat you need in a day to follow the 30 percent of calories guideline. (See page 251 for a height, weight, and corresponding calorie recommended intake table.)

If you follow the Guide to Good Eating, choosing the low-fat foods within each food group, and limiting the fat used in preparing these foods, you'll probably meet that goal.

Trimming the Fat

- Use as little butter, margarine, and oil as possible (where possible use a high polyunsaturated or low-fat variety) on toast, sandwiches, vegetables, and, especially, in cooking. Use lemon juice or herbs on vegetables instead of butter.
- Instead of frying, try the low-fat cooking methods—broiling, baking, steaming, poaching, and boiling.
- Roast meats on a rack and sauté in a nonstick skillet. Sauté vegetables in 1 teaspoon oil and ¼ cup water.
- After browning meat, spoon off all the fat.
- Trim the visible fat from meat and remove the skin from poultry. Choose lean cuts and watch serving sizes of meat, too. Three or four ounces, about the size of a pack of cards, is a good portion.
- Keep salad dressings to a minimum and switch to low-fat dressings, and light mayonnaise.
- Serve low-fat relishes and sauces, like cranberry or mint sauce, with meat, rather than rich sauces or gravies.
- Substitute skim milk, 1% or 2% for whole milk and opt for

Safety Switch—to Reduce Fats

Choose	Instead of	Grams of Fat Saved
1 glass skim milk	1 glass whole milk	9
¼ cup grated low-fat mozzarella	¼ cup grated Cheddar	5
¼ cup creamed low-fat cottage cheese	¼ cup cream cheese	17
4 ounces chicken, no skin	4 ounces chicken, with skin	6
Bread with 1 teaspoon margarine	Bread with 1 tablespoon margarine	7
Salad, 1 tablespoon light mayonnaise	Salad, 2 tablespoons regular mayonnaise	15
1 pear or tomato	1 avocado	30
½ cup unbuttered popcorn	½ cup peanuts	38
Apple crisp	Apple pie	13
Bran muffin	Croissant	8

other low-fat dairy products—part-skim cheese, light sour cream, skim-milk yogurt.

· Snack on fresh fruits, vegetables and unbuttered popcorn; avoid chips, peanuts, french fries, rich desserts, whipped cream.

SALT—LICKING THE HABIT

Everyone thinks it makes peanuts taste better, but people may not be aware that salt may lead to a stroke, hypertension, or kidney failure. Americans consume 5,000 milligrams or more of sodium per day, much more than needed for the average person to stay healthy. Most of it is in the form of salt (sodium chloride).

The problem with sodium is that there's a lot around you don't see. It's in processed foods, sauces, snack foods, and many other surprising items. In fact, here's where your sodium intake comes from:

Sources of Sodium in the Average Diet

Processed foods	50%
Salt shaker	25%
Naturally occurring in foods and water	24%
Non-food items (e.g., medications)	1%

The recommendation is that you consume only 3,000 milligrams of sodium (note that salt is about 40 percent sodium) or less a day, about the equivalent of 1 ¼ level teaspoons of salt. Here's how you might try cutting down.

Salt Shakers

- The taste for salt is acquired and can be unacquired. Think about the salt you use and always taste *before* you add salt, gradually decreasing the amount.
- Don't automatically add salt to cooking water. Add it, if necessary, after tasting, just before serving.
- Take the salt shaker off the table or use a pepper shaker for the salt (smaller holes) instead.
- Season foods with lemon juice, vinegar, a pinch of sugar, mustard, herbs, spices, peppers, ginger, garlic, onion, or wine instead of salt.

Safety Switch—to Reduce Sodium

Generally speaking, foods made from scratch are better for you than processed or convenience foods, because *you* can control the amount of fat, salt, and other ingredients.

Choose	Instead of
Tomato paste	Tomato sauce
Canned whole tomatoes	Stewed tomatoes
Garlic	Garlic salt
Onion	Onion salt
Homemade Chicken Stock (page 62)	Bouillon cubes
Homemade soups	Dehydrated soups
Unsalted crackers	Salted crackers
Shredded wheat	Rice Krispies
Regular or quick-cooking oatmeal	Ready-to-serve oatmeal
Fresh, frozen, or low-sodium canned vegetables	Canned vegetables
Unsalted nuts	Salted nuts
Old Fashioned Pickled Beets (page 165)	Olives and dill pickles
Tortilla Chips (page 31)	Potato chips, corn chips
Low-salt Bagel Thins (page 37)	Pretzels
Unsalted popcorn	Salted popcorn
Homemade Ketchup (page 169)	Ketchup

- Watch out for such high salt foods as processed luncheon meats, bacon, sausages, smoked meats or fish, potato chips, pretzels, salted crackers, pickles, soy sauce, MSG (monosodium glutamate), canned or dried soups, and processed cheese.
- Read labels and avoid sodium compounds as well as salt, if you can. For example, MSG is very high in sodium.

SUGAR—SWEET SURRENDER

The average American consumes about 2½ pounds of sugar a week, enough to make your fillings ache. As with salt, the problem is not only the sugar you eat directly in desserts or tea and coffee, but the hidden sugar in prepared foods, from cereal to ketchup. Sugar is a simple carbohydrate that supplies energy to the body but little else in the way of nutrition. The high calorie count can lead to weight gain, one of the risk factors in heart disease. Also, if you are consuming a lot of sugar, you may be missing out on more nutritious foods, especially good snack foods like fruit, raw vegetables, and whole grains.

To kick the sugar habit, see the tips in the shopping section (pages 241–243) and the recipe modification section (pages 171–172).

FIBER—NATURALLY RIGHT

Fiber is a substance in food that is not digested or is partially digested. Your grandparents called it roughage and knew it helped keep them regular. Now there is growing evidence that certain types of fiber, such as in oat bran, may help lower blood cholesterol, as well. Fiber may also help protect the body against certain types of cancer, particularly colorectal cancer.

To increase your fiber intake, eat more fruits, vegetables, and whole grain breads and cereals. Be sure to include a variety, since different types of fiber perform different functions in the body. As a bonus, fiber-rich foods are nutritious and are usually low in calories and fat too. A complete list of fiber-rich foods is on page 252.

How much is enough? The National Cancer Institute recommends that healthy Americans consume 20 to 30 grams of fiber a day with an upper limit of 35 grams. Fiber supplements are not recommended. Too much fiber isn't healthy either, as food then passes through the intestines too quickly and some vitamins and minerals will not be absorbed. It's important to increase fiber levels slowly, and to drink plenty of liquids (8 to 12 cups a day of water, milk, juice, or other beverages) so that you don't suffer any discomfort. The recipe section of this book also includes suggestions for fiber.

Tips for Increasing the Fiber in Your Diet:

- Have four to five servings of fruits and vegetables a day.
- Eat the edible skins of fruits and vegetables and choose whole fruits over juices.
- Use whole-wheat flour. In most recipes you can substitute half of the all-purpose flour with whole-wheat flour.
- Choose whole-wheat foods when buying bread, pasta, English muffins, spaghetti, pita bread, hamburger buns, crackers.
- Add chickpeas or kidney beans to soups, salads, casseroles.
- Add bran or wheat germ to muffins, cereals, casserole toppings, meat loaf, cookies. Oat bran is particularly good for lowering blood cholesterol.
- Add dried fruits (prunes, raisins) and nuts to your cereals; use them to top fruit or ice cream desserts.
- Have fruits and vegetables for snacks as well as in meals.
- Choose breakfast cereals with at least 2 grams fiber per serving.

Safety Switch—to Increase Fiber

Choose	*Instead of*
Fresh orange	Orange juice
Whole-wheat bread	White bread
Cereals with 2 grams or more fiber/serving	Cereals with less than 2 grams fiber/serving
Bran muffin	White bun
Chili	Hot dog
Lentil or bean soup	Noodle soup
Baked beans	Pasta
Spinach salad	Iceberg lettuce salad
Potato with skin	Potato without skin
Raw vegetables and dip	Chips and dip
Fruit desserts	Puddings, pastries

POTASSIUM—A CAUTIONARY NOTE

Potassium, a mineral found in fruits, juices, milk, and most vegetables, helps the body get rid of sodium, and may be involved in controlling blood pressure. Some medication for high blood pressure, and other medications, may cause a loss of potassium. Check with your doctor if you are on medication. The list on page 252 gives food sources of potassium.

The Life-style Factors

Good food alone will not keep your heart healthy. There are a few other adjustments you may need to make in your life.

SMOKING—BUTT OUT

To put it bluntly, don't smoke. Three hundred fifty thousand people in America will die of smoke-related cardiovascular ailments this year. Most will die of a heart attack, and if you smoke a pack of cigarettes a day, your risk of a heart attack doubles. Smoke even more and your risk rises higher. Smoking is probably the single most preventable cause of heart disease.

EXERCISE—WORK OUT

Modern conveniences make it easy to lead a fairly sedentary existence. Unless you plan for exercise, you might not get it. Yet moderate exercise can greatly reduce your risk of heart disease—by halving your risk of hypertension, by lowering your blood cholesterol level, and by controlling your weight and your stress level.

Aerobic exercise, such as running, walking, swimming, cycling, and basketball, increases the body's ability to use oxygen and strengthens the heart muscle. Try for at least three thirty-minute periods of aerobic exercise per week. Checking with your doctor is a sensible first step.

ALCOHOL—HOLD OUT

Excess alcohol consumption can damage your body in many ways, including increasing your risk of heart disease. Alcohol can prevent your body from absorbing important nutrients. If you drink, try to limit your consumption.

In Good Company

Many of the recommendations of the American Heart Association are shared by other health organizations, like the American Cancer Society, which also suggests limiting total fat and increasing your fiber intake.

What this means to you is that the good food practices given here are recommended by a wide variety of health professionals. Eating for a healthy heart means eating for a better chance of overall health. And that means eating for a better, and perhaps longer, life for you and your family.

Sample Daily Menu Plans

The following menus do not exceed 2,000 calories per day and follow the American Heart Association's recommendations of not more than 300 milligrams of cholesterol and 3,000 milligrams of sodium per day. Their fat content does not exceed 30 percent of the total calories. Persons who need to eat more than 2,000 calories should follow these menus, simply increasing the portions by the appropriate amount to meet their energy needs.

Recipes for dishes noted with asterisks appear in this book and can be found by using the index.

Menu 1
28% of Calories from Fat

	Sample Daily Menu with a Restaurant Lunch			
	Grams Fat	Milligrams Cholesterol	Milligrams Sodium	Calories
Breakfast				
Cantaloupe (½)	Trace	0	12	93
Buttermilk, Bran, and Blueberry Muffin*	8	31	111	189
Fruit-flavored 2% yogurt (½ cup)	2	7	88	131
Restaurant lunch				
Apple juice (½ cup)	Trace	0	4	62
Sliced chicken sandwich (sliced chicken from ½ breast, lettuce, 2 slices bread, and 1 teaspoon mayonnaise)	5	74	384	313
Tossed green salad with oil and vinegar dressing (1 teaspoon oil and 1 tablespoon vinegar)	5	0	5	56
2% milk (1 cup)	5	19	129	128
Dinner				
Mexican Rice and Bean Casserole*	5	12	371	275
Broccoli spears (1 cup)	Trace	0	9	48
Spinach Salad with Sesame Seed Dressing*	9	0	48	116
Slice toast (1)	Trace	Trace	142	76
Margarine (2 teaspoons—for broccoli and toast)	8	0	66	66
2% milk (1 cup)	5	19	129	128
Applesauce-Raisin Squares*	3	11	6	73
TOTALS	55	173	1504	1754

*Recipes included.

Menu 2
26% of Calories from Fat

	Grams Fat	Sample Daily Menu with a Brown-Bag Lunch		
	Grams Fat	Milligrams Cholesterol	Milligrams Sodium	Calories
Breakfast				
Orange juice (½ cup)	Trace	0	2	59
Whole-wheat cereal	Trace	0	—	169
Sliced banana (1)	Trace	0	1	105
Slice toast (1)	Trace	Trace	142	76
Margarine (1 teaspoon)	4	0	33	33
2% milk (1 cup)	5	19	129	128
Brown-bag lunch				
Gouda cheese (1½ ounce)	13	52	376	164
Bagel (1)	2	0	245	200
Margarine (1 teaspoon)	4	0	33	33
Carrot and celery sticks	Trace	0	0	37
Easy Oat Bran and Date Cookie* (1)	4	8	64	97
Apple juice (½ cup)	Trace	0	4	62
Dinner				
Linguine with Salmon and Chives*	12	23	149	400
Tossed Seasonal Greens*	2	0	13	30
Roll (1)	2	2	313	156
Margarine (1 teaspoon)	4	0	33	33
Pineapple-Orange Sorbet*	Trace	0	1	93
2% milk (1 cup)	5	19	129	128
TOTALS	57	123	1667	2003

*Recipes included.

Menu 3
27% of Calories from Fat

	Sample Daily Menu with an At-Home Lunch			
	Grams Fat	Milligrams Cholesterol	Milligrams Sodium	Calories
Breakfast				
Grapefruit (½)	Trace	0	0	39
Bran flakes	Trace	0	291	139
Slice whole-wheat toast (1)	Trace	Trace	132	61
Peanut butter (1 tablespoon)	8	0	3	95
2% milk (1 cup)	5	19	129	128
At-home lunch				
Pasta and Fresh Vegetable Salad*	6	0	77	165
Tuna fish canned in water (½ cup)	1	48	468	135
Roll (1)	2	2	313	156
Margarine (1 teaspoon)	4	0	33	33
2% milk (1 cup)	5	19	129	128
Dinner				
Pork Chops with Rosemary and Orange*	9	67	70	201
Garlic-Parsley Potatoes*	2	0	22	119
Stir-Fry Ratatouille*	7	0	12	107
Grated Carrot and Green Pea Salad*	1	2	79	71
Sliced peaches (1 cup)	Trace	0	10	115
Plain biscuits (2)	2	Trace	48	57
TOTALS	52	157	1816	1749

*Recipes included.

Menu 4
25% of Calories from Fat

	Sample Daily Menu with a Brown-Bag Lunch			
	Grams Fat	Milligrams Cholesterol	Milligrams Sodium	Calories
Breakfast				
Orange slices (1 orange)	Trace	0	0	62
Slices toast (2)	Trace	Trace	284	152
Partly skimmed mozzarella cheese (2 ounces)	9	35	282	154
Brown-bag lunch				
Classic Tuna Salad with Fresh Dill sandwich*	5	21	559	238
Cucumber slices (½ cup)	Trace	0	1	7
Pear	Trace	0	0	100
2% milk (1 cup)	5	19	129	128
Buttermilk Apple Cake*	5	1	152	174
Dinner				
6 ounces Grilled Tandoori Chicken* with rice (1 cup)	14	88	127	440
Green beans (1 cup)	Trace	0	4	46
Winter Fruit Compote with Figs and Apricots*	1	0	6	148
2% milk (1 cup)	5	19	129	128
TOTALS	44	183	1673	1777

*Recipes included.

Guidelines for Nutrient Ratings of Recipes

In our rating system, each serving of food must provide the amount as listed in the following chart for each nutrient. Percent of Recommended Daily Allowance is also given. Nutrient analysis was done using CBORD nutrition accounting software system.

Nutrient	Good Source	Percent of Recommended Daily Allowance	Excellent Source	Percent of Recommended Daily Allowance
Vitamin A (International Units)	600	12	1200	24
Thiamine (milligrams)	0.25	17	0.45	30
Riboflavin (milligrams)	0.40	24	0.75	44
Niacin (milligrams)	2.50	13	4.50	23
Vitamin C (milligrams)	7.5	13	15.0	25
Calcium (milligrams)	150.0	15	300.0	30
Phosphorus (milligrams)	150.0	15	300.0	30
Iron (milligrams)	2.0	11	4.0	22
Dietary fiber (grams)	2.0		4.0	

Daily Total Protein, Fat, and Carbohydrate Intake According to Percentage of Total Calories According to the American Heart Association's Dietary Recommendations

Calorie Intake	Percent Calories from Protein	Grams Protein per Day	Percent Calories from Fat	Grams Fat per Day	Percent Calories from Carbohydrate	Grams Carbohydrate per Day
1,200	15	45	30	40	55	165
1,500	15	56	30	50	55	206
1,800	15	68	30	60	55	248
2,100	15	79	30	70	55	289
2,300	15	86	30	77	55	316
2,600	15	98	30	87	55	357
2,900	15	109	30	97	55	399
3,200	15	120	30	107	55	440

Unless otherwise stated, all recipes in this book were tested and analyzed using 2% milk, 2% yogurt, 2% cottage cheese, and a soft margarine. Because everyone's taste for salt varies and we hope you will gradually reduce your taste for salt, most of the recipes in this book call for no salt or salt to taste, and have been analyzed without any or using a minimum of salt.

MICROWAVE NOTE: Recipes have been tested in a 700-watt full-size microwave oven with a turntable. If your oven is different, cooking times may have to be adjusted slightly. If you don't have a turntable you may have to rotate dishes once or twice during cooking.

Appetizers and Snacks

An appetizer or small first course makes a meal more special. Appetizers are my favorite part of restaurant meals; I will often pass on dessert in favor of an interesting salad or soup and will sometimes order two appetizers rather than a main course.

Some appetizers or hors d'oeuvres, such as meat or chicken liver pâtés and creamy cheeses, can be terribly high in fat, cholesterol, sodium, and calories and can quickly add to our daily calories. On the other hand, there are many terrific-tasting appetizers that aren't too heavy in calories or other elements we should keep to a minimum. Try the Shrimp Mousse with Dill (page 35) or Spiced Meatballs with Coriander Dipping Sauce (page 39) or others in this section, or any of the soup or salad recipes for starters, which your family and guests will ask for again and again.

Appetizer or First Course

When planning menus try to make sure each course has different foods and that the whole meal is a pleasing combination of colors, textures, seasonings, flavors, and temperature. If you have a filling first course such as Fettuccine and Mussel Salad (page 81), plan a light main course of perhaps some poultry and a green vegetable. If you have a main course that is high in fat and calories choose a light first course such as a soup without cream.

As well as the recipes in this section, consider a soup, salad, pasta, or fish for a first course.

Crackers, etc.

When buying crackers it pays to spend a few minutes reading the labels. Many crackers are high in salt and contain hydrogenated vegetable oils (palm or coconut), which means they have saturated fats.

Melba toast and crispbreads are two kinds of crackers without hydrogenated vegetable oil.

For dips and spreads, instead of crackers use raw vegetables, whole-wheat pita bread rounds (tear into smaller pieces), Low-Salt Bagel Thins (page 37), Quick Homemade Melba Toast, or Tortilla Chips.

Tortilla Chips

These are a healthy alternative to store-bought tortilla chips, which are high in calories, fat, and sodium. Use fresh, frozen, or canned tortillas (whole wheat if you can find them) for these crisp easy-to-make chips.

Dip each tortilla in water; drain off excess. Cut into 6 wedges and place on baking sheet. Bake in 500°F oven for 5 minutes. Let cool and store in airtight container for up to 2 weeks. (One ounce of chips has about 1 gram fat, 62 calories.)

Quick Homemade Melba Toast

Choose fine-grained bread such as whole wheat, pumpernickel, or sandwich bread. Cut in very thin slices (remove crusts if you want) and arrange in a single layer on a cookie sheet. Bake in 250°F oven for 20 to 30 minutes or until crisp. Time will vary depending on how old the bread and how thick the slices.

Raw Veggies for Snacks

If you keep a supply of cut-up celery, carrots, broccoli, or cauliflower in the refrigerator they will often be chosen for snacks over cookies and chips.

Vegetables such as broccoli, which are high in vitamin C, will lose most of their vitamin C if stored in water; instead, store them in a plastic bag with a few drops of water.

Salmon Spread with Capers

MAKES ABOUT 1¼ CUPS

PER SERVING
(1 tablespoon)

17 calories
1 g fat
3 mg cholesterol
50 mg sodium

2 g protein
0 g carbohydrate

NUTRITION NOTE

Be sure to crush salmon bones and include them as they are an excellent source of calcium; also include the juices because they contain omega-3 fatty acids, which may help in reducing the risk of heart disease.

I keep a can of salmon on the shelf and a bottle of capers in the refrigerator in case someone drops in unexpectedly. Then I can make this in a few seconds to serve as a spread with crackers or pita bread, or use to stuff vegetables, such as cherry tomatoes or snow peas. Scallions, chives, sweet peppers, or fresh dill can be used instead of celery. Choose sockeye salmon for its bright red color.

1 7½-ounce can salmon, preferably red sockeye
⅓ cup capers, drained
⅓ cup finely chopped celery
2 tablespoons low-fat plain yogurt or light sour cream
1 teaspoon lemon juice
Hot pepper sauce
2 tablespoons chopped fresh parsley

In small bowl, flake salmon along with juices and well-mashed bones. Add capers, celery, yogurt or sour cream, and lemon juice; mix well. Add hot pepper sauce to taste. Spoon into serving bowl and sprinkle with parsley.

Spinach-Onion Dip

MAKES 2¼ CUPS

PER SERVING
(1 tablespoon) (made with
low-fat plain yogurt)

10 calories
 0 fat
 1 mg cholesterol
96 mg sodium

 1 g protein
 1 g carbohydrate

This is a good creamy yet low-fat base for many dips. Instead of spinach, you can add other vegetables, herbs, or seasonings (see Variations). Serve this dip surrounded with fresh, crisp vegetables, such as carrots, celery, sweet peppers, blanched snow peas, asparagus, broccoli, or cauliflower. It's best to make it at least 4 hours in advance so that flavors can develop.

1 10-ounce package fresh spinach (or frozen chopped, thawed)
1 cup low-fat cottage cheese
1 tablespoon lemon juice
½ cup light sour cream or low-fat plain yogurt
½ cup chopped fresh parsley
¼ cup chopped scallion, including 2 inches green tops
1 teaspoon salt
Freshly ground pepper

Trim stems and coarse leaves from spinach. Rinse spinach, cook, covered, over medium heat for 3 minutes or until wilted. (If using frozen, no need to cook.)

Thoroughly drain, squeezing out excess moisture; coarsely chop and set aside.

In blender or food processor, process cottage cheese with lemon juice until blended. Add spinach, sour cream, parsley, scallion, salt, and pepper to taste; process just until mixed.

Cover and refrigerate for at least 4 hours or overnight to blend flavors.

VARIATIONS

PARSLEY-ONION DIP: Instead of spinach, substitute 1 cup coarsely chopped fresh parsley.

FRESH BASIL-ONION DIP: Instead of spinach, substitute ½ cup coarsely chopped fresh basil leaves.

DILL DIP: Instead of spinach, substitute ¼ cup coarsely chopped fresh parsley and ⅓ cup chopped fresh dill (or 1 tablespoon dried dillweed).

Compare

Many dips are made with mayonnaise or cream cheese as a base; these are much higher in fat and calories. Just as good-tasting, if not better, dips can be made using cottage cheese and/or yogurt.

One Cup	Grams Fat	Calories	Milligrams Cholesterol
Low-fat yogurt (1.57% BF)	4	158	16
2% cottage cheese	5	214	20
Light sour cream (7% BF)	13	220	47
Sour cream (14% BF)	46	475	94
Light mayonnaise	80	928	140
Mayonnaise	176	1632	120
Cream cheese*	80	832	256

*Although cream cheese is lower in total fat than mayonnaise, it is not recommended because it is higher in cholesterol and saturated fat.

ARTICHOKE-ONION DIP: Instead of spinach, substitute 1 cup drained, coarsely chopped canned unmarinated artichoke hearts.

SHRIMP, CRAB, OR CLAM DIP: Instead of spinach, add 1 cup rinsed and drained crab, small shrimp, or clams.

CURRY DIP: Instead of spinach, add 1 teaspoon each curry powder and ground cumin; mix well then season with more to taste.

Broccoli and Mushroom Dip

MAKES 2¼ CUPS

Chopped broccoli adds color, flavor, and fiber to this low-calorie dip.

PER SERVING
(1 tablespoon) (made with low-fat plain yogurt)

12 calories
0.5 g fat
0 mg cholesterol
22 mg sodium

1 g protein
1 g carbohydrate

2 cups chopped broccoli (include stalks)
1 tablespoon vegetable oil
1 clove garlic, minced
1 small onion, chopped
¼ pound mushrooms, coarsely chopped

¾ cup low-fat cottage cheese
¼ cup low-fat plain yogurt or light sour cream
Salt and freshly ground pepper

In pot of boiling water, cook broccoli just until tender-crisp (3 minutes). Drain and refresh under cold water; drain again and set aside.

In nonstick skillet, heat oil over medium heat; add garlic, onion, and mushrooms, and cook, shaking pan to prevent sticking, for 5 minutes or until onion is tender. Set aside.

In food processor, combine cottage cheese and yogurt; process until smooth. Add mushroom mixture and broccoli; season with salt and pepper to taste. Process with on/off motion just until mixed. Cover and refrigerate for up to 2 days.

Shrimp Mousse with Dill

MAKES ABOUT 4 CUPS

PER SERVING
(1 tablespoon)

12 calories
0.5 g fat
9 mg cholesterol
28 mg sodium

1.5 g protein
0.5 g carbohydrate

Serve as part of a light salad plate, or surround with crackers, Melba toast, or fresh vegetables for a delicious appetizer spread.

1 envelope unflavored gelatin
½ cup cold water
⅓ cup minced scallions including 2 inches green tops or chives
½ cup chopped fresh dill (not packed)
1 tablespoon lemon juice
½ teaspoon salt
½ teaspoon granulated sugar
Dash hot pepper sauce
2 tablespoons tomato paste
¾ cup low-fat plain yogurt
½ cup light sour cream
½ cup finely chopped celery
1¾ cups small cooked salad shrimp, 12 ounces, coarsely chopped
Dill sprigs

In microwave-safe bowl or small saucepan, sprinkle gelatin over cold water; let stand until softened, about 5 minutes. Microwave at high (100%) power for 40 seconds or warm over medium heat until gelatin is dissolved; let cool slightly.

In bowl combine scallions, dill, lemon juice, salt, sugar, hot pepper sauce, tomato paste, yogurt, sour cream, celery, and gelatin; mix well. Stir in shrimp and refrigerate until mixture begins to set. Spoon into lightly oiled 4 cup mold or, alternatively, spoon into serving bowl. Cover and refrigerate until firm, at least 3 hours.

To unmold, run a knife around mousse to loosen from mold. Invert onto serving platter. Cover with hot, damp tea towel for 1 minute. Hold mold and platter securely and give a strong shake to release mousse. Remove mold. Or, just serve in the bowl. Either way, garnish with sprigs of fresh dill.

Compare ¼ Cup Shrimp Mousse with Dill Made with:

	Grams Fat	Milligrams Cholesterol	Calories
Low-fat yogurt and light sour cream	2	21	48
Mayonnaise (½ cup) and whipping cream (¾ cup)	8	48	108

This type of spread is often made with mayonnaise and whipping cream. I prefer a lighter version made with yogurt and sour cream.

Snacks and Nibbles

These can quickly add up to lots of fat and calories. For example, if you consume about 2,000 calories a day you should have no more than 66 grams of fat.

High-Fat Snacks	Grams Fat
Peanuts (½ cup)	35
Potato chips (1 small bag)	14
Cheddar cheese (1½ ounce, a 2-inch cube)	15

Lower-Fat Alternative Snacks	
Popcorn (unbuttered) (1 cup)	0
Shrimp Mousse with Dill (¼ cup) (page 35)	2
Skim-milk cheese (1½ ounce)	3
Fresh vegetables with Spinach-Onion Dip (¼ cup) (page 33)	1

Italian Tomato Bruschetta

MAKES 4 SERVINGS, 2 SLICES EACH

PER SERVING (2 slices)*

105 calories
  2 g fat
  1 mg cholesterol
190 mg sodium

  3 g protein
 19 g carbohydrate

*including Parmesan

Traditionally, this Italian-style garlic bread is made by toasting thick slices of Italian bread, then rubbing them with a cut clove of garlic and drizzling with a top-quality (first-pressed, dense, and green-colored) olive oil. Sometimes the toast is topped with diced tomato or cheese. Here's a low-calorie, low-fat version that is equally delicious. Serve for a first course or as a snack after bridge or tennis, as an hors d'oeuvre on tiny toasted bread rounds, or as part of a soup-and-salad meal. To prepare for a group, use the round Italian bread. Cut in half horizontally; prepare, and then cut into wedges to serve.

> 8 slices French or Italian bread, ½-inch thick
> 2 cloves garlic, halved
> 1 teaspoon olive oil
> 2 tablespoons minced onion
> 1 large tomato, diced
> Pinch dried oregano
> Pinch freshly ground pepper
> 2 teaspoons freshly grated Parmesan cheese (optional)

Under broiler or in toaster oven, toast bread on both sides until brown. Rub one side of hot toast with cut side of garlic.

While bread is toasting, heat oil in nonstick skillet over medium-high heat; add onion and cook, stirring, until tender. Add tomato, oregano, and pepper; stir to mix.

Spoon tomato mixture over garlic side of hot toast and serve immediately. Alternatively, sprinkle with Parmesan and (if using) broil for 1 minute.

Low-Salt Bagel Thins

MAKES 20 PIECES

If you love crisp, salty snacks such as potato chips, here is a healthy alternative. How good they are depends on how thin you can slice the bagel.

PER SERVING (1 piece)

14 calories
0.5 g fat
0 mg cholesterol
15 mg sodium

0 g protein
2 g carbohydrate

1 bagel
2 teaspoons soft margarine, melted
1 teaspoon dried oregano

Using very sharp serrated knife, slice bagel into very thin rounds. Arrange in single layer on baking sheet; brush with margarine. Sprinkle with oregano. Bake in 350°F oven for 12 minutes. Let cool and store in airtight container for up to 1 week.

Mussels on the Half Shell

MAKES ABOUT 6 FIRST-COURSE SERVINGS, 50 TO 60 PIECES

PER SERVING
(9 mussels)

114 calories
6 g fat
33 mg cholesterol
197 mg sodium

10 g protein
5 g carbohydrate

GOOD: vitamin C, iron, niacin

These mussels look great on an hors d'oeuvre platter, aren't difficult to make, and are inexpensive compared to crab or shrimp. Mussels can be purchased ahead and stored for 1 to 2 days in a bowl or paper bag in the refrigerator. Don't store in a plastic bag.

3 pounds mussels (in shells)
¼ cup white wine or water
2 tablespoons vegetable oil
2 tablespoons lemon juice
3 cloves garlic, minced
½ cup chopped fresh parsley
2 medium tomatoes, diced

Scrub mussels and discard any that do not close when tapped; cut off any hairy beards. In large heavy saucepan, bring wine or water to boil. Add mussels, cover, and cook over medium-high heat for 5 to 7 minutes or until mussels open. Discard any that do not open.

NUTRITION NOTE

Mussels aren't nearly as high in cholesterol as previously thought; about 3½ ounces of mussels (meat only) has 50 milligrams cholesterol.

Remove from heat; reserve 2 tablespoons of cooking liquid. When mussels are cool enough to handle, using small knife, separate mussels from shell and set aside; reserve half the shells.

In bowl, combine reserved cooking liquid, oil, lemon juice, garlic, parsley, and tomatoes; add mussels and stir gently. Cover and refrigerate for 3 hours.

To serve, place a mussel in each half shell; spoon tomato mixture over. Arrange on a platter and pass with drinks, or arrange on individual plates and serve as first course.

Spiced Meatballs with Coriander Dipping Sauce

MAKES 1 CUP SAUCE, 25 MEATBALLS

PER SERVING
(1 meatball)

28 calories
 1 g fat
 7 mg cholesterol
 9 mg sodium

 2 g protein
 2 g carbohydrate

Middle Eastern seasonings of cinnamon, allspice, and garlic, plus crunchy water chestnuts and juicy raisins, make these meatballs the best I've tasted; salt will never be missed. Bake rather than fry them; not only is there less fat as a result, it's also much easier. Fresh coriander, also called cilantro, is available at some supermarkets and most Oriental grocery stores. Because the flavor is quite different, don't substitute the dried coriander; instead add chopped fresh basil, dill, or curry powder to taste.

MEATBALLS

¼ cup raisins
½ pound lean lamb, trimmed of visible fat, ground
⅓ cup minced water chestnuts
2 tablespoons minced scallions including 2 inches green tops
1 clove garlic, minced
½ teaspoon ground allspice
½ teaspoon ground cinnamon
Freshly ground pepper

CORIANDER DIPPING SAUCE

¾ cup plain 2% yogurt
¼ cup minced fresh coriander leaves, lightly packed
Freshly ground pepper

Meatballs: Soak raisins in hot water for 15 minutes; drain and chop. In bowl, combine raisins, lamb, water chestnuts, scallions, garlic, allspice, cinnamon, and pepper to taste; mix well.

Shape into 25 bite-size balls. Arrange in single layer in ungreased baking dish. Bake, uncovered, in 400°F oven for 20 minutes.

(continued)

Coriander Dipping Sauce: Meanwhile, in small bowl combine yogurt, coriander, and pepper to taste; cover and refrigerate for at least 30 minutes for flavors to develop. Serve hot meatballs with toothpicks for dipping into sauce.

Marinated Mushrooms

MAKES 10 APPETIZER SERVINGS

PER SERVING

39 calories
2 g fat
0 mg cholesterol
29 mg sodium

2 g protein
5 g carbohydrate

GOOD: niacin, fiber

Pass these zippy mushrooms with drinks or serve as part of a relish tray or salad plate.

⅔ cup tarragon vinegar
⅓ cup vegetable oil
2 tablespoons granulated sugar
1 teaspoon dried basil
1 teaspoon dried thyme
½ teaspoon salt
2 tablespoons water
Dash hot pepper sauce
¼ teaspoon dried hot pepper flakes (optional)
1 clove garlic, minced
Freshly ground pepper
1 medium onion, sliced
1½ pound medium mushrooms

In large bowl, combine vinegar, oil, sugar, basil, thyme, salt, water, hot pepper sauce, dried hot pepper flakes (if using), garlic, and pepper to taste; stir until well mixed.

Separate onion into rings. Rinse mushrooms and trim bases. Add onions and mushrooms to vinegar mixture; mix lightly. Cover and refrigerate for at least 8 hours, stirring occasionally. Drain before serving.

VARIATION

MARINATED MUSHROOMS AND ARTICHOKES: Drain one 14-ounce can artichoke hearts. Cut in half and add to mushroom mixture before marinating.

Mushroom-Stuffed Zucchini Cups

For a light, refreshing, hot hors d'oeuvre follow recipe on page 41 using very thin zucchini cut into bite-size pieces. Serve on platter along with Spiced Meatballs with Coriander Dipping Sauce (page 39) and cherry tomatoes.

Marinated Spiced Carrots

MAKES ABOUT 10 APPETIZER SERVINGS

PER SERVING

27 calories
0 g fat
0 mg cholesterol
13 mg sodium

0.5 g protein
6 g carbohydrate

EXCELLENT: vitamin A

These are a favorite with the bridge club I used to play with. The members have been serving these along with the Marinated Mushrooms (page 40) at their year-end party for the last twenty years. A few cherry tomatoes on the platter look nice and add extra color.

1 pound small carrots, scraped
½ cup granulated sugar
½ cup white vinegar
½ cup water
1 tablespoon mustard seeds
3 whole cloves
1 3-inch stick cinnamon, broken

Cut carrots into 3-inch-long, very thin sticks. Blanch in boiling water for 3 minutes; drain and cool under cold water. Drain again and place in bowl.

In saucepan, combine sugar, vinegar, water, mustard seeds, cloves, and cinnamon; bring to boil. Reduce heat and simmer for 10 minutes; pour over carrots. Let cool, then cover and refrigerate for at least 8 hours or overnight. Drain well; discard cloves and cinnamon.

Seafood Lettuce Rolls with Nuoc Cham Dipping Sauce

MAKES 5 SERVINGS OF 3 ROLLS EACH,
AND ⅓ CUP SAUCE

PER SERVING
(without sauce)

138 calories
6 g fat
54 mg cholesterol
85 mg sodium

17 g protein
3 g carbohydrate

GOOD: calcium
EXCELLENT: niacin

These surprise packages are an intriguing and delicious first course. Serve with Coriander Dipping Sauce (page 40) or Nuoc Cham Dipping Sauce. If you enjoy Vietnamese cooking, serve the lettuce rolls with a nuoc cham dipping sauce and include a small spoonful of cooked rice vermicelli noodles in the rolls. Thin strips of cooked pork can be used instead of salmon.

SEAFOOD LETTUCE ROLLS

1 head Boston or leaf lettuce
1 7½-ounce can salmon
1 dried red chili pepper or 1 fresh hot pepper
½ cup low-fat plain yogurt
1 cup small shrimp
2 cups alfalfa sprouts
Fresh coriander (cilantro) leaves (optional)

NUOC CHAM DIPPING SAUCE

2 dried red chili peppers
1 clove garlic, minced
1 tablespoon granulated sugar
1 tablespoon lime juice
3 tablespoons water
2 tablespoons bottled fish sauce

Seafood Lettuce Rolls: Cut large lettuce leaves in half down center vein. In bowl, flake salmon along with juices and well-mashed bones. Split chili pepper in half lengthwise, discard seeds and vein; finely chop and mix into yogurt.

On narrow end of each lettuce piece, place 1 tablespoon flaked salmon, top with 1 or 2 shrimp, then approximately 2 tablespoons alfalfa sprouts, a dollop of yogurt, and 1 or 2 coriander leaves (if using). Roll into cylinder shape.

Nuoc Cham Dipping Sauce Split peppers in half, discard seeds and membranes; chop finely. In small dish combine peppers, garlic, granulated sugar, lime juice, water, and bottled fish sauce (available in Oriental food stores).

Warm Vegetable Salad with Tomato-Shallot Dressing

MAKES 8 SERVINGS

PER SERVING

100 calories
8 g fat
0 mg cholesterol
40 mg sodium

3 g protein
7 g carbohydrate

EXCELLENT: vitamin A, vitamin C, fiber

Warm vegetables over cool greens is a very pleasing combination. You can prepare the vegetables and dressing in advance, then just before serving quickly blanch vegetables and add dressing. It's a lovely dinner-party first course or a light lunch.

½ pound spinach (see Note)
1 small Belgian endive
1 cup green beans, cut 2 inches long and sliced lengthwise
1 cup julienne-cut carrots
1 cup small cauliflower florets
1 cup small broccoli florets
3 tablespoons sunflower seeds

TOMATO-SHALLOT DRESSING

¼ cup vegetable oil
¼ cup water
¼ cup lemon juice
2 shallots, minced
1 tablespoon chopped fresh basil (or ½ teaspoon dried)
½ teaspoon Dijon mustard
Salt and freshly ground pepper
3 medium tomatoes, peeled and diced

Trim, rinse, and dry spinach; tear into large pieces. Separate endive leaves. On 6 salad plates, arrange spinach and endive leaves.

Tomato-Shallot Dressing: In food processor or mixing bowl, combine oil, water, lemon juice, shallots, basil, and mustard; mix well. Season with salt and pepper to taste.

Five minutes before serving, in large pot of boiling salted water, blanch green beans, carrots, cauliflower, and broccoli for 2 minutes; drain. Spoon warm vegetables onto greens; stir tomatoes into dressing and spoon dressing over vegetables. Sprinkle with sunflower seeds. Serve immediately before vegetables cool.

Note: This salad is best made with fresh leaf spinach (usually bought by the bunch) available in the summer and fall. One 10-ounce package of fresh spinach can also be used.

Green Bean Appetizer Salad with Fresh Tomato-Chive Dressing

Serve this as a light first course in the summer and fall when green beans and tomatoes are at their sweetest and best flavor. It's also a great way to use up any leftover cooked beans.

Line salad plates with leaf lettuce. Arrange crisp-cooked, chilled beans and sliced raw mushrooms over lettuce. Spoon Fresh Tomato-Chive Dressing (page 82) over beans (sprinkle feta cheese on top if not already added to dressing). Garnish with lemon wedges or chopped fresh herbs such as coriander (cilantro), dill, or basil.

Curried Chicken Croustades

MAKES 40 APPETIZERS

PER SERVING
(1 croustade)

30 calories
1 g fat
6 mg cholesterol
56 mg sodium

3 g protein
3 g carbohydrate

Serve these savory tidbits at a cocktail party or make larger croustades and serve for a luncheon dish. In this recipe tiny shells of bread are toasted and filled with curried chicken. Both parts can be made in advance, then reheated before serving. The croustades are perfect low-calorie, low-fat containers for savory fillings. Use the leftover bread trimmings to make bread crumbs for Herb-Breaded Chicken (page 229), Fish Fillets with Herbed Crumbs (page 117), or any other recipe.

40 thin slices bread (about 2 loaves)
Curried Chicken filling for crêpes (page 104)

Using 2-inch cookie cutter or glass, cut out 40 rounds of bread. Press bread rounds into very small tart tins (about 1½ inches in diameter). Bake in 300°F oven for 20 minutes or until toasted. Remove from oven and let cool. (Croustades can be prepared in advance and stored in covered container for up to 1 week or frozen for up to 2 months.)

Fill croustades with Curried Chicken mixture and place on baking sheet. Heat in 400°F oven for 15 minutes or until hot.

Quick, Low-Calorie, Low-Fat Hors d'Oeuvres

CUCUMBER CANAPÉS: Use round cucumber slices as the base for canapés. If you wish, scoop out a tiny portion of cucumber from center to form a hollow; top with a spoonful of:

- Shrimp Mousse with Dill (page 35);
- Salmon Spread with Capers (page 32);
- Classic Tuna Salad with Fresh Dill (page 68);
- or Curried Chicken (page 104).

MINI-PITAS: Cut small (1½-inch) pita bread rounds in half so that you have 2 pockets. Line pocket with a soft leaf lettuce and fill with any of the fillings listed with Cucumber Canapés.

VEGETABLE CANAPÉS: Fill hollowed-out cherry tomatoes, zucchini rounds, snow peas, or mushroom caps with any of the spreads listed, or with the dip recipes in this book.

Use Belgian endive spears for dipping.

Soups

Homemade soup is such a treat and so easy to make that I wish I always had some on hand. In this section there are elegant soups to serve as first courses at a dinner party—such as Cream of Parsnip Soup with Ginger (page 55) or Fresh Beet Soup with Yogurt (page 58)—or there's a Chunky Vegetable-Bean Soup (page 52), which is a wonderfully warming main-course dish. Or serve soup for lunch; new wide-mouth unbreakable Thermos containers make soups easy to pack for lunch. Soups are easy to prepare, make good use of leftovers, and can be made ahead of time.

Canned and Packaged Soups

Canned and packaged soups are very high in sodium. If you only use them, your family will acquire a taste for heavily salted soups. To increase the nutrients and decrease the sodium of packaged or canned soup, use them as a base, and add more vegetables, such as grated carrot, grated zucchini, chopped green beans, broccoli, cubed potatoes, and/or chopped onion.

The main nutritional advantage to homemade chicken stock (besides its better flavor) is that it is low in sodium. However, if you add salt, the sodium level will be close to that of commercial soups. Anyone on a low-sodium diet should use homemade stock without adding salt. If you use stocks from a can or cube, remember that they are high in salt, so don't add any more. Doubling the ratio of water to stock powder, a stock cube, or canned stock will halve the sodium content.

Whenever possible, add skim, 1%, or 2% milk instead of water to canned soups; this way you increase the soup's protein and calcium content.

I often add leftover cooked rice or noodles, chicken or meats, or an extra mushroom or scallion to soups.

Compare 1 Cup of Homemade and Canned Soups:

	Grams Fat	Milligrams Sodium
Asparagus and Potato Bisque (page 50)	1	52
Canned cream of asparagus (with water added)	3	996
Mushroom Bisque with Tarragon (page 51)	5	257
Canned cream of mushroom (with water added)	9	1,091

Tips for Healthier Soups

TO GET THE MAXIMUM FLAVOR WITH THE LEAST AMOUNT OF FAT:

The most effective way to reduce fat in soups is to cut down the amount of butter, margarine, or oil you put in them. Many recipes call for more of these than is necessary.

- When making a vegetable soup, if you cook the vegetables first in margarine (¼ cup margarine has 56 grams fat), the margarine is absorbed by the vegetables. Instead cook vegetables in only 1 teaspoon margarine and some chicken stock, or better still in only chicken stock.
- Another way is to substitute light cream or milk for heavy or whipping cream. (A quarter cup of light cream will add 8 grams fat; whipping cream 20 grams fat.) If you do need more fat for flavor, add it at the end of cooking—just before serving. This will give the maximum flavor for the least amount of fat.

  Traditional high-fat and high-cholesterol soup thickeners are whole milk, cream, egg yolks, and high-fat cheese. Instead, thicken soups with rice, noodles, potato, legumes, puréed vegetables, low-fat cheese, 2% milk, or low-fat plain yogurt.

Compare the Sodium in 1 Cup of:

Chicken stock diluted from can	
Chicken stock from a cube	740+ mg
Chicken stock from powder	
Basic Chicken Stock (unsalted) (page 62)	4 mg

TO GET THE MAXIMUM FLAVOR WITH THE LEAST
AMOUNT OF SODIUM:

- Instead of using salt to add flavor to soups, use onion or celery, herbs (thyme, rosemary, oregano, chives, parsley, to name just a few), lemon juice, a pinch of sugar, pepper, nutmeg, or garlic. Also use more of the vegetable itself, i.e., if you are making carrot soup, add extra carrots.
- If you add salt, add it at the end of cooking just before serving—you'll need less. Keep in mind if you add ¼ teaspoon salt to 1 cup homemade soup, you add 581 milligrams sodium.

Turkey Noodle Soup

MAKES 6 SERVINGS, ¾ CUP EACH

PER SERVING

91 calories
3 g fat
32 mg cholesterol
137 mg sodium

11 g protein
5 g carbohydrate

GOOD: vitamin C
EXCELLENT: vitamin A, niacin

Whenever you roast a turkey or chicken, make this comforting soup from the leftovers. Don't be put off by the long list of ingredients; it's really quite easy to prepare. I usually start the stock simmering while I'm making dinner one night, let it simmer for a few hours that evening then finish it the next night. If you prefer, add rice instead of noodles.

If you don't have a leftover turkey or chicken carcass, substitute 6 cups chicken stock for the stock here.

For a main course soup and to increase fiber add 1 19-ounce can chickpeas or kidney beans, drained. Other good additions: green peas, chopped fresh spinach, asparagus, chopped broccoli, diced potato, squash, or turnip.

STOCK

1 carcass from roast chicken or turkey
7 cups water
1 bay leaf
1 stalk celery, chopped
1 medium onion, quartered

SOUP

¼ cup broken noodles (½-inch pieces)
1 stalk celery (including leaves), chopped
1 carrot, chopped
3 scallions, sliced
⅓ cup grated zucchini
1 teaspoon dried basil
1 teaspoon dried thyme
Dash hot pepper sauce
Salt and freshly ground pepper

In stockpot or large saucepan, combine carcass, water, bay leaf, celery, and onion. Simmer, covered, for 4 hours. Strain, reserving stock. Let bones cool, then pick out any meat and add to stock.

Bring stock to boil; add noodles and simmer for 5 minutes. Add celery, carrot, scallions, zucchini, basil, and thyme; simmer for 10 minutes. Stir in hot pepper sauce; season with salt and pepper to taste.

Mussel, Clam, and Fish Chowder

MAKES 6 SERVINGS, 1¾ CUPS EACH

Serve this wonderfully warming seafood stew for lunch, dinner, or as late-night party fare. If fresh mussels and clams aren't available, use canned or bottled ones. Shrimp can be added, but that will raise the cholesterol level. Some fish markets sell fresh fish pieces, often called chowder bits or pieces. These are usually inexpensive and ideal for this recipe; remove any skin or bones before adding.

(continued)

PER SERVING

185 calories
3 g fat
65 mg cholesterol
467 mg sodium

21 g protein
19 g carbohydrate

GOOD: fiber, niacin, iron
EXCELLENT: vitamin A, vitamin C

2 teaspoons vegetable oil
1 medium onion, chopped
1 stalk celery, chopped
1 carrot, chopped
2 cloves garlic, minced
1 bay leaf
1 teaspoon dried thyme
1 teaspoon dried basil
1 19-ounce can tomatoes (undrained)
2 cups water
2 potatoes, diced
1 pound mussels (in shells)
1 pound small clams (in shells) or one 6½-ounce can
1 pound fresh white flesh fish (cod, haddock, monkfish)
½ cup dry white wine
Salt and freshly ground pepper
1 cup chopped fresh parsley

In large saucepan, heat oil over medium heat; cook onion, celery, and carrot, stirring, for 5 minutes. Add garlic, bay leaf, thyme, basil, tomatoes, water, and potatoes; bring to simmer. Cover and cook over low heat for 25 minutes or until vegetables are tender. Remove bay leaf.

Meanwhile, scrub mussels and clams under cold running water; cut off any hairy beards from mussels. Discard any clams or mussels that do not close when tapped. Add clams to saucepan; simmer for 5 minutes. Add mussels, fish (if using monkfish cut into chunks), and wine. Simmer for 5 minutes or until clams and mussels open; discard any that don't open. Season with salt and pepper to taste. Just before serving sprinkle with parsley. (Chowder can be prepared up to 1 day in advance, refrigerated, and reheated.)

Asparagus and Potato Bisque

MAKES 6 SERVINGS, ¾ CUP EACH

Potato helps to thicken this soup without adding the extra calories or preparation time of a butter/flour–thickened soup. It's delicious served hot or cold, but when serving hot, substitute either light cream or milk for the yogurt, since yogurt tends to curdle easily when heated.

PER SERVING*

103 calories
  1 g fat
  4 mg cholesterol
 39 mg sodium

  5 g protein
 19 g carbohydrate

GOOD: fiber, niacin
EXCELLENT: vitamin C

*made with yogurt and
unsalted chicken stock

1 large potato, peeled and diced
1 small onion, chopped
1½ cups water or chicken stock
1 pound asparagus
2 teaspoons lemon juice
1 cup 2% milk
½ cup low-fat plain yogurt, light cream, or milk
Salt, freshly ground pepper, and nutmeg

In saucepan, combine potato, onion, and water or chicken stock; cover and simmer until potato is nearly tender, 5 to 10 minutes.

Meanwhile, trim asparagus of tough ends, then cut into about 1½-inch lengths. Add to potato mixture; cover and simmer for 5 minutes or until asparagus are tender.

Using slotted spoon, remove asparagus tips and let cool in cold water to prevent further cooking. Drain and reserve for garnish.

In food processor or blender, purée asparagus-potato mixture; add lemon juice. Pour into bowl; cover and refrigerate until chilled. Stir in milk and yogurt; season with salt, pepper, and nutmeg to taste. Serve cold or reheat. Garnish each serving with reserved asparagus tips.

Mushroom Bisque with Tarragon

MAKES 4 SERVINGS, ¾ CUP EACH

PER SERVING

107 calories
  5 g fat
  7 mg cholesterol
257 mg sodium

  6 g protein
 10 g carbohydrate

GOOD: vitamin C,
niacin

Easy to make, this creamy soup tastes so much better than anything out of a can.

½ pound mushrooms
1 tablespoon margarine
2 tablespoons minced onion
2 tablespoons all-purpose flour
1 cup chicken stock, hot
1½ cups 2% milk
1 teaspoon dried tarragon
⅓ cup minced fresh parsley
Salt and freshly ground pepper

(continued)

Thinly slice 4 mushroom caps and set aside; coarsely chop remaining mushrooms (if using food processor, use on-off turns).

In saucepan, melt margarine over medium heat; add onion and cook for 2 minutes, stirring occasionally. Add chopped mushrooms and cook for 4 minutes, stirring often; sprinkle with flour and stir until mixed. Whisk in hot chicken stock and bring to boil, whisking constantly. Reduce heat to low and add milk, tarragon, parsley, and reserved sliced mushrooms; simmer, uncovered, for 4 minutes.

Season to taste with salt and pepper.

Chunky Vegetable-Bean Soup

MAKES 8 SERVINGS, ¾ CUP EACH

PER SERVING

147 calories
2 g fat
2 mg cholesterol
566 mg sodium

9 g protein
25 g carbohydrate

GOOD: vitamin C, iron
EXCELLENT: fiber,
vitamin A, niacin

Onion and potato are the basis for this soup—the potato helps to thicken it, the onion adds flavor. You can add any seasonal fresh vegetables—broccoli, mushrooms, zucchini, carrots, tomatoes—that you have on hand. Instead of canned kidney beans, you can add ¼ cup uncooked noodles, or rice or barley, along with the potato.

1 large onion, chopped
1 large potato, peeled and cubed
4 cups chicken stock
2 stalks celery, diced
¼ pound green beans, cut in 1-inch pieces
¼ small cabbage, thinly sliced, and/or ½ 10-ounce package spinach, coarsely sliced
1 carrot, grated or chopped
¼ cup chopped sweet red pepper
1 teaspoon dried dillweed (or ¼ cup chopped fresh)
1 19-ounce can kidney beans, drained
Salt, cayenne, and freshly ground pepper
¼ cup grated Parmesan cheese (optional)

In large heavy saucepan, combine onion, potato, and chicken stock; bring to a boil. Reduce heat and simmer for 10 minutes.

Add celery, green beans, cabbage and/or spinach, carrot, sweet

Compare 1 Cup of:

	Calories	Grams Fat	Milligrams Sodium*	Grams Protein	Grams Fiber
Canned Chunky Vegetable Soup	104	3	837	3	3
Canned Vegetable Soup	80	2	770	2	1
Homemade Chunky Vegetable-Bean Soup	147	2	566	9	7

*Sodium values based on using canned chicken stock, or stock made from a cube. If homemade, sodium is greatly reduced.

pepper, dillweed, and kidney beans; cover and simmer for 10 minutes or until vegetables are tender.

Season with salt, cayenne, and pepper to taste. Sprinkle each serving with Parmesan (if using).

Chilled Cucumber-Chive Soup

MAKES 6 SERVINGS, ¾ CUP EACH

PER SERVING

85 calories
4 g fat
12 mg cholesterol
168 mg sodium

6 g protein
7 g carbohydrate

GOOD: vitamin C, calcium

Quick to prepare, this wonderful summer soup is perfect for lunch, a picnic, or a first course for an alfresco dinner. For packed lunches it's easy to transport in a Thermos.

½ cup low-fat cottage cheese
½ cup light sour cream
2 cups buttermilk
½ unpeeled English cucumber diced
½ cup chopped fresh parsley
⅓ cup diced red radishes
¼ cup chopped fresh chives or scallions
Salt and freshly ground pepper

In blender or food processor, process cottage cheese and sour cream until smooth; add buttermilk and process to mix.

Transfer to bowl; stir in cucumber, parsley, radishes, and chives. Season with salt and pepper to taste. Refrigerate until chilled.

Jiffy Gazpacho

Don't throw away leftover tossed green salads made with an oil-and-vinegar dressing. Instead, purée in a blender or food processor and add tomato juice to taste. Refrigerate until cold, then serve in soup bowls, topped with finely chopped tomato, green pepper, and garlic croutons.

Fresh Corn Bisque with Scallions

MAKES 8 SERVINGS, ⅔ CUP EACH

PER SERVING

91	calories
4	g fat
0	mg cholesterol
150	mg sodium

2	g protein
14	g carbohydrate

GOOD: fiber, vitamin A

In fresh corn season, as markets overflow with locally grown corn on the cob, try this fresh-tasting, economical soup. The recipe can easily be halved, or you can freeze any extra in container sizes to suit your household.

2 tablespoons vegetable oil
1 medium onion, chopped
1 carrot, chopped
1 stalk celery, chopped
2 cloves garlic, minced
½ teaspoon ground turmeric
1 bay leaf
4 cups water
5 ears of corn, husked, about 5 cups (see Note)
½ teaspoon salt
Cayenne pepper
¼ cup chopped scallions or fresh coriander (cilantro or Chinese parsley)

In large saucepan or soup kettle, heat oil over medium heat. Add onion, carrot, celery, and garlic; cook, stirring, for 2 minutes. Stir in turmeric and cook for 1 minute. Add bay leaf and water; bring to simmer.

Cut corn kernels from cobs and set aside. Add cobs to saucepan; cover and simmer for 10 minutes. Add corn kernels and simmer for

10 minutes longer. Discard corn cobs and bay leaf. Reserve about 1 cup corn kernels.

In blender or food processor, purée mixture in batches. Return to saucepan and add reserved corn kernels, salt, and cayenne to taste. Serve hot or cold and garnish with scallions or coriander.

Note: To make the soup using frozen or drained canned (two 19-ounce cans) kernel corn: After adding bay leaf and water, simmer for 10 minutes. Add 4 cups kernel corn, simmer 5 minutes; discard bay leaf. In blender or food processor purée in batches. Return to saucepan and add 1 cup corn kernels. Simmer 5 minutes. Season and garnish as in above recipe.

Cream of Parsnip Soup with Ginger

MAKES 5 SERVINGS, ⅔ CUP EACH

PER SERVING

111 calories
3 g fat
3 mg cholesterol
194 mg sodium

3 g protein
17 g carbohydrate

GOOD: fiber, vitamin C

This splendid soup is the creation of Doug Andison, my friend and good cook. He microwaves parsnips and leeks separately in large amounts, then freezes them in smaller portions so he can prepare this soup easily at the last minute. He also likes to press the gingerroot through a garlic press instead of grating or chopping and might use cream instead of 2% milk.

1 medium onion (or 2 whites of leeks), chopped
4 medium parsnips, peeled and cubed (about 10 ounces)
1 cup water
1 tablespoon soft margarine
2 tablespoons all-purpose flour
1 cup chicken stock
1½ teaspoons grated fresh gingerroot
¾ cup 2% milk
Salt and white pepper

In saucepan, combine onion, parsnips, and water; simmer, covered, for 8 to 10 minutes or until parsnips are tender. Purée in blender or food processor and set aside.

In saucepan, melt soft margarine over medium heat; stir in flour and cook for 1 minute. Stir in chicken stock and cook, stirring, until mixture comes to boil and thickens.

Add puréed parsnip mixture, gingerroot, milk, and salt and pepper to taste. Stir to mix well and heat through. Serve hot or cold. (If too thick, thin with more milk or chicken stock.)

Harvest Pumpkin and Zucchini Soup

MAKES 8 SERVINGS, ¾ CUP EACH

PER SERVING

99 calories
4 g fat
2 mg cholesterol
202 mg sodium

3 g protein
13 g carbohydrate

GOOD: vitamin C, niacin

This is a delightful fall soup. If you don't peel the zucchini, the soup will be green in color; if peeled it will be pumpkin-colored. You can use nearly any kind of squash instead of pumpkin. I've even made it using spaghetti squash—it always tastes terrific.

3 cups peeled, cubed pumpkin or squash
3 cups cubed zucchini
2 medium potatoes, peeled and cubed
1 large onion, sliced
2 cups chicken stock
2 tablespoons vegetable oil
2 tablespoons chopped fresh parsley
2 cloves garlic, chopped
¾ cup 2% milk
1 teaspoon dried basil (or 2 tablespoons chopped fresh)
Fresh mint leaves or chopped fresh parsley

In large saucepan, combine pumpkin, zucchini, potatoes, onion, chicken stock, oil, parsley, and garlic. Cover and simmer, stirring occasionally, for 45 minutes or until vegetables are tender. If stock simmers down, add water to reach original level.

In food processor or blender, purée mixture in batches; return to saucepan. Add milk and basil; heat until hot. Garnish each serving with mint leaves or parsley.

Zucchini and Watercress Vichyssoise

MAKES 8 SERVINGS, ¾ CUP EACH

PER SERVING

80 calories
1 g fat
3 mg cholesterol
214 mg sodium

4 g protein
14 g carbohydrate

GOOD: vitamin C,
niacin

This light, elegant, quick-to-prepare soup is perfect for the first course of a dinner party. Serve it hot in the spring when the first crop of watercress appears, or chilled in the summer for a refreshing starter.

1 pound zucchini (about 4 small), sliced
1 large potato, peeled and diced
1 medium onion, chopped
2 cups chicken stock
1 tablespoon lemon juice
½ cup lightly packed watercress leaves
1½ cups 2% milk
Salt and freshly ground pepper
Watercress leaves

In saucepan, combine zucchini, potato, onion, and chicken stock; cover and simmer until vegetables are tender, 15 to 20 minutes.

In food processor or blender, purée hot mixture with lemon juice and watercress until smooth. Stir in milk, and salt and pepper to taste; reheat if necessary and serve hot. Alternatively, cover and refrigerate until cold. To serve, thin with additional milk if too thick and garnish with watercress leaves.

MICROWAVE METHOD: In microwave-safe dish, combine zucchini, potato, and onion with 2 tablespoons of the chicken stock. Cover and microwave at high (100% power) until vegetables are tender, 10 to 13 minutes, rotating every few minutes and stirring after 6 minutes.

In food processor or blender, purée mixture until smooth, adding some of the remaining chicken stock if too thick to process. Return to dish and stir in remaining chicken stock, lemon juice, watercress, and milk. Add salt and pepper to taste and reheat or serve cold.

Fresh Beet Soup with Yogurt

MAKES 8 SERVINGS, ¾ CUP EACH

PER SERVING

75 calories
2 g fat
1 mg cholesterol
185 mg sodium

3 g protein
12 g carbohydrate

GOOD: fiber, vitamin C
EXCELLENT: vitamin A

This beautiful red soup has a wonderful fresh beet taste when made with small, tender beets. I once made the mistake of making it in the winter using large, old beets and it was not as good.

2 pounds small beets
1 tablespoon soft margarine
1 large onion, chopped
¼ cup lemon juice
2 tablespoons drained white horseradish
1 large carrot, grated
1 cup chicken stock
⅔ cup low-fat plain yogurt
Salt and freshly ground pepper
Yogurt and thin strips or slices lemon or orange rind

Rinse beets and trim, leaving 1 inch of the ends attached.

In large saucepan, cover beets with water and bring to boil; reduce heat and simmer, covered, for 20 to 30 minutes or until tender. Remove beets from saucepan; reserve cooking liquid. When beets are cool enough to handle (or under cold running water), slip off skins and stems. Cut beets in half.

In large saucepan, melt margarine over medium heat; add onion and cook until tender. Add 3 cups reserved cooking liquid, beets, lemon juice, horseradish, carrot, and chicken stock; simmer for 5 minutes.

In blender or food processor, purée mixture in batches and return to saucepan; stir in yogurt. Season with salt and pepper to taste. Reheat over medium-low heat being careful not to boil. Garnish each serving with a spoonful of yogurt and strips of orange or lemon rind.

Fresh Tomato Soup Provençal

MAKES 6 SERVINGS, ¾ CUP EACH

PER SERVING

50 calories
1 g fat
2 mg cholesterol
182 mg sodium

3 g protein
8 g carbohydrate

GOOD: fiber, vitamin A
EXCELLENT: vitamin C

Fresh herbs add a delightful flavor to this soup. If the herbs called for here aren't available, use other fresh herbs, such as dill instead of basil and oregano instead of thyme. For a lighter soup, omit milk and add a little more chicken stock.

3 large tomatoes, quartered (about 1¼ pound)
1 medium onion, sliced
1 clove garlic, chopped
1¼ cups chicken stock
2 tablespoons tomato paste
¼ cup chopped fresh parsley
¼ cup chopped fresh basil, or 1 teaspoon dried (see Note)
1 tablespoon chopped fresh thyme (or ½ teaspoon dried)
⅔ cup 2% milk
Salt and freshly ground pepper
Fresh thyme sprigs or basil leaves

In saucepan, combine tomatoes, onion, garlic, and chicken stock; cover and simmer for 15 minutes.

Transfer to blender or food processor; add tomato paste and process until smooth. Stir in parsley, basil, thyme, and milk; season with salt and pepper to taste.

Cover and refrigerate to serve chilled, or reheat over medium heat and serve hot. Garnish each serving with thyme sprigs or basil leaves.

Note: When substituting fresh herbs for dried, three times the amount of fresh is often used. However, with Tomato Soup Provençal I like a lot more fresh herbs than usual. The amount will also vary depending upon the type of herb and how hard you pack the fresh herbs when measuring.

Split Pea, Bean, and Barley Soup

MAKES 6 SERVINGS, 1 CUP EACH

PER SERVING

154	calories
3	g fat
0	mg cholesterol
401	mg sodium

6	g protein
27	g carbohydrate

GOOD: niacin, iron
EXCELLENT: fiber,
vitamin A

When you want something that is a light yet warming meal, this soup is just right. Serve it with toast or hot French bread and a green salad.

1 tablespoon vegetable oil
2 medium onions, chopped
½ cup dried green split peas
¼ cup dried lima beans
¼ cup pot barley
5 cups water
1 bay leaf
1 teaspoon celery seeds
1 unpeeled potato, diced
1 carrot, chopped
1 stalk celery (including leaves), chopped
1 teaspoon dried basil
1 teaspoon salt
½ teaspoon dried thyme
¼ teaspoon freshly ground pepper

In large heavy saucepan, heat oil over medium heat; add onions and cook, stirring, until tender.

Rinse split peas and lima beans, discarding any shriveled or discolored ones. Add to saucepan along with barley, water, bay leaf, and celery seeds. Bring to boil; reduce heat and simmer, covered, for 1½ hours.

Add potato, carrot, celery, basil, salt, thyme, and pepper; simmer for 30 minutes or until vegetables are tender. Remove bay leaf. If too thick, add water to reach desired thickness.

Chilled Carrot and Coriander Soup

MAKES 6 SERVINGS, ¾ CUP EACH

PER SERVING

58 calories
1 g fat
0 mg cholesterol
482 mg sodium

4 g protein
9 g carbohydrate

GOOD: fiber, niacin
EXCELLENT; vitamin A

Be sure to use tender young carrots when making this sweet, flavorful soup. Fresh coriander, also called cilantro, adds a special extra flavor; it's available at most Chinese food stores and many fruit and vegetable stores that sell fresh herbs. Coriander seeds can easily be ground in a coffee or spice grinder.

1 medium onion, chopped
1 pound young carrots, scraped and sliced
1 teaspoon ground coriander
3½ cups chicken stock
¼ cup chopped fresh coriander leaves or parsley
Salt and freshly ground pepper
Yogurt or light sour cream, sunflower seeds, coriander leaves, or parsley

In saucepan, combine onion, carrots, ground coriander, and chicken stock; cover and simmer until vegetables are tender, 15 to 20 minutes.

In food processor or blender, purée mixture until smooth. Stir in fresh coriander. Add salt and pepper to taste. Serve hot, or cover and refrigerate until cold.

Garnish each serving with spoonful of yogurt or sour cream, sprinkling of sunflower seeds and chopped fresh coriander leaves or parsley.

MICROWAVE METHOD: In microwave-safe dish, combine onion, carrots, ground coriander, and 2 tablespoons chicken stock. Cover and microwave at high (100%) power for 8 to 12 minutes or until carrots are tender. (Time will vary depending on thickness of slices and age of carrots.)

In food processor or blender, purée mixture until smooth. Stir in fresh coriander and remaining chicken stock; season with salt and pepper to taste. Reheat or refrigerate until cold.

Basic Chicken Stock

MAKES ABOUT 8 CUPS

<u>PER SERVING (1 cup)</u>

3 calories
0 g fat
3 mg cholesterol
4 mg sodium

0 g protein
0 g carbohydrate

As well as its much better flavor, the main reason for recommending homemade chicken stock is its low salt content. If you're not in the habit of making chicken stock, it can seem very time-consuming. Once you start making it you'll realize how easy it is. Any pieces of chicken can be used, even a whole chicken (giblets removed). Backs and necks are least expensive.

Remove the meat from the bones after the chicken is cooked, and use in salads like Tarragon Chicken Salad (page 64), in Curried Chicken Crêpes (page 104), Curried Chicken Croustades (page 44), sandwiches, or add to soups. Freeze homemade chicken stock in ice-cube trays or ½-cup containers and use in cooking whenever you want extra flavor without added salt. Use in soups, salad dressings, sauces, or stir-frys.

4 pounds chicken, whole or pieces
3 quarts cold water
2 carrots, chopped
2 medium onions, chopped
2 stalks celery including leaves, chopped
2 bay leaves
6 black peppercorns
2 sprigs fresh thyme (or pinch each dried thyme, basil, and marjoram)

In stockpot, combine chicken and water; bring to boil. Skim off any scum. Add carrots, onions, celery, bay leaves, peppercorns, and thyme; simmer, uncovered, for 4 hours.

Compare the Sodium in 1 Cup of:

Basic Chicken Stock	4 mg
Canned chicken broth	746 mg
Chicken broth from cube	762 mg

Sodium values are based on using stock made from a cube, powder, or canned. If using homemade chicken stock, sodium falls to 47 milligrams per serving.

Remove from heat and strain; cover and refrigerate stock until fat congeals on surface. Remove fat layer. Refrigerate for up to 2 days or freeze for longer storage.

VARIATIONS

TURKEY STOCK: Use turkey bones or carcass instead of chicken.

BEEF, VEAL, OR LAMB STOCK: Use beef, veal, or lamb bones instead of chicken. For added flavor, roast bones before simmering in water. Spread bones in roasting pan and bake in 400°F oven for 1 hour or until browned; transfer to stock-pot and continue as in Basic Chicken Stock recipe.

Salads and Dressings

My favorite salads are so simple that they hardly qualify as recipes. I love thick slices of juicy tomatoes sprinkled with fresh basil, coarsely ground pepper, and chopped chives. Other favorites are fresh, tender spinach leaves, sliced mushrooms, and balsamic vinegar, and Boston lettuce and Walnut Oil Vinaigrette.

Salad dressings are easy to make. Homemade dressings taste much better, and are less expensive and often healthier than store-bought. Commercial salad dressings tend to be high in fat, calories and sodium, while low-calorie dressings still have a significant amount of sodium. Both are generally made of poorer-quality fats and oils than you'd use at home.

For salad dressings I usually use safflower oil, olive oil, or a combination of both. For a special green salad with a delicious flavor, I love to add some walnut or other nut oil. (See page 87 for more information on oils.)

Tarragon Chicken Salad

MAKES 6 SERVINGS

This light and easy-to-make salad is lovely for a special lunch or dinner on a hot summer day. Serve on lettuce or with a green salad and chilled cooked asparagus or sliced tomatoes. Cook chicken in microwave or simmer in water and use liquid for stock (see Basic Chicken Stock, page 62).

PER SERVING

170 calories
8 g fat
61 mg cholesterol
91 mg sodium

21 g protein
4 g carbohydrate

EXCELLENT: niacin

3 cups cooked cubed chicken
1½ cups sliced celery
¼ cup chopped chives or scallions
½ cup low-fat plain yogurt
¼ cup light sour cream or light mayonnaise
1½ teaspoon dried tarragon
2 tablespoons toasted slivered almonds (see Note)
Salt and freshly ground pepper

In large bowl, combine chicken, celery, chives or scallions, yogurt, sour cream or mayonnaise, and tarragon; mix lightly. Cover and refrigerate for 1 hour or up to 24 hours. Just before serving, add almonds; season with salt and pepper to taste.

Note: To toast almonds, roast on pie plate in 350°F oven for 5 minutes or until golden.

VARIATION

CHICKEN SALAD SANDWICH DELUXE: Spread Tarragon Chicken Salad on pumpernickel, a bagel, or toasted Italian bread. Add any combination of alfalfa sprouts, watercress, or leaf lettuce and sliced tomato. Serve open-faced or top with bread.

Compare 1 Serving of Tarragon Chicken Salad Made with:

	Grams Fat	*Milligrams Sodium*	*Calories*
Yogurt (½ cup) plus sour cream (¼ cup)	8	91	170
Sour cream (¾ cup)	10	85	186
Mayonnaise (¾ cup)	27	207	331

White Bean, Radish, and Red Onion Salad

MAKES 8 SERVINGS, ½ CUP EACH

This looks attractive on red leaf lettuce. It goes well on a summer salad plate, a buffet dinner, or with barbecued hamburgers or lamb chops.

Remember this salad when you are making packed lunches. It will be a welcome change from sandwiches.

Red kidney beans or chickpeas can be used instead of white kidney beans. All are excellent sources of fiber. Instead of radishes you can use the same amount of chopped sweet green or red pepper, or tomato.

> 1 19-ounce can white kidney beans, drained
> ½ cup red onion, chopped
> 1 cup thinly sliced or diced cucumber
> ¾ cup sliced radishes
> 1 clove garlic, minced
> ½ cup chopped fresh parsley
> 3 tablespoons lemon juice or sherry vinegar
> 2 tablespoons vegetable oil
> Salt and freshly ground pepper
> Red leaf lettuce

In sieve or colander, rinse beans under cold water; drain and place in salad bowl. Add onion, cucumber, radishes, garlic, and parsley; toss to mix. Add lemon juice, oil, and salt and pepper to taste; toss. Salad can be prepared to this point, covered, and refrigerated for up to 2 days.

At serving time, arrange salad on bed of red lettuce.

Snow Pea and Red Pepper Buffet Salad

MAKES 8 SERVINGS

PER SERVING

80 calories
5 g fat
0 mg cholesterol
70 mg sodium

3 g protein
8 g carbohydrate

GOOD: fiber, niacin
EXCELLENT: vitamin C

This colorful dish is perfect for buffet meals any time of year. The salad can be prepared in advance; however to keep the snow peas' bright green color, add the dressing just before serving. To make a larger amount, double salad ingredients but use same amount of dressing.

¾ pound snow peas
2 tablespoons sesame seeds
½ pound mushrooms, sliced
1 small sweet red pepper, cut in thin strips

WALNUT ORANGE DRESSING

1 clove garlic, minced
½ cup orange juice
3 tablespoons cider or white wine vinegar
1 teaspoon granulated sugar
¼ teaspoon salt
2 tablespoons vegetable or walnut oil (see Note)
Freshly ground pepper

Top and string peas; blanch in boiling water for 2 minutes or until bright green and slightly pliable. Drain and rinse under cold water; dry thoroughly and set aside.

In ungreased skillet over medium heat, cook sesame seeds, shaking pan often, for 2 minutes or until lightly browned. Set aside.

Dressing: In food processor or bowl, combine garlic, orange juice, vinegar, sugar, and salt. With machine running or while mixing, gradually add oil.

In salad bowl, combine snow peas, mushrooms, and red pepper. Just before serving, add sesame seeds and enough dressing to lightly coat vegetables; toss to mix.

Note: Be sure to store walnut oil in refrigerator and use within a few months, as it can become rancid.

Roasted Red Pepper, Chèvre, and Arugula Salad

MAKES 5 SERVINGS

PER SERVING*

52 calories
3 g fat
10 mg cholesterol
142 mg sodium

3 g protein
4 g carbohydrate

GOOD: vitamin A
EXCELLENT: vitamin C

PER SERVING**

76 calories
6 g fat
10 mg cholesterol
117 mg sodium

3 g protein
4 g carbohydrate

*made with Ranch-Style
Buttermilk Dressing

**made with
Mustard-Garlic Vinaigrette

In the summer and early fall, look for locally grown arugula (out of season it is very expensive). This oak leaf–shaped salad green, with its nutty, peppery taste, is a delicious addition to any tossed salad. If not available, use red or green leaf lettuce and/or radicchio. Buy a soft chèvre or goat cheese, or substitute feta cheese.

> 1 sweet red pepper
> 4 cups arugula leaves, not packed
> 1 small head Boston lettuce, torn
> 1½ ounces chèvre, crumbled
> ¼ cup Ranch-Style Buttermilk Dressing (page 84) or
>   Mustard-Garlic Vinaigrette (page 83)
> Freshly ground pepper

On baking sheet, bake red pepper in 400°F oven for 20 to 30 minutes, turning once or twice, or until pepper is soft and skin is blackened and blistered (or grill until skin is blistered). Place in plastic bag, seal, and let pepper steam for 10 minutes. Scrape skin from peppers; discard seeds and cut pepper into about 1-inch long, thin strips.

In salad bowl, toss together red pepper, arugula, Boston lettuce, chèvre, and dressing; season with pepper to taste.

Classic Tuna Salad with Fresh Dill

MAKES 5 SERVINGS, ¼ CUP EACH

Use this easy-to-make tuna salad as part of a summer salad plate—served, perhaps, in a hollowed-out tomato or papaya half—for sandwich fillings, or as an hors d'oeuvre when stuffed in cherry tomatoes, mushrooms, or hollowed-out cucumber rounds. When buying canned tuna fish, choose tuna packed in water rather than tuna packed in oil because it is lower in fat. Both kinds have the

PER SERVING

86 calories
5 g fat
21 mg cholesterol
275 mg sodium

10 g protein
1 g carbohydrate

EXCELLENT: niacin

same amount of omega-3 fatty acids from fish oils. (Tuna is not usually packed in fish oil.)

1 6.5-ounce can tuna, packed in water
¼ cup diced celery
¼ cup chopped fresh dill
2 tablespoons chopped fresh parsley
2 tablespoons chopped chives or scallions
2 tablespoons light mayonnaise
2 tablespoons low-fat plain yogurt
½ teaspoon Dijon mustard

In bowl, mash tuna with juices. (If you only have tuna packed in oil, drain thoroughly and add more yogurt to taste.) Add celery, dill, parsley, chives, or scallions, mayonnaise, yogurt, and mustard; mix well.

Sliced Cucumbers with Chives, Yogurt, and Basil

MAKES 6 SERVINGS, ½ CUP EACH

PER SERVING

33 calories
2 g fat
4 mg cholesterol
101 mg sodium

1 g protein
4 g carbohydrate

Serve this cooling salad with curries, paella, seafood, or as part of a salad plate or buffet any time of year. If chives aren't available, substitute scallions, and fresh chopped dill can be used instead of basil.

1 English cucumber
¼ teaspoon salt
¼ cup light sour cream
¼ cup plain low-fat yogurt
2 tablespoons chopped chives
2 teaspoons lemon juice
1 tablespoon chopped fresh basil (or ¼ teaspoon dried)
¼ teaspoon granulated sugar
Freshly ground pepper

Peel cucumbers only if skin is tough or waxy. In food processor or by hand, thinly slice cucumbers. Place in colander and sprinkle with salt. Toss, then let stand for 30 to 40 minutes. Rinse under cold water, then pat dry.

In bowl, combine sour cream, yogurt, chives, lemon juice, basil, and sugar; mix well. Stir in cucumber; season with pepper to taste.

Serve in shallow bowl or on plate.

Italian Rice and Mozzarella Salad with Vegetables

MAKES 4 CUPS, ABOUT 6 SERVINGS

PER SERVING

187 calories
7 g fat
8 mg cholesterol
97 mg sodium

5 g protein
25 g carbohydrate

GOOD: vitamin A, vitamin C, niacin

This is a handy salad to have on hand for quick summer meals and is a great way to use up leftover cooked rice; use brown rice if you have it. It's not necessary to follow this recipe exactly; rather, use it as a guide and add whatever vegetables or cooked meats you have on hand. Chopped zucchini, cauliflower, or artichokes are nice additions.

3 cups cooked rice
¼ cup diced carrots
¼ cup diced celery
¼ cup diced sweet red or green pepper
½ cup fresh or frozen green peas
¼ cup chopped red onion
¼ cup chopped fresh parsley
¼ cup diced low-fat mozzarella
3 tablespoons cider vinegar
2 tablespoons olive or vegetable oil
2 tablespoons orange juice
1 tablespoon light mayonnaise
¼ teaspoon dried thyme (or 1 teaspoon fresh)
¼ teaspoon dried basil (or 1 teaspoon fresh)
¼ teaspoon dried oregano (or 1 teaspoon fresh)
Freshly ground pepper

In salad bowl, combine rice, carrots, celery, sweet pepper, peas, onion, parsley, and cheese; set aside. In small bowl, combine vinegar, oil, orange juice, mayonnaise, thyme, basil, and oregano; mix well. Pour over salad and toss to mix. Season with pepper to taste.

VARIATION

CURRIED RICE SALAD: Prepare Italian Rice Salad but substitute 2 teaspoons each curry powder and cumin for thyme, basil, and oregano. Add more curry to taste.

Tossed Seasonal Greens

MAKES 8 SERVINGS

PER SERVING

30 calories
2 g fat
0 mg cholesterol
13 mg sodium

1 g protein
3 g carbohydrate

GOOD: vitamin C

The best green salads are made up of an interesting and colorful variety of lettuce combined with a delicious dressing. The darker the green in lettuce, the higher the vitamins A and C content. Choose whichever lettuce is freshest in the market—leaf lettuce (red or green), romaine, Boston, butter, Bibb, mâche, chicory, radicchio, spinach, or Belgian endive. Try to choose spinach more often than lettuce for salads; it is higher in nutrients, particularly vitamins A and C, iron, and fiber. Add watercress or a seasonal fruit or vegetable, such as the suggestions which follow.

1 small head red leaf lettuce
1 small butter lettuce or romaine
1 small red onion, thinly sliced

HERB VINAIGRETTE
1 clove garlic, minced
2 tablespoons tarragon or white wine vinegar
1 teaspoon Dijon mustard
1 tablespoon olive or walnut oil
¼ cup water, orange juice, unsweetened pineapple juice,
   or chicken stock
1 scallion, minced
¼ cup chopped fresh parsley

Rinse lettuce leaves; spin dry or dry in paper or tea towels. Wrap in paper towels and refrigerate until needed.

Herb Vinaigrette: In food processor, blender, or bowl, combine garlic, vinegar, mustard, oil, and water; mix well. Stir in scallion and parsley.

(continued)

One way to reduce the fat in a salad dressing is to substitute another liquid for part of the oil. For example, in the Tossed Seasonal Greens with Herb Vinaigrette there is only 1 tablespoon oil and ¼ cup water, stock, or fruit juice.

Compare 1 Serving of:

	Grams Fat	Calories
Tossed Seasonal Greens	2	30
Seasonal greens using dressing made with ⅓ cup oil	9	93

Just before serving, tear lettuce into bite-size pieces and place in salad bowl. Separate red onion into rings; add to bowl. (Add any other seasonal salad ingredients if using.) Drizzle with dressing and toss to mix.

SEASONAL SALAD ADDITIONS

WINTER: Cherry tomatoes, sections of orange or grapefruit, sliced green apples, alfalfa sprouts, sunflower seeds

SPRING: Blanched and drained fiddlehead ferns, blanched asparagus, chives, watercress

SUMMER: Radish, cucumber, tomato, scallions, fresh basil or parsley, rose or geranium petals

FALL: Red, green, or yellow sweet peppers, cauliflower, broccoli, radicchio

Spinach Salad with Sesame Seed Dressing

MAKES 10 SERVINGS

PER SERVING

93	calories
7	g fat
0	mg cholesterol
39	mg sodium
3	g protein
6	g carbohydrate

GOOD: fiber, iron
EXCELLENT: vitamin A, vitamin C

Bright red strawberries are beautiful in this entertaining salad. In winter, use mandarin oranges, grapefruit sections, or sliced green apple instead of strawberries.

1 pound spinach
⅓ cup sliced almonds, blanched
2 cups sliced fresh strawberries

SESAME SEED DRESSING

1 tablespoon sesame seeds
¼ cup cider vinegar
3 tablespoons vegetable or walnut oil
3 tablespoons water
1 tablespoon granulated sugar
1 teaspoon poppy seeds
¼ teaspoon paprika
¼ teaspoon Worcestershire sauce
1 scallion, minced

Trim, rinse, and dry spinach; tear into bite-size pieces (you should have about 10 cups, lightly packed). Place in salad bowl and set aside.

Sprinkle almonds on baking sheet and roast in 350°F oven for 5 minutes or until golden brown; set aside.

Sesame Seed Dressing: Place sesame seeds in ungreased skillet, stir over medium-high heat until lightly browned. In bowl or jar, combine sesame seeds, vinegar, oil, water, sugar, poppy seeds, paprika, Worcestershire, and scallion; mix well.

Just before serving, pour dressing over spinach and toss well to coat. Add strawberries and almonds; toss lightly.

Carrot and Cracked-Wheat Salad with Yogurt-Herb Dressing

MAKES 4 LARGE SERVINGS

PER SERVING

152 calories
5 g fat
13 mg cholesterol
69 mg sodium

6 g protein
22 g carbohydrate

GOOD: fiber, vitamin C
EXCELLENT: vitamin A

Bulgur or cracked wheat, available at some supermarkets and most health food stores, is a nutty-tasting grain that is delicious in salads or as a vegetable. It's a good source of fiber. Save any leftover dressing and use as a dip with vegetables or as a sauce with fish.

½ cup bulgur or cracked wheat
½ cup chopped scallions
½ cup chopped celery
½ cup grated carrot
Salt and freshly ground pepper
½ head Boston or romaine lettuce

YOGURT-HERB DRESSING

½ cup low-fat plain yogurt
½ cup light sour cream
1 teaspoon Dijon mustard
1 teaspoon each dried oregano and basil (or 2 tablespoons chopped fresh)
Salt and freshly ground pepper
Sliced tomatoes, cucumber, mushrooms, and radishes, and chopped fresh parsley

In bowl, cover bulgur with very hot water. Let stand for 1 hour; drain well. Add scallions, celery, and carrot.

Yogurt-Herb Dressing: Combine yogurt, sour cream, mustard, oregano, basil, and salt and pepper to taste; mix well. Pour just enough dressing over bulgur mixture to moisten, reserving remaining dressing; toss to mix. Cover and refrigerate for at least 1 hour or up to 2 days.

Just before serving, toss salad again; add salt and pepper to taste. On large platter, arrange lettuce leaves. Mound bulgur salad in center.

Garnish with slices of tomato, cucumber, mushrooms, and radishes; sprinkle with parsley. Pass extra dressing separately.

VARIATION

FOR A MAIN-COURSE SALAD: Add slices of chicken, Classic Tuna Salad with Fresh Dill (page 68), or strips of low-fat cheese to a platter of Carrot and Cracked Wheat Salad with Yogurt-Herb Dressing. To complete it, choose from what you have on hand—such as florets of broccoli or cauliflower.

Note: To cook bulgur or cracked wheat, in saucepan combine with twice as much water and simmer for 15 minutes or until tender but not mushy.

To serve as a vegetable, add seasonings such as salt, pepper, lemon juice, or herbs, and vegetables.

To use in salads, drain well, cool, and combine with dressing and chopped vegetables.

To use in stuffings, combine with onion and herbs, such as sage and thyme.

Grated Carrot and Green Pea Salad

Green peas—fresh, frozen, or canned are an excellent source of dietary fiber. Add them to soups, stir-frys, and pasta dishes or this salad. (If you are using canned peas, look for the low-sodium type since the regular ones are high in sodium.)

For a quick, easy high-fiber salad combine cooked frozen green peas, grated carrot, diced celery, chopped scallion, and fresh parsley. Mix equal parts of light sour cream and yogurt, add ½ teaspoon or more Dijon mustard, and freshly ground pepper to taste; mix lightly with carrot mixture.

Sliced water chestnuts or artichoke hearts are good additions.

Danish Potato Salad with Dill

MAKES 6 SERVINGS, ¾ CUP EACH

PER SERVING

169 calories
4 g fat
6 mg cholesterol
225 mg sodium

5 g protein
31 g carbohydrate

GOOD: fiber, niacin
EXCELLENT: vitamin C

Dijon mustard and fresh dill add extra flavor to this summer salad. If fresh dill isn't available, use 1 teaspoon dried dillweed and ½ cup chopped fresh parsley. The potatoes, including the skin, are a good source of fiber. Without the skin, though, the amount of fiber is reduced by half.

2 pounds potatoes
1 cup low-fat plain yogurt
3 tablespoons light mayonnaise
¼ cup minced scallion
1 teaspoon curry powder
1 teaspoon Dijon mustard
½ teaspoon salt
⅓ cup chopped fresh dill
Freshly ground pepper

Watercress (optional)

Scrub potatoes and cook in large pot of boiling water until tender. Drain and let cool slightly; peel, only if skins are tough, and cut into thin slices.

In bowl, mix together yogurt, mayonnaise, scallion, curry powder, mustard, and salt. Add potatoes, dill, and pepper to taste; stir gently. Garnish each serving with watercress (if using).

Compare a ¾-Cup Serving of Salad Made with:

	Grams Fat	Milligrams Cholesterol	Milligrams Sodium	Calories
Low-fat plain yogurt (plus 3 tablespoons light mayonnaise)	4	6	291	169
Light mayonnaise	16	24	631	269
Mayonnaise	33	25	407	420

Curried Vermicelli Noodle Salad

MAKES 10 SERVINGS

PER SERVING

200 calories
10 g fat
0 mg cholesterol
117 mg sodium

6 g protein
25 g carbohydrate

GOOD: fiber, vitamin C, niacin, iron

This salad is easy to prepare, especially in large quantities, and is perfect for buffets or hot-weather dining. Vermicelli, very thin noodles, are available in the pasta section of most supermarkets. I prefer rice vermicelli, sometimes called rice sticks, which are clear, very thin noodles often sold in the Chinese food section of the supermarket. If unavailable, use 4 cups cooked thin noodles.

½ pound vermicelli noodles
½ cup pine nuts
1 cup coarsely chopped fresh parsley

CURRY DRESSING

1 cup pearl onions
¼ cup olive oil
2 teaspoons curry powder
1½ teaspoons ground coriander
½ teaspoon ground cardamom
¼ teaspoon ground turmeric
½ teaspoon minced garlic
1½ cups beef or chicken stock
½ cup golden raisins

In large pot of boiling water, cook vermicelli according to package directions or for 3 to 5 minutes, just until al dente (tender but firm). Don't overcook because noodles become mushy. Rinse under cold water, drain well, and set aside.

On a pie plate, bake pine nuts in 350°F oven for 5 minutes or until golden. Set aside.

Curry dressing: In saucepan of boiling water, blanch pearl onions for 3 minutes; drain. Let cool slightly, then peel.

In saucepan, heat oil over medium heat. Add curry powder, coriander, cardamom, and turmeric; cook for 3 minutes, stirring occasionally. Add garlic, pearl onions, stock, and raisins. Simmer for 5 minutes or until onions are tender. Remove from heat and let cool.

Toss noodles with dressing. (Salad can be covered and refrigerated for up to 1 day.) Just before serving, add pine nuts and parsley; toss well.

Shell Pasta Salad with Salmon and Green Beans

MAKES 8 SERVINGS

PER SERVING

241 calories
7 g fat
22 mg cholesterol
108 mg sodium

18 g protein
24 g carbohydrate

GOOD: iron
EXCELLENT: niacin

This is one of my favorite pasta salads. Salmon is an excellent source of omega-3 polyunsaturated fatty acids, which some studies have found help to lower blood pressure and to reduce the risk of heart disease. And fresh dill adds a wonderful flavor. Use fresh basil to taste if dill's not available. In a pinch, use 1 teaspoon dried basil or dill plus ½ cup finely chopped fresh parsley.

½ pound small pasta shells or macaroni
¼ pound green beans
½ cup low-fat cottage cheese
½ cup low-fat plain yogurt
1 tablespoon fresh lemon juice
½ cup coarsely chopped fresh dill
2 7½-ounce cans salmon, drained
Freshly ground pepper
Boston or red leaf lettuce

In large pot of boiling water, cook pasta until al dente (tender but firm). Drain and rinse under cold water; drain again and set aside.

Cut green beans into 1½-inch lengths and blanch in boiling water for 2 minutes. Drain and rinse under cold water; drain thoroughly and set aside.

In food processor or through sieve, purée cottage cheese. Combine with yogurt and lemon juice; mix well.

In bowl, combine pasta, green beans, yogurt mixture, and dill; stir to mix. Discard skin from salmon and break into chunks; add to salad and stir gently to mix. Add pepper to taste. Line serving plates with lettuce leaves and mound salad on top.

Tortellini with Tuna Salad

MAKES 8 SERVINGS, ¾ CUP EACH

PER SERVING

278 calories
6 g fat
13 mg cholesterol
172 mg sodium

16 g protein
40 g carbohydrate

GOOD: fiber, iron
EXCELLENT: vitamin C,
niacin

Pasta salads are great for lunch, picnics, buffets, and light suppers. You don't really need a recipe; just add any of the usual salad ingredients, such as cooked or raw vegetables (except for lettuces), to cooked noodles or any type of pasta and toss with a dressing.

¾ pound tortellini, meat or cheese
1 cup fresh or frozen peas
½ sweet red pepper, diced
½ cup chopped red onion
1 6.5 ounce can tuna, packed in water, drained
1 14-ounce can unmarinated artichoke hearts, drained and quartered (optional)
½ cup chopped fresh parsley
¼ cup chopped fresh basil (or 2 teaspoons dried)

DRESSING

1 clove garlic, minced
1 teaspoon Dijon mustard
3 tablespoons lemon juice or white wine vinegar
¼ cup orange juice
3 tablespoons olive oil
¼ cup low-fat plain yogurt
¼ cup finely chopped fresh basil (see Note)
Salt and freshly ground pepper

In large pot of boiling water, cook tortellini until al dente (tender but firm); drain and rinse under cold water. Drain thoroughly. Thaw peas under cold water.

In salad bowl, combine pasta, peas, sweet pepper, onion, tuna, artichokes (if using), parsley, and basil; toss lightly to mix.

Dressing: In blender, food processor or bowl, combine garlic, mustard, lemon and orange juice; mix well. With machine running or while mixing, gradually add oil. Add yogurt, basil, and salt and pepper to taste; mix. Pour over salad and toss to mix. Cover and refrigerate for up to 2 days.

Note: If fresh basil isn't available, use 1 teaspoon dried plus ½ cup chopped fresh parsley.

Pasta and Fresh Vegetable Salad

MAKES 10 SERVINGS

PER SERVING

165 calories
6 g fat
0 mg cholesterol
77 mg sodium

5 g protein
24 g carbohydrate

EXCELLENT: vitamin A, vitamin C, fiber

This is the kind of salad I often make during the summer using whatever vegetables I have on hand. It's great with cold meats, salmon or tuna salad, poached fish, or chicken and sliced tomatoes. It keeps well for a few days in the refrigerator and is fine for lunches or picnics.

½ pound macaroni, rotini, or any pasta (about 3 cups)
1 sweet green pepper, chopped
4 small carrots, thinly sliced
4 scallions, chopped
6 radishes, sliced
½ head cauliflower, cut in small florets
1 cup chopped fresh parsley

ITALIAN VINAIGRETTE DRESSING

¼ cup cider or tarragon vinegar
¼ cup vegetable oil
¼ cup orange juice
2 teaspoons Dijon mustard
1 tablespoon grated Parmesan cheese
1 clove garlic, minced
1 teaspoon dried basil
1 teaspoon dried oregano
¼ teaspoon salt
¼ teaspoon freshly ground pepper

In large pot of boiling water, cook pasta until al dente (tender but firm). Drain and rinse under cold water; drain thoroughly.

In large bowl, combine cooked pasta, green pepper, carrots, scallions, radishes, cauliflower, and parsley.

Italian Vinaigrette Dressing: In bowl or food processor, combine vinegar, oil, orange juice, mustard, cheese, garlic, basil, oregano, salt, and pepper; mix well. Pour over salad and toss to mix. Cover and refrigerate for up to 2 days.

Alfresco Summer Supper (22% of Calories from Fat):

	Grams Fat	Calories
Chilled Cucumber-Chive Soup (page 53)	4	85
Pasta and Fresh Vegetable Salad (page 80)	6	165
Sliced cold chicken breast (no skin) (4 ounces)	4	187
Whole-wheat rolls	2	156
1 teaspoon margarine	4	33
Sliced peaches and blueberries	0	90
Milk (skim, 8 ounces)	0	90
TOTALS	20	806

Fettuccine and Mussel Salad

MAKES 8 SERVINGS

PER SERVING

308 calories
8 g fat
25 mg cholesterol
178 mg sodium

15 g protein
43 g carbohydrate

GOOD: iron
EXCELLENT: fiber,
vitamin C, niacin

This easy-to-make salad is delicious with any kind of cooked pasta, from linguine to spaghetti noodles to shells. Serve as a first course, with soup for a light dinner, or as part of a buffet supper. When cooking the pasta for dinner, cook extra to use another day in a salad. Rinse the cooked pasta under cold water to prevent it sticking together.

¾ pound fettuccine
3 pounds mussels (in shells)
¼ cup water
1½ cups frozen peas, thawed
1 sweet red or green pepper, chopped
4 scallions, chopped
1 cup chopped fresh parsley
¼ cup lemon juice
¼ cup vegetable or olive oil
2 cloves garlic, minced
Salt and freshly ground pepper

In large pot of boiling water, cook fettuccine until al dente (tender but firm). Drain and rinse under cold water; drain thoroughly and set aside. You should have about 5 cups.

(continued)

Scrub mussels under cold running water and remove any hairy beards. Discard any that do not close when tapped. In large heavy saucepan, combine water and mussels. Cover and bring to boil over high heat; reduce heat and simmer for 5 to 8 minutes or until mussels open. Discard any that do not open. Let cool; reserve ½ cup cooking liquid and remove meat from shells. Discard shells.

In large salad bowl, combine fettuccine, mussels, peas, sweet pepper, scallions, and parsley.

In small bowl or food processor, combine reserved mussel cooking liquid, lemon juice, oil, and garlic; mix well. Pour over pasta mixture and toss to mix. Season with salt and pepper to taste. Cover and refrigerate until chilled.

Fresh Tomato-Chive Dressing

MAKES 2 CUPS

PER SERVING
(1 tablespoon)

12 calories
1 g fat
1 mg cholesterol
17 mg sodium

0 g protein
0 g carbohydrate

This light dressing is particularly good on appetizer salads or spooned over cold cooked vegetables. In order to get the most fiber, don't peel or seed tomatoes. If you prepare the dressing in advance, add cheese just before serving.

2 medium tomatoes, diced
2 tablespoons cider or white wine vinegar
2 tablespoons vegetable oil
2 teaspoons Dijon mustard
1 clove garlic, minced (optional)
3 tablespoons chopped chives or scallion
Freshly ground pepper
¼ cup crumbled feta cheese

In small bowl, combine tomatoes, vinegar, oil, mustard, garlic (if using), chives, and pepper to taste; mix well. Cover and refrigerate for up to 3 days. Just before serving, stir in cheese.

Mustard-Garlic Vinaigrette

MAKES ABOUT ⅔ CUP

PER SERVING
(1 tablespoon)

50 calories
 5 g fat
 0 mg cholesterol
17 mg sodium

 0 g protein
0.5 g carbohydrate

By adding water to reduce the fat, and mustard and garlic to increase the flavor, we have a lower-calorie, yet flavorful, dressing.

1 clove garlic, minced
2 teaspoons Dijon mustard
2 tablespoons lemon juice
¼ cup water
½ teaspoon granulated sugar
¼ cup vegetable oil
1 teaspoon grated Parmesan cheese
Freshly ground pepper

In blender, food processor, or mixing bowl, combine garlic, mustard, lemon juice, water, and sugar; mix well. With machine running or while mixing, gradually add oil. Add Parmesan; season with pepper to taste.

VARIATION

WALNUT OIL VINAIGRETTE: Prepare Mustard-Garlic Vinaigrette but substitute walnut oil for vegetable oil and omit Parmesan cheese.

Compare 1 Tablespoon of:

	Grams Fat	Calories
Mustard-Garlic Vinaigrette	5	50
Standard vinaigrette recipe (4 parts oil; 1 part vinegar)	10	95

Ranch-Style Buttermilk Dressing

MAKES 1⅓ CUPS

PER SERVING
(1 tablespoon)

17 calories
1 g fat
2 mg cholesterol
47 mg sodium

0.5 g protein
1 g carbohydrate

Even though this dressing contains mayonnaise, it is much lower in fat and calories than most creamy dressings. Use it with tossed green salads, coleslaw, or chilled cooked vegetables.

1 cup buttermilk
⅓ cup light mayonnaise
1 small clove garlic, minced
½ teaspoon granulated sugar
½ teaspoon dried dillweed
¼ teaspoon dry mustard
Pinch freshly ground pepper
2 tablespoons chopped fresh parsley

In small bowl or jar, combine buttermilk, mayonnaise, garlic, sugar, dillweed, mustard, pepper, and parsley; mix well. Cover and refrigerate for up to 4 days.

VARIATIONS

BLUE-CHEESE DRESSING: Add 2 tablespoons crumbled blue cheese.

FRESH HERBS: Add 2 tablespoons chopped fresh dill, or 1 tablespoon chopped fresh basil, or 2 teaspoons chopped fresh tarragon.

WATERCRESS: Add ¼ cup chopped watercress leaves.

SCALLION OR CHIVE: Add 2 tablespoons chopped scallion or chives (or to taste).

CELERY: Add 1 teaspoon celery seed and 2 tablespoons chopped celery leaves.

CUMIN: Add ½ teaspoon dried ground cumin.

CURRY: Add 1 teaspoon curry powder.

TOMATO: Add 2 tablespoons tomato paste.

Yogurt-Orange Dressing

MAKES ABOUT 1 CUP

PER SERVING
(2 tablespoons)

55 calories
4 g fat
1 mg cholesterol
14 mg sodium

1 g protein
5 g carbohydrate

This quick and easy dressing is delicious with a fruit salad.

⅔ cup low-fat plain yogurt
2 tablespoons vegetable oil
2 tablespoons frozen orange-juice concentrate
1 tablespoon packed brown sugar
1 teaspoon grated orange rind

In small bowl, combine yogurt, oil, orange juice, sugar, and orange rind; mix thoroughly. Cover and refrigerate for up to 2 days.

Creamy Herb Dressing

MAKES ½ CUP

PER 2-TABLESPOON
SERVING (made with
cottage cheese)

22 calories
0.5 g fat
2 mg cholesterol
10 mg sodium

3 g protein
2 g carbohydrate

Use this light yet creamy dressing on pasta salads, vegetable salads, and lettuce salads. Because the flavors develop upon standing, if you want to use the dressing immediately increase the mustard, oregano, and basil to ½ teaspoon each or more to taste.

¼ cup low-fat cottage cheese or light sour cream
¼ cup low-fat plain yogurt
¼ teaspoon Dijon mustard
¼ teaspoon dried oregano (or 1 tablespoon chopped fresh)
¼ teaspoon dried basil (or 1 tablespoon chopped fresh)
Salt and freshly ground pepper

In blender or food processor, process cottage cheese until smooth. Add yogurt, mustard, oregano, and basil. Add salt and pepper to taste; process to mix. Cover and refrigerate for 4 hours or up to 3 days.

Hidden Fat

Salads aren't always a light meal when it comes to considering the fat content. Lunch of a roll and salad can add up to more than half the amount of fat you need in a day.

The fat content in salads comes mainly from the oil in the dressing and can be very deceptive. The amount of oil in the Tomato, Broccoli, and Pasta Salad (page 130) is at least half the amount that you would find in most salad recipes of this type. And, even with a reduced amount of oil and a small amount of low-fat cheese, the fat content is higher than some of the meat, chicken, and fish recipes in this book. A tossed green salad with 2 tablespoons of a standard oil-and-vinegar dressing per serving has 20 grams of fat. This is ⅓ the fat most women require in a day.

The amount of dressing (2 tablespoons) used in the following chart is a conservative amount of salad dressing. If you like a lot of dressing, you could easily be using double this amount. If this is the case you could be eating 30 grams of fat just in a salad, which is about half the daily fat requirement for someone consuming 1,800 calories a day.

If you spread your bread or roll with 1 tablespoon butter or margarine you are adding another 11 grams of fat.

Next time you make a salad at home or at a salad bar estimate how much dressing you use and compare two tablespoons (a portion in a small ladle or a heaping dessert spoonful) with:

	Grams Fat	Milligrams Sodium	Calories
Mustard-Garlic Vinaigrette (page 83)	10	34	100
Standard home vinaigrette	20	125*	190
Italian (store-bought)	16	570	160
Italian Reduced Calorie (store-bought)	1	420	12
Ranch-Style Buttermilk Dressing (page 84)	2	94	34
Ranch Style (store-bought)	14	250	140
Blue Cheese (page 84)	4	132	44
Blue cheese (store-bought)	14	306	142
Light Blue Cheese (store-bought)	6	390	80
Creamy Herb Dressing (page 85)	1	10	22
Mayonnaise-type dressing (store-bought)	12	164	120

*Based on ½ teaspoon salt per 1 cup dressing.

WAYS TO REDUCE FAT IN SALAD DRESSINGS

OIL-BASED DRESSING: Replace half of the oil you usually use with water, fruit juice, or chicken stock.

MAYONNAISE OR SOUR CREAM–BASED DRESSING: You can reduce the fat in your diet considerably by using yogurt instead of mayonnaise and sour cream in salads. If you're used to all mayonnaise or sour cream, make the change gradually by using half mayonnaise or sour cream and half yogurt, gradually changing to nearly all yogurt. Or, use light mayonnaise or a mixture of half light mayonnaise and either low-fat plain yogurt or light sour cream.

Note: Light sour cream has half the fat of regular sour cream. If you use a small amount of dressing, it isn't going to make a great deal of difference in this recipe whether you use cottage cheese or light sour cream—either is much lower in fat than oil. One-quarter cup dressing made with sour cream has 4 grams fat; light sour cream has 2 grams fat; cottage cheese has 1 gram fat.

CHOOSING AN OIL FOR SALAD DRESSINGS

Oils are made up of a combination of different fats; some are much more saturated than others. The flavor should also be considered when choosing an oil.

Choose: Safflower, walnut, olive, sunflower, soybean, corn, canola (has the least amount of saturated fat), sesame (strong flavor, so use in small amounts).

Sesame oil has a distinct, strong nutty flavor and is used sparingly, usually combined with another oil as a flavoring to a stir-fry or salad dressing.

Because walnut and olive oils are heavier you can use a smaller amount and often combine them with another oil (such as safflower); these oils are nice for salads. I find corn oil not appealing for salads; it is better for cooking.

Avoid: Coconut oil (high in saturated fat), palm oil (high in saturated fat), or vegetable oil (when the kind of oil isn't stated on a container, it is likely to be palm or coconut).

WHEN MAKING SALADS OR CHOOSING FROM A SALAD BAR

High-fat foods to avoid or choose less of:

- most important is salad dressing—don't use any more than absolutely necessary
- avocado
- bacon bits
- olives
- high-fat cheese (cheddar, blue cheese)
- nuts

High-sodium foods to avoid or choose less of:

- anchovies
- olives
- salted or prepared croutons
- bacon bits

High-cholesterol foods to avoid or choose less of:

- egg yolks

Note: If salad is the main course, a certain amount of protein foods, such as cheese or egg, is acceptable.

Meat and Poultry

People often tell me about how healthfully they are eating and how their diet has changed over the years. One of the first things they say is that they don't eat red meat anymore.

Red meat has been given bad press; there is no reason to eliminate it from your diet completely. Meat is an important source of complete protein, useable iron, B vitamins (thiamin, niacin, and B_{12}) and minerals, but it also contains a high proportion of saturated fats. For this reason, the selection of meats, the size of the servings, and the method of cooking become very important.

Compare the Fat in One Serving of:

12 ounces rib roast, including fat: (244 milligrams cholesterol)	72 g
6 ounces roast beef, including fat	36 g
1 tablespoon butter or margarine (for a roll)	11 g
2 tablespoons mayonnaise (for a salad)	22 g
TOTAL	69 g
3 ounces top round steak (lean only)	5 g
1 teaspoon butter or margarine (for a roll)	4 g
1 tablespoon light mayonnaise (for a salad)	5 g
TOTAL	14 g

Recommended Cuts

BEEF: round, flank, sirloin-tip roast, sirloin steak (if well trimmed), tenderloin, and rump

Compare These Beef Cuts and Portion Sizes:

	3-ounce Portion			8-ounce Portion		
	Grams Fat	Milligrams Cholesterol	Calories	Grams Fat	Milligrams Cholesterol	Calories
Rib roast, roasted lean and fat	18	61	256	48	163	683
Rib roast, roasted lean only	10	60	196	27	160	523
Steak inside (top) round (lean and fat)	5	57	154	13	152	411
Steak inside (top) round (lean only)	3	57	144	8	152	384

PORK: choose lean cuts or those easy to trim, loin roast, tenderloin and loin chops, pork steaks (choose ham and bacon less often because of their high salt and fat content)

LAMB: cuts from leg and loin section

VEAL: lower in fat than beef and other red meats but slightly higher in cholesterol; all cuts are lean except those from the breast, i.e., stewing veal

Which meat has the most fat? Whether or not beef has more fat than pork is not really the issue. *What is most important is the kind of cut you buy, the way you cook it, and the amount you eat.* A lean cut of pork has less fat than a prime rib roast. Pork spareribs have more fat than top round steak. Try to choose a lean cut, remove all visible fat, cook it without adding any fat—and eat only one serving.

If you do buy high-fat cuts, then choose a cooking method with which you can pour off the fat. For example, if you buy regular ground beef, use it in spaghetti sauce so that you can brown the meat first then pour off the fat before adding other ingredients. If you use stewing veal, make the dish a day ahead and refrigerate. The next day you can easily remove the fat that will have hardened on top of the dish.

When possible, choose lean or medium ground beef. Ground pork varies in fat content and often isn't very different from regular ground beef. When compared with beef, pork looks fattier because the meat is only ground once; beef is ground twice so it is more uniform in color.

Amount to Serve

How do I know what a 3- or 4-ounce portion of meat is? The easiest way is to *buy* only that much. For example, if you are cooking for 4 people, buy only 1 pound of ground meat, stewing beef, pork chops, or boneless chicken breasts. For 4 servings, buy about 1½ pounds of bone-in meats, 2 pounds of chicken.

When you are cooking roasts or bone-in cuts it is more difficult to judge amounts; for a rough estimate, consider a 3½-ounce serving of meat to be about the size of a deck of playing cards. Many adults, especially men, are used to larger meat portions than 3 ounces.

How to make the recommended serving size of meat, i.e., 3 ounces, not look skimpy:
· The meat portion should only take up one-fourth of the dinner plate. Increase the amount and variety of vegetables you serve.
· Slice meat thinly, it will look like more. For example 3 ounces of thinly sliced flank steak will look as if there is more meat than the same weight of sirloin steak in a single piece 1-inch thick.
· Choose dishes in which meat is combined with vegetables, such as stews, stir-frys, and casseroles.
· Serve as a sauce over pasta—see Spaghetti Sauce recipes (page 223).
· Guide to Good Eating recommends that we have two 2-ounce servings of meat or meat alternatives a day. If one serving is small, for example a thin slice of meat in a sandwich at lunch, then the serving size at dinner can be larger.

Selecting Poultry

Turkey, chicken, Cornish game hens, quail, or partridge are good choices. Avoid self-basting turkeys because they are injected with saturated fats. Duck and goose are very high in fat. Removing the skin from poultry significantly reduces fat content.

Cooking Methods to Reduce Fat

· Avoid frying meats—instead, grill, broil, stew, stir-fry, braise, or roast on a rack.
· If you are going to fry, use a nonstick skillet and use as little high-polyunsaturated margarine or vegetable (not palm or co-conut) oil as possible.
· Make a stew one day in advance; cover and refrigerate. When cold, remove fat that has solidified on top.

Family Favorite Shepherd's Pie

MAKES 5 SERVINGS

PER SERVING

324 calories
 12 g fat
 60 mg cholesterol
 95 mg sodium

 20 g protein
 35 g carbohydrate

GOOD: fiber, iron
EXCELLENT: vitamin A,
vitamin C, thiamin,
niacin

My mother always made shepherd's pie from leftover Sunday roast beef, gravy, and mashed potatoes. However, since we seldom have roasts, I make shepherd's pie using ground meat—either beef, pork, or lamb. If you don't have leftover mashed potatoes, boil 5 medium potatoes; drain and mash with milk.

1 pound very lean ground beef, pork, or lamb, or a combination
    of these
2 medium onions, chopped
2 cloves garlic, minced
1 carrot, minced (optional)
⅓ cup tomato paste (see Note)
⅔ cup water
1 teaspoon dried thyme
2 teaspoons Worcestershire sauce
Freshly ground pepper
Paprika
2 cups mashed potatoes

In skillet over medium heat, cook beef, stirring to break up meat, until brown; pour off fat. Add onions, garlic, and carrot (if using); cook until tender. Add tomato paste, water, thyme, Worcestershire sauce, and pepper to taste. Simmer for 5 minutes, stirring up any brown bits on bottom of pan.

Spoon meat mixture into 8-cup baking or microwave-safe dish; spread mashed potatoes evenly on top. Sprinkle with paprika to taste. Bake in 375°F oven for 35 minutes or until heated through, or microwave at high (100%) power for 9 minutes.

Note: This dish is equally good made with 1 8-ounce can tomato sauce instead of tomato paste and water, but it is higher in sodium.

Compare the Sodium in One Serving of Shepherd's Pie:

Made with tomato paste plus water	95 mg
Made with tomato sauce	342 mg

Beef and Tomato Stir-Fry

MAKES 4 SERVINGS

Make this easy, tasty dish in the summer and fall when garden-fresh tomatoes are plentiful. Serve over rice or noodles. In winter substitute green peppers, broccoli, or snow peas instead of tomatoes and cook until crisp-tender, adding water if necessary to prevent burning.

¾ pound top round or flank steak
2 tablespoons cornstarch
2 tablespoons sherry
1 tablespoon low-sodium soy sauce
2 tablespoons vegetable oil
1 medium onion, thinly sliced
2 cloves garlic, minced
4 tomatoes, cut in wedges
4 scallions, cut in thin 2-inch-long strips

Cut beef across the grain into thin strips; cut strips into 2-inch lengths. In bowl, combine cornstarch, sherry, and soy sauce; mix until smooth. Add beef and toss to coat.

In wok or nonstick skillet, heat oil over high heat. Add beef and stir-fry for 2 minutes; add onion and stir-fry for 1 minute or until beef is browned. Add garlic and tomatoes; stir-fry until tomatoes are heated through, 1 to 2 minutes. Stir in scallions and serve immediately.

Ginger-Garlic Marinated Flank Steak

MAKES 4 SERVINGS

This is a favorite in our household. If I'm organized, I try to marinate it early in the day. The steak can marinate for two days and, once cooked, it is good hot or cold. (In other words, if no one arrives home for dinner—your kids get invited out and your husband has to work late—you can cook it the next day. Or, if only one person shows up, you can cook it and serve the rest the next

PER SERVING (using either marinade)

134	calories
4	g fat
49	mg cholesterol
38	mg sodium
23	g protein
1	g carbohydrate

GOOD: iron
EXCELLENT: niacin

day.) If you're cooking for two, have it hot the first night and cold the second.

> 1 pound flank steak
> Ginger-Garlic Marinade (page 72) or Italian Herb Marinade (page 73)

Lightly score (cut) beef about ⅛-inch deep in diagonal slashes. Place in shallow dish. Pour marinade over; cover and refrigerate for at least 2, or up to 48 hours, turning meat once or twice.

Remove meat from marinade and broil or grill for 4 to 5 minutes on each side or until desired doneness. Cut diagonally across the grain into thin slices. Serve hot or cold.

Note: If you're cooking for one, buy a flank steak and cut it into three portions. Use one portion for the Ginger-Garlic Marinated Flank Steak (page 93), one for the Beef and Tomato Stir-Fry (page 93), and one for the Stir-Fry for One (page 239). Flank steak is one of the leanest cuts of beef. It's delicious when marinated, then grilled or broiled and cut diagonally across the grain into thin slices. When served this way, it's also an economical cut of beef because 1 pound will serve 4 people. (One pound of porterhouse steak of the same thickness looks very skimpy when divided into four portions.)

Ginger-Garlic Marinade

Most marinade recipes call for more oil than necessary. Even though the marinade is poured off before cooking, I recommend keeping the oil at a minimum. Use this marinade with fish, shrimp, chicken, turkey, beef, pork, or lamb.

> 2 tablespoons rice or cider vinegar
> 2 tablespoons water
> 1 tablespoon vegetable oil
> 1 tablespoon grated fresh gingerroot (or 1 teaspoon ground ginger)
> 1 teaspoon granulated sugar
> 1 clove garlic, minced

Combine vinegar, water, oil, ginger, sugar, and garlic; mix well. Makes about ⅓ cup, enough for a 1-pound steak.

Italian Herb Marinade

Use with beef, pork, lamb, chicken, or turkey.

> ¼ cup red wine vinegar
> 1 tablespoon vegetable oil
> 2 tablespoons chopped fresh parsley
> 1 teaspoon dried marjoram or oregano (or 1 tablespoon chopped fresh)
> 1 teaspoon dried thyme (or 1 tablespoon chopped fresh)
> 1 bay leaf, crumbled
> 1 small onion, minced
> 2 cloves garlic, minced
> Freshly ground pepper

In small bowl mix together vinegar, oil, parsley, marjoram, thyme, bay leaf, onion, garlic, and pepper to taste. Makes about ⅓ cup, enough for one 1-pound steak.

Easy Oven Beef and Vegetable Stew

MAKES 8 SERVINGS

This is the easiest stew to make and tastes wonderful. Make it on the weekend and you'll probably have enough left over for a meal during the week. Or make it during the week to transport to ski cabin or cottage. The flavor of a stew is usually better the second day. Make it a day in advance and refrigerate. Any fat will solidify on top and can easily be removed.

(continued)

PER SERVING

235 calories
5 g fat
43 mg cholesterol
325 mg sodium

20 g protein
27 g carbohydrate

GOOD: fiber, iron
EXCELLENT: vitamin A,
vitamin C, niacin

1½ pounds beef round or rump, cut into cubes
¼ cup all-purpose flour
6 small onions
2 large potatoes, peeled or unpeeled, cut in chunks
    (1 pound)
3 large carrots, cut in chunks
3 cloves garlic, minced
2 cups diced turnip
3 cups water
1¼ cups beef stock or canned bouillon
1 8-ounce can tomato sauce (see Note)
1 teaspoon dried thyme
½ teaspoon dried oregano
¼ teaspoon freshly ground pepper
1 bay leaf
½ teaspoon grated orange rind (optional)

Remove all visible fat from beef; cut beef into 1-inch cubes.

In large casserole or Dutch oven, toss beef with flour. Add onions, potatoes, carrots, garlic, turnip, water, beef stock, tomato sauce, thyme, oregano, pepper, bay leaf, and orange rind; stir to mix.

Bake, covered, in 325°F oven for 3 hours, stirring occasionally (if you remember). Remove bay leaf.

Note: If you are on a sodium-restricted diet, substitute tomato paste and water for the tomato sauce and use homemade or low-sodium beef stock (117 mg sodium is from stock).

Compare the Sodium in One Serving of:

Easy Oven Beef and Vegetable Stew	325
Canned beef and vegetable stew	1,064

Beef and Pasta Casserole for a Crowd

MAKES 14 SERVINGS

PER SERVING

378 calories
13 g fat
67 mg cholesterol
295 mg sodium

29 g protein
36 g carbohydrate

GOOD: fiber, riboflavin
EXCELLENT: vitamin A,
vitamin C, niacin,
calcium, iron

This is the type of dish to serve to a crowd at the cottage or ski cabin. It's also perfect to take to a potluck supper or for a teenager's party.

1 pound short pasta (penne, fusilli, rotini)
1 teaspoon vegetable oil
2 pounds very lean ground beef
3 medium onions, finely chopped
2 cloves garlic, minced
1/2 pound mushrooms, sliced
2 stalks celery, sliced
1 sweet green pepper, chopped
1 13-ounce can tomato paste
1 quart water
1 teaspoon dried oregano
1 teaspoon dried basil
1/4 cup chopped fresh parsley
1 10-ounce package fresh spinach, rinsed, cooked, drained, and chopped
1 pound low-fat mozzarella cheese, cut in small cubes
Salt and freshly ground pepper
1 cup fresh bread crumbs
1/2 cup freshly grated Parmesan cheese

In large pot of boiling water, cook pasta until al dente (tender but firm), about 10 minutes or according to package directions. Drain and rinse under cold running water; drain and set aside.

In large nonstick skillet or Dutch oven, heat oil over medium heat. Add beef, onions, and garlic; cook, stirring, for a few minutes or until beef is no longer pink. Drain off fat. Add mushrooms, celery, and green pepper; cook for 5 minutes, stirring occasionally. Stir in tomato paste, water, oregano, basil, and parsley; simmer, covered, for 30 minutes.

Combine meat sauce, spinach, pasta, and mozzarella cheese; season to taste with salt and pepper. Spoon into lightly greased 4-quart casserole. Sprinkle with bread crumbs, then Parmesan. The recipe may be prepared up to 2 days in advance, covered, and refrigerated. Remove from refrigerator 1 hour before baking. Bake, uncovered, in 350°F oven for 45 minutes or until bubbly.

Grilled Butterflied Leg of Lamb with Lemon and Garlic

MAKES 8 SERVINGS

PER SERVING*

196 calories
10 g fat
88 mg cholesterol
63 mg sodium

26 g protein
1 g carbohydrate

GOOD: iron
EXCELLENT: niacin

*based on using only lean part of lamb

I love lamb, and this is one of my favorite ways to cook it. I either barbecue or broil this cut; when it's cooked medium-rare, lamb is delicious cold the next day.

3 cloves garlic, minced
½ teaspoon grated lemon rind
½ teaspoon dried crushed rosemary (or 1 tablespoon chopped fresh)
¼ teaspoon freshly ground pepper
2 tablespoons lemon juice
2 tablespoons olive or vegetable oil
1 3-pound boned and butterflied leg of lamb (see Note)

In small bowl or food processor, combine garlic, lemon rind, rosemary, pepper, and lemon juice. Gradually pour in oil and mix until blended.

Trim visible fat from lamb. Place lamb in shallow dish; pour marinade over, turning to coat both sides. Cover and let stand at room temperature for 1 to 2 hours or refrigerate overnight (bring to room temperature before cooking).

Remove lamb from marinade, reserving marinade. On greased grill 4 inches from hot coals (at high setting if a gas grill), or under broiler, grill or broil lamb for 15 minutes, brushing with marinade several times. Turn and cook for 12 minutes longer or until meat is pink inside.

Remove from heat and let stand for 10 minutes. To serve, slice thinly across the grain.

Compare One Serving of:

Grilled Lamb with Lemon and Garlic Using:	Grams Fat	Calories
Lamb leg, lean and fat, untrimmed	25	354
Lamb leg, lean only, trimmed after slicing	10	196

Note: Butterflied legs of lamb are boned then cut open, but not all the way through, so the meat can be spread apart like two butterfly wings. Be sure to trim all fat from lamb.

Lamb Loins with Rosemary and Peppercorns

MAKES 4 SERVINGS

PER SERVING (using lamb loins)

170 calories
7 g fat
90 mg cholesterol
93 mg sodium

25 g protein
0 g carbohydrate

GOOD: iron
EXCELLENT: niacin

Fork-tender lamb loins, often available in the frozen food section of the supermarket, are a special treat and one of the leanest cuts of lamb. Lamb loins cook quickly and are best served rare or medium-rare. Be careful not to overcook as they will be too dry and sometimes tough.

1 pound boneless lamb loins (or 2 pounds loin lamb chops)
1½ teaspoons dried peppercorns, crushed (or ¼ teaspoon freshly ground)
1 tablespoon fresh rosemary (or 1 teaspoon dried)
2 tablespoons chopped fresh mint (optional)
2 cloves garlic, minced
2 tablespoons dry sherry or red wine vinegar
1 tablespoon low-sodium soy sauce

If using loin chops, remove any visible fat.
Place lamb in shallow dish.
In small bowl, combine peppercorns, rosemary, mint (if using), garlic, sherry, and soy sauce; mix well and pour over lamb. Cover and marinate at room temperature for 30 minutes or refrigerate for at least 1, or up to 6, hours.
Remove from marinade. Broil or grill over hot coals 3 to 4 minutes for tenderloins; 6 minutes for loins or until meat is still pink inside, turning once or twice. Cut diagonally into thin slices.

Pork Chops with Rosemary and Orange

MAKES 4 SERVINGS

PER SERVING*

201 calories
9 g fat
67 mg cholesterol
70 mg sodium

22 g protein
6 g carbohydrate

EXCELLENT: vitamin C, thiamin, niacin

*made with center-cut loin chops

This fast and easy recipe also works well using veal or turkey scallopine. For my son (who doesn't like sauces), I don't pour any over his serving. My daughter quietly scrapes the rosemary off hers. My husband and I like it the way it is, so everyone is happy.

1 pound fast-fry or thinly sliced, center-cut loin pork chops, bone in
2 oranges
2 teaspoons soft margarine
2 teaspoons dried rosemary
Salt and freshly ground pepper

Trim visible fat from pork chops. Peel and slice one orange; squeeze juice from other and set aside.

Heat heavy-bottomed or nonstick skillet over high heat; add margarine and heat until sizzling. Add pork chops and cook for about 2 minutes or until brown on bottom; turn. Sprinkle with rosemary, and salt and pepper to taste. Cook until brown on other side. Remove chops to side plate.

Add reserved orange juice and slices; cook for 1 to 2 minutes, stirring to scrape up brown bits on bottom of pan. To serve, arrange chops on plates and pour juice and orange slices over.

Brochette of Pork with Lemon and Herb Marinade

MAKES 4 SERVINGS

Herbs and lemon add tangy flavor to this easy-to-prepare pork dish. Use pork tenderloin or any other lean cut of pork. Zucchini or blanched slices of carrot can be used instead of the vegetables here. And, pineapple chunks packed in their own juice can be used instead of fresh pineapple.

PER SERVING

235 calories
12 g fat
67 mg cholesterol
58 mg sodium

23 g protein
8 g carbohydrate

GOOD: fiber, riboflavin, iron
EXCELLENT: vitamin C, thiamin, niacin

1 pound boneless lean pork
Grated rind and juice of 1 lemon
2 large cloves garlic, minced
2 teaspoons dried basil (or 2 tablespoons fresh)
1 teaspoon dried thyme (or 1 tablespoon fresh)
2 tablespoons chopped fresh parsley
1 tablespoon vegetable or olive oil
1 sweet green pepper, cut in squares
2 medium onions, quartered and separated into pieces
16 cherry tomatoes or fresh pineapple chunks

Trim all visible fat, then cut pork into 1-inch cubes. In bowl, combine lemon rind and juice, garlic, basil, thyme, parsley, and oil. Add pork and toss to coat well. Cover and marinate in refrigerator for 4 hours or overnight.

Alternately thread pork, green pepper, onions, and cherry tomatoes or pineapple onto skewers. On greased grill about 4 inches over hot coals or under broiler, grill brochettes, turning often, for 15 minutes or until pork is no longer pink inside.

Cauliflower and Ham Gratin

MAKES 4 SERVINGS

PER SERVING

219 calories
10 g fat
21 mg cholesterol
533 mg sodium

15 g protein
18 g carbohydrate

GOOD: fiber, vitamin A, thiamin
EXCELLENT: vitamin C, niacin, calcium

Ham and cauliflower are a wonderful combination. Dill adds extra flavor and red pepper adds color and crunch.

½ head cauliflower
1½ tablespoons soft margarine
2 tablespoons all-purpose flour
1 cup skim milk
¼ cup grated Parmesan cheese
¼ cup grated low-fat mozzarella cheese
¼ cup chopped fresh dill (see Note)
Freshly ground pepper
½ cup diced cooked ham (2 ounces)
½ sweet red pepper, coarsely chopped
⅓ cup fresh bread crumbs

(continued)

Cut cauliflower into florets, about 2-inches each. In large pot of boiling water, blanch cauliflower for 5 minutes or until tender-crisp; drain and set aside.

In saucepan, melt margarine; add flour and cook over low heat, stirring, for 1 minute. Pour in milk and bring to simmer, stirring constantly. Simmer, stirring, for 2 minutes. Add Parmesan and mozzarella cheeses, dill, and pepper to taste; cook, stirring, until cheese melts.

In lightly greased 11- by 7-inch shallow baking dish, arrange cauliflower, ham, and sweet pepper; pour sauce evenly over. Sprinkle with bread crumbs. Bake in 375°F oven for 30 minutes or until bubbly.

Note: If fresh dill is unavailable, use ¼ cup chopped fresh parsley plus 1 teaspoon dried dillweed.

Compare These Two Ham Dinners:

Dinner 1: 29% of Calories from Fat	Grams Fat	Milligrams Cholesterol	Milligrams Sodium	Calories
Cauliflower and Ham Gratin (page 101)	10.1	21	533	219
Green beans	0.1	0	8	17
Sliced tomatoes	0.1	0	5	12
Whole-wheat bun	1.0	1	197	90
Margarine (1 teaspoon)	3.6	0	32	34
Milk, skim (8 ounces)	0	5	133	90
TOTALS	15.0	27	908	462
Dinner 2: 47% of calories from fat				
Ham steak (4 ounces, lean)	8.7	65	1571	187
Cauliflower	0.1	0	4	14
with cheese sauce* (¼ cup)	9.9	33	271	126
Green beans	0.1	0	8	17
Whole-wheat bun	1.0	1	197	90
Butter (1 teaspoon)	3.6	11	39	34
Milk, whole (8 ounces)	9	35	126	159
TOTALS	32.4	145	2,216	627

*Cheese sauce made with whole milk and Cheddar cheese.

Grilled Tandoori Chicken

MAKES 6 SERVINGS

This Indian yogurt-and-spice marinade makes the chicken moist and full of flavor. Serve with rice and a green vegetable such as asparagus, green beans, or broccoli or see the Summer Barbecue menu.

1½ teaspoon Dijon mustard
2 tablespoons vegetable oil
¼ cup low-fat plain yogurt
1½ teaspoons minced fresh gingerroot
¼ teaspoon cumin seeds
¼ teaspoon coriander seeds
¼ teaspoon ground turmeric
2 tablespoons lemon juice
2 tablespoons chopped canned green chili, 1 fresh green chili, seeded and chopped, or ¼ teaspoon dried red pepper flakes or to taste
1 2½-pound chicken, cut in pieces or chicken breasts

Place mustard in mixing bowl or food processor; add oil, drop by drop, whisking or processing until well blended. Stir in yogurt; set aside.

Using mortar and pestle, spice grinder, or coffee grinder, pound or grind gingerroot, cumin and coriander seeds, and turmeric to form a paste; add lemon juice and mix well. Stir into yogurt mixture along with chopped chili.

Cut any visible fat from chicken and remove skin. Using knife, make very small cuts in meat. Arrange in shallow dish or place in plastic bag; pour yogurt-spice mixture over chicken and stir to coat all pieces. Cover and refrigerate for at least 8 hours or up to 24 hours.

On greased grill 4 to 6 inches from hot coals or under broiler, grill chicken for 15 to 20 minutes on each side (15 minutes if top is down on barbecue) or until chicken is tender and juices run clear when chicken is pierced with fork. Watch carefully and turn to prevent burning.

Barbecued Lemon Chicken

MAKES 4 SERVINGS

PER SERVING

148 calories
4 g fat
73 mg cholesterol
64 mg sodium

27 g protein
0 g carbohydrate

EXCELLENT: niacin

This simple way to cook chicken is one of my husband's favorites—the chicken is moist, juicy, and very delicious. In the winter, my friend Janet Dey cooks chicken this way in her fireplace barbecue.

4 boneless chicken breasts
Juice of 1 lemon
2 teaspoons olive oil
1 clove garlic, minced
½ teaspoon dried oregano
Pinch cayenne pepper

Cut any visible fat from chicken and remove skin. In shallow dish, arrange chicken in single layer.

In small dish, combine lemon juice, oil, garlic, oregano, and cayenne; mix well. Pour over chicken and turn to coat both sides. Let stand at room temperature for 20 minutes or cover and refrigerate overnight.

On greased grill, cook chicken over hot coals for 4 to 5 minutes on each side or until meat is no longer pink inside.

Curried Chicken Crêpes

MAKES 4 SERVINGS, 2 CRÊPES EACH

PER SERVING (2 crêpes)

244 calories
7 g fat
58 mg cholesterol
347 mg sodium

25 g protein
18 g carbohydrate

EXCELLENT: niacin

This is a delicious dish to consider when you want a make-ahead dish for brunch, lunch, or dinner. If you keep crêpes in your freezer and have any leftover cooked chicken or turkey, these can be a quick and easy dinner. Cooked turkey, shrimp, or pork can be used instead of chicken.

2 teaspoons soft margarine
½ medium onion, chopped
½ cup diced celery
1 tablespoon all-purpose flour
1½ teaspoons (approximately) curry powder
¼ teaspoon salt

½ cup chicken stock
1 ½ cup diced cooked chicken (about ¾ pound boneless chicken
    breasts)
¼ cup light sour cream
¼ cup low-fat plain yogurt
8 Basic Crêpes (page 183)
Yogurt, chutney, green grapes

In saucepan, melt margarine over medium heat; add onion and celery, and cook, stirring, until onion is softened. Add flour, curry powder, and salt; cook, stirring, for 1 minute.

Whisk in chicken stock and bring to simmer while whisking. Reduce heat to low and simmer, stirring, for 2 minutes. Remove from heat and stir in chicken, sour cream, and yogurt. Taste and add more curry powder if desired.

Place 2 or 3 large spoonfuls of chicken mixture across center of each crêpe. Roll up and place seam-side down in lightly greased shallow baking dish.

Bake in 375°F oven for 20 minutes or microwave at high (100%) power for 2 minutes or until heated through. Garnish each serving with a spoonful of yogurt, another of chutney, and some grapes.

Old-Fashioned Chicken or Turkey Pot Pie

If you have leftover cooked chicken or turkey, and any crisp-cooked vegetables such as carrots, green beans, zucchini, or leeks, combine them with sliced fresh mushrooms, frozen peas, and Cream Sauce (page 163). Season with a touch of tarragon and sherry; spoon into baking dish.

Cover with mashed potatoes and bake in 375°F oven for 30 minutes or until hot and bubbly, and potatoes are golden.

Using mashed potatoes made with skim milk and without butter or margarine instead of pastry as a topping for a chicken or meat pie reduces the fat by about half.

Curried Chicken and Tomato Casserole

MAKES 10 SERVINGS

PER SERVING

198 calories
8 g fat
49 mg cholesterol
113 mg sodium

20 g protein
13 g carbohydrate

GOOD: calcium, iron
EXCELLENT: vitamin C,
niacin

For an easy yet elegant dinner, serve small dishes of raisins, peanuts, coconut, chutney, and yogurt, plus rice, along with this casserole. For a particularly delicious fresh flavor, grind the cumin and coriander seeds just before using. You can, however, substitute 2 tablespoons curry powder or more to taste, for the cumin and coriander seeds, turmeric, aniseed, and hot pepper flakes. Don't substitute canned tomatoes. The Sliced Cucumbers with Chives, Yogurt, and Basil (page 69) is particularly nice with this.

3 pounds chicken pieces (breasts, thighs)
2 tablespoons soft margarine
4 medium onions, chopped
3 tablespoons minced fresh gingerroot
¼ cup water
5 cloves garlic, minced
2 tablespoons cumin seeds, ground
2 tablespoons coriander seeds, ground
2 tablespoons ground turmeric
1 teaspoon aniseed
¼ teaspoon (approximately) hot pepper flakes
4 large tomatoes, seeded and coarsely chopped
1½ cups low-fat plain yogurt
Salt and pepper
1 teaspoon garam masala (see Note)
¼ cup chopped fresh coriander

Cut any visible fat from chicken and remove skin.

In large Dutch oven or skillet, heat margarine over medium-high heat; brown chicken pieces a few at a time and remove to plate. Add onions and cook for 3 minutes or until tender, stirring often. Add gingerroot, water, garlic, cumin, coriander, turmeric, aniseed, and hot pepper flakes; mix well and simmer for 1 minute. Add tomatoes and simmer for 2 minutes. Stir in yogurt.

Return chicken, including any juices, to pan and stir gently. Season with salt and pepper to taste; add more hot pepper flakes if desired. Cover and simmer for 25 to 30 minutes or until chicken is tender and cooked through.

Compare One Serving of Curried Chicken and Tomato Casserole:

	Grams Fat	Calories
Including chicken skin	12	247
Without chicken skin	8	198

This recipe can be prepared in advance, cooled, covered and refrigerated for up to 2 days. To reheat, cook over medium heat, stirring occasionally, for about 20 minutes, or place uncovered in 350°F oven for 35 to 45 minutes or until heated through.

Just before serving, stir in garam masala and chopped coriander.

Note: Buy garam masala at specialty food shops, or make this version by using a spice grinder or coffee grinder to combine 4 peppercorns, 2 cardamom seeds, 2 cloves, ½-inch piece cinnamon stick, and a pinch each of cumin seeds and grated nutmeg.

Tarragon-Roasted Chicken

MAKES 6 SERVINGS

PER SERVING

155 calories
6 g fat
70 mg cholesterol
70 mg sodium

23 g protein
0 g carbohydrate

EXCELLENT: niacin

This is a delicious and easy way to cook chicken. Be sure to remove the skin when carving as it has a large amount of fat.

2 cloves garlic
1 3-pound chicken
2 teaspoons dried tarragon
¼ cup dry white wine
1 tablespoon vegetable oil

Cut 1 garlic clove in half. Rub cut sides on outside of chicken; place garlic in chicken cavity. Sprinkle half the tarragon in chicken cavity. Truss chicken. Use a cotton string to tie the legs and wings close to the body. (This prevents the legs and wings from becoming overcooked and dried out before the rest of the chicken is cooked.) Place in roasting pan.

Mince remaining garlic and combine with remaining tarragon,

wine and oil; drizzle over chicken. Roast in 350°F oven, basting frequently, for 1¼ hours or until juices run clear when chicken is pierced with fork.

Mushroom Onion Stuffing

MAKES 6 CUPS, ENOUGH FOR A 6-POUND CHICKEN (ABOUT 8 SERVINGS)

PER SERVING

59 calories
1 g fat
1 mg cholesterol
122 mg sodium

2 g protein
2 g carbohydrate

GOOD: fiber

This stuffing is good with chicken or turkey. Serve with cranberry sauce and nobody will notice if you don't have gravy.

3 cups fresh whole wheat bread crumbs
1½ cups coarsely chopped mushrooms
1 cup finely chopped celery
2 small onions, finely chopped
1 teaspoon dried thyme
1 teaspoon dried sage
¼ teaspoon freshly ground pepper

In large bowl, combine bread crumbs, mushrooms, celery, onions, thyme, sage, and pepper.

NOTE

Stuff a bird just before cooking. If you stuff it in advance, even if you refrigerate it, the center will take time to become cold and you run the risk of contamination. Fill cavity but don't pack it, it will expand during cooking. Fasten closed with skewers or sew closed using a needle and string or thread.

VARIATION

Instead of mushrooms or celery, add chopped apple or pear, cooked cranberries, or chopped dried apricots; or replace half of the bread crumbs with cooked wild rice.

Chicken and Shrimp Creole

MAKES 8 SERVINGS

PER SERVING

321 calories
5 g fat
105 mg cholesterol
638 mg sodium

30 g protein
38 g carbohydrate

GOOD: fiber, thiamin
EXCELLENT: niacin,
iron, vitamin C

For the most flavor, cook the shrimp for this dish in their shells, then peel and devein rather than peeling before cooking. If preparing in advance, use parboiled (converted) rice as some kinds of rice will get mushy when reheated. Cooked, sliced Italian sausage is a tasty addition or substitute for shrimp in this dish; however sausage is high in fat and would add about 10 grams of fat per serving.

1 ½ pounds boneless chicken
1 tablespoon vegetable oil
2 medium onions, coarsely chopped
3 cloves garlic, minced
1 each sweet red and green pepper, coarsely chopped
1 28-ounce can tomatoes, peeled or unpeeled (undrained)
4 cups chicken stock
1 teaspoon dried thyme
1 teaspoon dried oregano
¼ teaspoon cayenne pepper
2 cups parboiled (converted) rice
1 pound medium shrimp (fresh or frozen)
½ cup chopped fresh parsley

Cut any visible fat from chicken, remove skin, and cut into cubes. In large nonstick skillet or heavy pan, heat oil over medium heat; cook chicken for about 3 minutes or until lightly browned. Add onions and garlic; cook for 3 minutes or until softened. Stir in peppers; add tomatoes, breaking up with back of spoon. Add stock, thyme, oregano, and cayenne; bring to boil. Stir in rice; cover, reduce heat, and simmer for 25 minutes or until most of the liquid is absorbed.

Meanwhile, in saucepan of boiling water, cook shrimp for 3 minutes; drain. Peel and devein if necessary. Add shrimp to rice mixture and cook for 5 minutes or until shrimp are hot. Stir in parsley.

Stir-Fried Chicken with Broccoli

MAKES 8 SERVINGS

PER SERVING

171 calories
6 g fat
49 mg cholesterol
224 mg sodium

21 g protein
8 g carbohydrate

GOOD: iron
EXCELLENT: fiber,
vitamin A, vitamin C,
niacin

Stir-fries are perfect last-minute dishes that can easily be stretched to accommodate extra guests. Just add more broccoli or extra vegetables and cook more rice or noodles. If you have dried Chinese mushrooms on hand, use a few of them (soaked first) instead of fresh.

1½ pounds boned, skinned chicken breasts
2 tablespoons vegetable oil
2 tablespoons minced fresh gingerroot
2 medium onions, sliced
6 cups broccoli florets
1 cup thinly sliced carrots
½ pound mushrooms, sliced
¾ cup chicken stock
2 tablespoons sherry
2 teaspoons low-sodium soy sauce
2 teaspoons cornstarch
2 tablespoons water
4 cups sliced Chinese cabbage, or bok choy (see Note)

Cut chicken into thin strips about 1½ inches long; set aside.

In wok or large heavy skillet, heat oil over high heat. When stir-frying, it is very important to have oil very hot before adding any food. If food sticks, either the wok wasn't hot enough or you need a little more oil. If food starts to stick after adding vegetables, add a little water to prevent scorching. Gradually add chicken to wok with half of the gingerroot; stir-fry for 2 minutes. Remove from wok and set aside. Add onion and stir-fry for 2 minutes; set aside with chicken.

Add broccoli, carrots, mushrooms, and remaining gingerroot to wok; stir-fry for 2 minutes, adding a little water to prevent sticking if necessary.

Mix together chicken stock, sherry, and soy sauce; pour over broccoli mixture. Cover and let steam for 2 minutes. Stir in reserved onion and chicken. Mix cornstarch with water; stir into wok and bring to boil. Add Chinese cabbage; stir and cook for 1 minute or until tender crisp.

Note: If bok choy is not available locally, use thinly sliced green cabbage.

Szechuan Orange-Ginger Chicken

MAKES 4 SERVINGS

PER SERVING

220 calories
10 g fat
66 mg cholesterol
58 mg sodium

24 g protein
6 g carbohydrate

EXCELLENT: vitamin C, niacin

This popular recipe is much easier and faster to make than it looks. Chinese dishes from the Szechuan region of China usually have a spicy, hot flavor; if you prefer a milder taste, use less chili paste—the dish is delicious either way. Serve with rice.

1 pound boned skinned chicken breasts
1 sweet green pepper
1 sweet red pepper
1 orange
1 teaspoon bottled chili paste (see Note)
2 tablespoons sherry
1 teaspoon granulated sugar
1 teaspoon cornstarch
2 tablespoons vegetable oil
1 teaspoon minced garlic
1 tablespoon minced fresh gingerroot

Cut chicken into 1-inch squares; set aside. Halve green and red peppers and remove ribs and seeds; cut into 1-inch squares.

Using vegetable peeler, remove rind from orange (orange part only, no white). Cut rind into thin julienne strips about 1½ inches long; set aside. Squeeze orange and reserve ¼ cup juice.

In small bowl, combine reserved orange juice, chili paste, sherry, sugar, and cornstarch; stir until smooth.

In wok, heat oil over high heat; add chicken and stir-fry for 2 minutes or until no longer pink. Remove chicken. Add orange rind, garlic, and gingerroot; stir-fry for 10 seconds. Add peppers and stir-fry for 1 minute. Add chili paste mixture and bring to boil. Return chicken to wok and stir until heated through.

Note: Bottled chili paste is available in some supermarkets and most Oriental grocery stores. You can substitute dried chili peppers to taste or the kind of hot chili sauce found in Oriental grocery stores. The seeds in fresh or dried peppers are very hot; if you want a milder taste omit seeds.

Make-Ahead Paella

MAKES 8 SERVINGS

PER SERVING

309 calories
8 g fat
115 mg cholesterol
429 mg sodium

31 g protein
30 g carbohydrate

GOOD: fiber, thiamin
EXCELLENT: niacin, vitamin C, iron

This is one of my favorite dishes for entertaining—it looks spectacular, tastes delicious, and can be mostly prepared in advance. It's great any time of year for a sit-down dinner or special buffet. There are many versions of this Spanish specialty—do vary the seafood to your own tastes and to what's available. Saffron adds a delicate flavor and a beautiful yellow color but is terribly expensive and sometimes hard to find. If unavailable add 1 tablespoon turmeric.

12 littleneck or Manila clams (in shells)
1 pound mussels (in shells)
2 pounds chicken breasts (or 1 pound boneless)
1 tablespoon vegetable oil or margarine
½ pound hot Spanish or Italian sausage
4 cloves garlic, minced
1½ cups parboiled (converted) rice
3 cups water or clam cooking liquid
1½ cups coarsely chopped tomato
1 sweet green pepper, cut in ½-inch pieces
1 bay leaf
1 teaspoon saffron threads
¼ teaspoon ground turmeric
¼ teaspoon freshly ground pepper
Cayenne pepper
¾ pound medium shrimp, cooked peeled and deveined (see Note)
1 cup peas, fresh or frozen

Scrub clams and mussels under cold running water; cut off any hairy beards from mussels. Discard any clams or mussels that do not close when tapped. Refrigerate mussels until needed. Steam clams over boiling water until shells open (about 5 minutes); reserve cooking liquid, discard any that don't open. Refrigerate until needed.

Cut any visible fat from chicken breasts and remove skin; cut into bite-size pieces. In large nonstick skillet, heat oil over medium-high heat, brown chicken. Transfer chicken to paella pan or large shallow casserole.

Add sausage to skillet and cook until no longer pink in color (time will vary depending on type of sausage); remove from skillet and cut into ¼-inch-thick slices; discard excess fat; add to pan with chicken.

In same skillet, cook garlic for 1 minute; stir in rice. Add clam cooking liquid or water, tomatoes, green pepper, bay leaf, saffron, turmeric, pepper, and cayenne to taste; bring to boil. Reduce heat and simmer for 15 minutes; pour over chicken.

(Recipe can be prepared ahead to this point, covered, and refrigerated for up to 1 day. Return all ingredients to room temperature before continuing with recipe.)

Add mussels and bake, covered, in 425°F oven for 20 minutes. Stir in shrimps, clams, and peas; bake for 15 minutes or until heated through and mussels open (discard any mussels that don't open).

Note: Cook shrimp in boiling water for 3 minutes. Drain and cool under cold water; peel and devein.

Grilled Turkey Scallopini with Herbs and Garlic

MAKES 4 SERVINGS

This is a favorite dish of mine for summer entertaining. It's extremely fast and easy, yet a little different. Because turkey is tender and this is a fairly strong-flavored marinade, it doesn't need hours of marinating and can be prepared at the last minute or an hour or 2 in advance. Veal scallopini or boneless chicken breasts can be used instead of turkey.

(continued)

PER SERVING

162 calories
6 g fat
57 mg cholesterol
120 mg sodium

25 g protein
1 g carbohydrate

EXCELLENT: niacin

3 cloves garlic, minced
½ teaspoon dried thyme
½ teaspoon dried rosemary
½ teaspoon dried oregano
2 tablespoons olive oil
2 tablespoons lemon juice
¼ teaspoon salt
Freshly ground pepper
1 pound turkey scallopini (see Note)

In food processor or small bowl, combine garlic, thyme, rosemary, oregano, oil, lemon juice, salt, and pepper to taste; mix well. Brush over both sides of turkey. (Grill immediately or cover and let stand at room temperature for 30 minutes or refrigerate for up to 2 hours.) On lightly greased grill 4 inches from hot coals, grill turkey for 2 minutes on each side or just until cooked through.

Note: If turkey scallopini aren't available in your store, slice partially frozen turkey breast meat thinly, then pound between two pieces of waxed paper into ¼-inch thick slices or use veal scallopini.

If using boneless chicken breasts, do not pound; increase grilling time to 7 to 10 minutes per side.

Fish

Fish is an original fast food that's easy to cook at home. Not only does it taste good but it is very nutritious. It is an excellent source of high-quality protein, and is high in vitamins A, D, and B-complex, and low in fat, particularly saturated fat. Fish contains the beneficial omega-3 type of fat, which according to the latest research helps to reduce the incidence of heart disease. Most fish is lower in cholesterol than meat or poultry.

For many years shellfish were banned on diets prescribed to lower blood cholesterol, because of a supposed high cholesterol count. But better testing techniques can now discriminate between the different sterols, and show that cholesterol isn't present in shellfish in so large an amount as to be of concern. Shrimp is the shellfish that is highest in cholesterol but as long as you don't have it too often or are not on a low-cholesterol diet, it can still be enjoyed in small amounts.

The two most important factors in preparing tasty fish are, above all, to buy good-quality fish, either fresh or frozen, and not to overcook it. You can substitute one kind of fish for another in the recipes here. Buy whatever kind is freshest and use in the recipe that appeals most to you.

Buying Fish

Odor and appearance are the clues to the freshness of seafood. There should be no strong fishy odor, and the eyes should be bright and bulging, not sunken into the head. The skin should spring back when pressed lightly. When I buy fish I ask the salesperson what fish came in that day and choose from these.

STORAGE

Wash, pat dry, and cover with an airtight wrapper. Fish can be refrigerated for about 2 days or in a freezer as long as 3 months.

Cooking Fish

Fish and shellfish are naturally tender. They should be cooked for a short time at a high temperature. To determine the length of cooking time, measure the thickness of the fish at its thickest part. Cook fresh fish 10 minutes per inch of thickness, adding 5 minutes if wrapped in foil; frozen fish requires 20 minutes per inch, plus 10 minutes if wrapped in foil. Cooking time may vary depending on the cooking method used. Don't overcook. Overcooked fish becomes dry, tough, and rubbery and loses its flavor. Fish is cooked when the flesh is opaque and it flakes easily.

OVEN STEAMING FISH

This method is the easiest and requires the least cleanup. Place fish on the foil and season with lemon juice and/or herbs. Wrap fish in foil and place on cookie sheet. Bake in 450°F oven for required time (see above), depending on thickness.

STEAMING FISH

If you don't have a fish steamer you can:

1. Use a wok with a lid. Place fish on a heat-proof plate. Add a small amount of water to the bottom of a wok and bring to a boil. Set 2 chopsticks above water level in the wok and place the plate on the chopsticks. Cover. The steam will circulate around the fish and cook it gently;
2. Use a roasting pan. Place a rack in the roaster and a heatproof

plate on top of the rack. Add water to below the level of the plate. To prevent the fish from falling apart, wrap in cheesecloth or lettuce leaves. Cover with a lid or foil. Cook for 10 minutes per inch of thickness.

MICROWAVING FISH

One of the best reasons for owning a microwave is to cook fish. It takes only minutes to cook and is very moist. Arrange fish in a microwave dish with the thickest part facing the outside of the dish. Season with pepper, lemon juice, or herbs (always add salt after microwaving not before). Place plastic wrap over dish with a small corner turned back for steam to escape. One pound of fresh or thawed fillets in a single layer at high setting takes about 4 to 5 minutes (10 to 12 for frozen). Times will vary depending on thickness. Rotate dish during cooking.

Fish Fillets with Herbed Crumbs

MAKES 4 SERVINGS

PER SERVING*

187 calories
  8 g fat
 70 mg cholesterol
145 mg sodium

25 g protein
 3 g carbohydrate

GOOD: iron
EXCELLENT: niacin

*based on cod fillets

Here's an easy-to-make and tasty way to serve fish fillets. It's really quick if you make your bread crumbs and chop the parsley in a blender or food processor, then melt the margarine and cook the fish in a microwave.

    1 pound fish fillets
    ⅓ cup fresh bread crumbs
    1 tablespoon margarine, melted
    ¼ cup chopped fresh parsley
    1 teaspoon dried thyme
    ¼ teaspoon freshly ground pepper

In shallow baking dish or microwave-safe dish, arrange fillets in single layer. Combine bread crumbs, margarine, parsley, thyme, and pepper; mix well and sprinkle over fish.

(continued)

Bake uncovered in 450°F oven for 10 minutes per inch of thickness for fresh fish, 20 minutes per inch for frozen or until fish flakes easily when tested with fork.

MICROWAVE METHOD: Microwave, uncovered, at high (100%) power for about 4 minutes for fresh fish or until fish flakes easily when tested with fork. If using frozen, defrost first then sprinkle with bread crumbs.

Fish Fillets with Basil and Lemon

MAKES 4 SERVINGS

PER SERVING*

164 calories
6 g fat
70 mg cholesterol
112 mg sodium

25 g protein
0 g carbohydrate

EXCELLENT: niacin

*using cod

This is so simple and easy, yet results in the best-tasting fish. If buying frozen fillets, try to buy the kind that have been frozen in a single layer or individually wrapped. If using the kind that have been frozen in a block, defrost the fish and separate into fillets before cooking. If buying fresh, choose whatever kind of fillets are freshest. About 1 tablespoon of any fresh herbs, such as chopped fresh dill, thyme, or tarragon, can be substituted for the basil.

1 pound fish fillets
1 tablespoon lemon juice
2 teaspoons margarine, melted
½ teaspoon dried basil
Freshly ground pepper
Fresh herbs or chopped fresh parsley

In microwave-safe or conventional baking dish, arrange fillets in a single layer. In small dish, combine lemon juice, margarine, and basil; drizzle over fish. Sprinkle lightly with pepper to taste.

Bake, uncovered, in 450°F oven for 8 to 10 minutes (10 minutes per inch thickness for fresh fish) or until fish is opaque and flakes easily with fork. Sprinkle with fresh herbs or parsley.

MICROWAVE METHOD: Cover with plastic wrap and turn back corner to vent. Microwave at high (100%) power for 3½ to 4½ minutes or until fish is opaque and flakes easily with fork.

Fish Facts

Recent research has shown not all fish and shellfish are high in cholesterol. Mollusks—oysters, scallops, clams, and mussels—are not as high in cholesterol as are crustaceans—shrimp, crab, and lobster. Cod is higher in cholesterol than many other fish. If using sole the cholesterol drops to about 60 grams, if using halibut to about 55 grams per serving.

Quick and Easy Salmon Steaks with Watercress Sauce

MAKES 4 SERVINGS

PER SERVING

295 calories
 11 g fat
 66 mg cholesterol
396 mg sodium

 43 g protein
  3 g carbohydrate

GOOD: thiamin, calcium, iron
EXCELLENT: niacin

Fresh salmon steaks are a wonderful treat and I like them best when simply cooked—either poached, steamed, or microwaved. The only way to ruin good-quality fish is to overcook it. If fillets or steaks are ¾- to 1-inch thick, you'll be much less likely to overcook them than if they are thin. Cooking times in this recipe are based on 1-inch-thick steaks. The easiest and fastest is the microwave. In summer, dress them up with this watercress sauce; in winter serve with the Fresh Dill Cream Sauce (page 163).

4 5-ounce salmon steaks, 1-inch thick
2 teaspoons lemon juice
Freshly ground pepper
Watercress sprigs

WATERCRESS SAUCE

1 cup low-fat cottage cheese
¼ cup low-fat plain yogurt
¼ cup chopped fresh watercress leaves
2 tablespoons chopped fresh parsley
1 tablespoon chopped fresh chives
2 teaspoons grated Parmesan cheese

On lightly oiled large piece of foil, arrange salmon in single layer. Sprinkle with lemon juice, and pepper to taste. Fold foil over salmon and seal; place on baking sheet. Bake in 400°F oven for about 15 minutes or until fish is opaque and flakes easily with fork.

MICROWAVE METHOD: In microwave-safe dish arrange salmon in single layer. Sprinkle with lemon juice, and pepper to taste. Cover with plastic wrap; fold back corner to vent. Microwave at high (100%) power for 5 minutes or until fish is opaque and flakes easily with fork.

Watercress Sauce: In food processor, combine cottage cheese, yogurt, chopped watercress, parsley, chives, and Parmesan; process until well mixed. Or pass cottage cheese through a sieve and combine with remaining ingredients.

Arrange salmon on plates and garnish with sprig of watercress. Pass sauce separately.

Dilled Snapper Fillets with Cucumber-Yogurt Sauce

MAKES 4 SERVINGS

PER SERVING

127 calories
3 g fat
74 mg cholesterol
134 mg sodium

21 g protein
3 g carbohydrate

EXCELLENT: niacin

Any kind of fish fillets—salmon, sole, sea bass—can be used; just choose whatever is freshest. If at all possible, try to use fresh dill instead of dried because the flavor is quite different.

4 5-ounce red snapper fillets
1½ teaspoon lemon juice
1 clove garlic, minced
2 tablespoons chopped fresh dill (or 1 teaspoon dried)

CUCUMBER-YOGURT SAUCE

¼ cup low-fat plain yogurt
¼ cup light sour cream
½ cup finely chopped cucumber
1 tablespoon chopped scallion
Freshly ground pepper

On broiler pan or in microwave-safe dish, arrange fillets in single layer with thickest part to outside. Brush with lemon juice; sprinkle with garlic and dill. Broil for 6 to 8 minutes or microwave, covered loosely with waxed paper, at high (100%) power for 4 to 5 minutes or until fish is opaque and flakes easily when tested with fork.

Cucumber-Yogurt Sauce: Meanwhile, in small dish, combine yogurt, sour cream, cucumber, scallion, and pepper to taste; mix well. Spread over fish and broil for 2 minutes or microwave at high (100%) power for 1 minute or until sauce is hot.

Barbecued Skewered Halibut with Red Peppers and Snow Peas

MAKES 4 SERVINGS

PER SERVING

164 calories
6 g fat
64 mg cholesterol
109 mg sodium

24 g protein
3 g carbohydrate

GOOD: fiber, iron
EXCELLENT: vitamin A, vitamin C, niacin

These easy-to-make kabobs look festive, taste great and, as an added bonus, make the fish go further. Serve over rice along with Tomato Salsa Sauce (page 126) or Cucumber-Yogurt Sauce (page 120). Be sure to soak the wooden skewers in water for at least 30 minutes to prevent charring.

    1 pound halibut or swordfish steaks
    Juice of 1 lime
    1 tablespoon olive oil
    2 tablespoons chopped fresh coriander, parsley, or dill
    Freshly ground pepper
    1 sweet red pepper
    20 snow peas

Cut fish into 1-inch cubes; place in a single layer in a shallow dish. Sprinkle with lime juice, oil, and coriander; cover and refrigerate for at least 30 minutes or up to 4 hours, turning once or twice.

Seed and cut red pepper into 1-inch squares. String snow peas and blanch in boiling water for 1 minute or until bright green and easily bent.

Thread fish on water-soaked wooden skewers alternating with red pepper, and snow peas folded in half. Grill over medium-hot coals, turning once or twice, for 12 to 18 minutes or until fish is opaque.

Linguine with Salmon and Chives

MAKES 4 SERVINGS

PER SERVING

400	calories
12	g fat
23	mg cholesterol
149	mg sodium

22	g protein
49	g carbohydrate

GOOD: calcium
EXCELLENT: niacin

Tender-crisp cooked vegetables, such as asparagus, green peas, or mushrooms, can be added to this quick and easy supper dish. Scallions can be used instead of chives; cooked fresh salmon instead of the canned, which is used along with its juices. Although this adds to the fat content, these juices are an excellent source of omega-3 fatty acids, which current research indicates may help to reduce heart disease.

½ pound linguine or any noodles
4 teaspoons soft margarine
1 small onion, chopped
2 tablespoons all-purpose flour
1 cup skim milk
⅓ cup chopped fresh chives
Freshly ground pepper
1 7½-ounce can salmon
2 tablespoons grated Parmesan cheese

In large pot of boiling water, cook linguine until al dente (tender but firm); drain, reserving ¼ cup cooking liquid. Return linguine to pan.

Meanwhile, in saucepan, melt margarine over medium heat; add onion and cook until tender. Stir in flour; mix well. Add milk and cook, whisking, until mixture comes to boil, thickens, and loses any raw-flour taste. Stir in chives, pepper to taste, and add reserved cooking liquid.

Flake salmon and add along with juices and chive mixture to pot with linguine; mix lightly. Sprinkle Parmesan cheese over each serving.

Fettuccine with Mussels, Leeks, and Tomatoes

MAKES 4 SERVINGS

PER SERVING

540 calories
 10 g fat
 87 mg cholesterol
527 mg sodium

 29 g protein
 82 g carbohydrate

GOOD: vitamin A,
riboflavin, calcium
EXCELLENT: fiber,
vitamin C, thiamin,
niacin, iron

This gorgeous dish is perfect for a special little dinner. As well as being easy to make, it tastes and looks wonderful, too.

3 pounds mussels (in shells)
2 leeks
¾ pound fettuccine
2 tablespoons olive oil
4 cloves garlic, chopped
½ teaspoon dried thyme
4 tomatoes, coarsely chopped
¼ cup dry white wine
1 cup coarsely chopped fresh parsley
Freshly ground pepper

Scrub mussels under cold running water; cut off any hairy beards. Discard any that do not close when tapped.

Trim leeks, discarding dark green parts. Slice in half lengthwise and rinse well. Cut into thin 1½-inch-long strips and set aside.

In large pot of boiling water, cook fettuccine until al dente (tender but firm); drain and return to pot.

Meanwhile, in large heavy saucepan, heat oil over medium heat; cook garlic and thyme for 1 minute. Add mussels, leeks, tomatoes, and wine; cover and bring to boil. Reduce heat and simmer for 5 to 8 minutes or until leeks are tender and mussels open (discard any that don't open).

Pour tomato mixture over fettuccine; add parsley, and pepper to taste. Toss to mix and serve on dinner plates or in large individual bowls.

Tuscan-Style Capellini with Clams and Garlic

MAKES 4 SERVINGS

PER SERVING

293 calories
7 g fat
17 mg cholesterol
78 mg sodium

10 g protein
46 g carbohydrate

GOOD: fiber, niacin
EXCELLENT: vitamin C, iron

In Italy, this popular pasta dish is made with tiny tender clams that have about 1-inch shells. Unfortunately, they're harder to find elsewhere. Try to time cooking of pasta so it is ready the same time the clams are. If using dried pasta, start it before cooking clams; if using fresh or very fine pasta, cook clams first.

2 pounds small size clams (in shells)
3 cloves garlic, minced
2 tablespoons olive oil
¼ cup dry white wine
½ pound capellini or spaghetti noodles
1 cup chopped fresh parsley
Salt and freshly ground pepper

Scrub clams under cold running water: discard any that do not close when tapped.

In large heavy saucepan, cook garlic and oil over medium-high heat for 1 minute; add wine and clams. Cover and cook until clams open (time will vary from 2 to 10 minutes depending on size of clams); discard any that do not open. Meanwhile, in large pot of boiling water, cook capellini until al dente (tender but firm); drain.

Pour clam mixture over hot pasta and toss with parsley. Season with salt and pepper to taste.

Teriyaki Cod Fillets

MAKES 4 SERVINGS

These fillets are absolutely delicious when microwaved. Any kind of fish can be used in this recipe, but I like cod or salmon the best.

2 tablespoons dry sherry
2 tablespoons water
1 tablespoon low-sodium soy sauce (see Note)

PER SERVING

173 calories
  6 g fat
 76 mg cholesterol
144 mg sodium

 27 g protein
  1 g carbohydrate

EXCELLENT: niacin

1 tablespoon vegetable oil
2 teaspoons grated gingerroot
1 teaspoon granulated sugar
1 clove garlic, minced
1 pound cod fillets, ¾-inch thick

In shallow microwave-safe or conventional dish, combine sherry, water, soy sauce, oil, gingerroot, sugar, and garlic; stir to mix. Add fish fillets and arrange in single layer; marinate at room temperature for 20 minutes or refrigerate for up to 4 hours, turning once or twice.

Remove fillets from marinade and transfer marinade to small saucepan. Place fillets in single layer in steamer; cover and steam for 5 to 8 minutes or until fish is opaque and flakes easily when tested with fork. Meanwhile, heat marinade over low heat until warm; drizzle over fish before serving.

MICROWAVE METHOD: Cover dish (fish and marinade) with vented plastic wrap and microwave at high (100%) power for 5 minutes or until fish is opaque and flakes easily when tested with fork.

Note: Soy sauce is very high in sodium. Low-sodium soy sauce is available at many supermarkets. If not, make your own by diluting regular soy sauce with an equal amount of water. There are two kinds of light soy sauce. One kind is basically lighter in color and is used in dishes for which you don't want the darker color. Another, newer version, lite soy sauce, is sodium-reduced. Naturally brewed soy sauce is lower in sodium than chemically brewed.

Grilled Halibut Steaks with Tomato Salsa Sauce

MAKES 4 SERVINGS, 1¼ CUPS SAUCE

As well as its delicious taste when barbecued, halibut is a good choice for grilling because it doesn't fall apart. However, other kinds of firm-fleshed fish, such as salmon or swordfish, can be substituted. Instead of a rich cream sauce, dress grilled fish with a

PER SERVING

234 calories
10 g fat
75 mg cholesterol
176 mg sodium

32 g protein
3 g carbohydrate

GOOD: vitamin C
EXCELLENT: vitamin A,
niacin

light, fresh Mexican salsa. This fairly mild tomato and cucumber salsa does not overpower the delicate flavor of fish. For extra spiciness, add chopped hot peppers to taste.

1½ pounds halibut steaks, about ¾-inches thick

TOMATO SALSA SAUCE
⅓ cup finely diced cucumber
⅓ cup finely diced sweet red pepper
2 tablespoons finely diced red onion
1 small ripe tomato, finely diced
2 teaspoons red wine vinegar
2 teaspoons chopped fresh coriander (optional)
½ teaspoon Worcestershire sauce
Dash hot pepper sauce
1 teaspoon olive oil

Tomato Salsa Sauce: In bowl, combine cucumber, red pepper, onion, tomato, vinegar, coriander (if using), Worcestershire sauce, hot pepper sauce, and oil; stir to mix. In food processor, purée half of the salsa mixture; combine with remaining salsa.

On greased grill or in broiler, grill fish, turning once, for about 4 minutes on each side or until fish is opaque and flakes easily when tested with fork. Place on serving platter or plates and spoon salsa over.

MICROWAVE METHOD: Place steaks in single layer in microwave-safe dish; cover with vented plastic wrap and microwave at high (100%) power for 4 to 5 minutes or until fish is opaque and flakes easily when tested with a fork.

Swordfish Steaks with Lime and Coriander

MAKES 4 SERVINGS

Fresh lime juice and coriander complement the flavor of most fish. Swordfish is particularly good for barbecuing because its firm flesh doesn't fall apart. Other fresh firm-fleshed fish steaks, such as

PER SERVING

150 calories
6 g fat
64 mg cholesterol
108 mg sodium

23 g protein
0 g carbohydrate

EXCELLENT: vitamin A, niacin

halibut or salmon, are also delicious cooked this way. If fresh coriander isn't available, substitute other herbs, such as fresh parsley, dill, rosemary, or oregano. Serve with Tomato Salsa Sauce (page 126).

1 pound swordfish, halibut, or salmon steaks, about ¾-inch thick
Juice of 1 lime
1 tablespoon olive oil
2 tablespoons chopped fresh coriander (or ½ teaspoon ground)
Freshly ground pepper

Lime wedges
Fresh coriander sprigs

Place fish in single layer in shallow dish. Sprinkle with lime juice, oil, and coriander; cover and refrigerate for at least 15 minutes or up to 4 hours, turning once or twice.

Broil or grill fish for 5 to 8 minutes or until fish is opaque and flakes easily when tested with fork. If grilling, turn halfway through. (Time will vary depending upon thickness of fish, about 10 minutes per inch of thickness.) Sprinkle with pepper to taste. Garnish each serving with lime wedges and sprigs of fresh coriander.

Meatless Main Courses

To make our diet more healthy we need to rely more on vegetable protein and less on animal protein. Legumes (beans, peas, lentils), nuts, seeds, and grains can provide protein, vitamins, and minerals, and are higher in fiber and lower in saturated fat than animal protein.

Protein is made up of twenty-two amino acids. Eight of these amino acids can't be produced by the body and must be obtained from food. These are called essential amino acids. All animal products contain all the essential amino acids. Plant foods are missing an essential amino acid. Therefore, it is important to combine a plant food with an animal food or two plant foods that together contain all the essential amino acids. When this happens they are called complementary proteins. Good combinations of plant foods are:

> legumes and grains (e.g., baked beans and whole-wheat bread)
> legumes and nuts (e.g., tossed salad with chickpeas and walnuts)
> legumes and low-fat dairy products (e.g., bean casserole with low-fat mozzarella topping)
> grains and low-fat dairy products (e.g., cereal and skim milk)

When we serve a meatless meal, we can use some low-fat cheese and eggs and still keep our saturated fat content down to the recommended level. It's important to consider our diet over a day or week. It's when we eat meats, high-fat cheese, and eggs on a daily basis that the fat and cholesterol levels will be too high. See other sections of this book for more meatless main-course dishes.

How Much Pasta to Cook?

For a main-course pasta dish which includes a number of ingredients along with pasta, I usually plan on about ½ pound for 4 servings. If it is a dish with only a light sauce such as pesto with pasta I use more. One-half pound of spaghetti noodles yields about 4 cups when cooked.

The easiest way to measure it is to weigh the uncooked pasta. If you don't have scales you can estimate by dividing up the package according to total weight (i.e., divide a 1-pound package in half to get ½ pound).

I usually try to cook more pasta than I need and use the extra to make a pasta salad or I mix it with any extra sauce and reheat it for breakfast or lunch.

Bean Casserole with Tomatoes and Spinach

MAKES 4 SERVINGS, 1½ CUPS EACH

PER SERVING

319 calories
4 g fat
0 mg cholesterol
727 mg sodium

18 g protein
55 g carbohydrate

GOOD: thiamin, calcium
EXCELLENT: fiber, vitamin A, vitamin C, niacin, iron

It seems that something that tastes as good as this should be harder to make. My son, Jeff, really likes this and says the Five-Grain Soda Bread (page 180) is perfect with it. Serve as a quick dinner or lunch along with a green salad. For a change of pace I sometimes cook a pound of ground beef along with the onions and add chili powder.

1 tablespoon soft margarine or vegetable oil
1 clove garlic, minced
2 medium onions, sliced
1 14-ounce can whole tomatoes
1 19-ounce can red kidney beans, drained
1 16-ounce can romano beans, drained
½ teaspoon dried oregano
1 10-ounce package fresh spinach or 1 bunch stems removed
Freshly ground pepper

NUTRITION NOTE

Choose whole canned tomatoes not stewed because stewed are higher in sodium. If possible choose a low-salt or low-sodium canned tomato.

In large heavy saucepan or casserole, heat margarine over medium heat; cook garlic and onions, stirring occasionally, for 3 minutes or until softened.

Add tomatoes, breaking up with back of spoon. Add kidney and romano beans, and oregano; bring to simmer.

Rinse, add spinach, cover, and simmer until spinach is wilted, about 2 minutes. Season with pepper to taste.

Tomato, Broccoli, and Pasta Salad

MAKES 6 SERVINGS

This salad is perfect for buffets, or with a green salad or soup for a main course. (For other main-course salads see salad section, page 64.) I like it with rigatoni, the large, tubular-shaped pasta, because it goes well with large chunks of tomato and broccoli; however, any other pasta can be substituted. The broccoli is added just before serving because otherwise, the acid in the salad dressing will cause the broccoli to lose its bright green color.

PER SERVING

229 calories
13 g fat
11 mg cholesterol
116 mg sodium

9 g protein
20 g carbohydrate

GOOD: fiber, vitamin A, niacin, calcium
EXCELLENT: vitamin C

¼ pound rigatoni or other pasta
3 cups broccoli florets
1 cup chopped scallions
3 tomatoes, cut in wedges
¼ pound low-fat mozzarella cheese, cubed
⅓ cup minced fresh parsley

MUSTARD VINAIGRETTE

3 tablespoons lemon juice
3 tablespoons water
2 cloves garlic, minced
1 teaspoon Dijon mustard
¼ cup vegetable oil
Salt and freshly ground pepper

In large pot of boiling water, cook pasta until al dente (tender but firm). Drain and rinse under cold water; drain again and set aside.

In another pot of boiling water, blanch broccoli for 2 minutes.

Drain and rinse under cold water. Drain again and wrap in paper towel; set aside.

In salad bowl, combine pasta, scallions, tomatoes, cheese, and parsley.

Mustard Vinaigrette: In food processor or mixing bowl, combine lemon juice, water, garlic, mustard, and oil; mix well. Pour over salad and toss to mix. Add salt and pepper to taste.

Cover and refrigerate for 30 minutes or up to 4 hours. Just before serving, add broccoli and toss to mix.

Rotini with Fresh Tomatoes, Basil, and Parmesan

MAKES 4 SERVINGS

PER SERVING*

368 calories
11 g fat
8 mg cholesterol
198 mg sodium

14 g protein
55 g carbohydrate

GOOD: niacin, calcium, iron
EXCELLENT: fiber, vitamin A, vitamin C

*meatless version

You can use any kind of pasta in this easy recipe. To preserve the fresh flavor and texture of the tomatoes they are quickly cooked over high heat. Once you have cooked the pasta, the whole mixture cooks in less than 5 minutes. Adding chicken, turkey, or ham to this dish will increase the protein. Adding ham will also increase the sodium (to 703 mg).

½ pound rotini (corkscrew shape) or any tubular pasta
2 tablespoons vegetable oil or margarine
4 scallions, chopped
4 tomatoes, coarsely chopped
3 cloves garlic, minced
1 cup strips or cubes cooked ham, turkey, or chicken (optional), about 5 ounces
1 cup coarsely chopped fresh parsley
¼ cup coarsely chopped fresh basil (or 1 teaspoon dried)
½ cup grated Parmesan cheese
Salt and pepper

In large pot of boiling water, cook pasta until al dente (tender but firm); drain. (If sauce isn't ready, rinse pasta under warm water for a few seconds to prevent it sticking together.)

Meanwhile, in large heavy saucepan or Dutch oven, heat oil over high heat. Add onions, tomatoes, and garlic; cook, stirring, for 2 to 3 minutes or until tomatoes are just heated through but still hold their shape. Stir in rotini, ham (if using), parsley, basil, and Parmesan. Reduce heat to medium; cook, stirring gently, for about 2 minutes or until heated through. Season with salt and pepper to taste.

Barley, Green Pepper, and Tomato Casserole

MAKES 6 SERVINGS

PER SERVING

304 calories
14 g fat
40 mg cholesterol
615 mg sodium

16 g protein
31 g carbohydrate

GOOD: fiber, vitamin A, iron
EXCELLENT: vitamin C, niacin, calcium

NUTRITION NOTE

Cheese is a good source of protein and calcium; however, it (particularly Cheddar) is high in fat. If this is part of a meatless meal, it can fit into a 30% fat diet. If you are serving this with meat, you should reduce the cheese by half and use a low-fat cheese such as low-fat mozzarella or feta.

Serve this as a main course along with a tossed salad and whole-wheat toast or pita bread. Crumbled feta cheese is a nice addition.

1 cup pot barley
3 cups vegetable or chicken stock, or water, hot
2 medium onions, chopped
1 sweet green pepper, chopped
2 large tomatoes, cut in chunks
1 teaspoon dried oregano
Salt and freshly ground pepper
2 cups shredded Cheddar cheese

In baking dish, combine barley, stock or water, onions, green pepper, tomatoes, oregano, and salt and pepper to taste; stir to mix. Cover and bake in 350°F oven for 45 minutes. Stir in cheese and bake, uncovered, for 25 minutes longer or until barley is tender and most liquid has been absorbed.

Fettuccine with Pesto Sauce

MAKES 4 MAIN-COURSE SERVINGS,
8 SIDE-DISH SERVINGS

PER SERVING*

542 calories
12 g fat
10 mg cholesterol
247 mg sodium

20 g protein
88 g carbohydrate

GOOD: vitamin C,
calcium, iron
EXCELLENT: fiber,
niacin

*as a main course

Pesto sauce is a fragrant fresh basil sauce that is absolutely perfect over pasta. This version has a full, pungent basil flavor yet omits the pine nuts and is much lower in oil than the classic recipe. Freeze extra pesto sauce in ice-cube containers; when frozen transfer to plastic bag. Use a cube to flavor soups, salad dressings, and sauces.

1 pound fettuccine
Freshly ground pepper
Grated Parmesan cheese

PESTO SAUCE

2 cloves garlic
1 cup fresh basil leaves, lightly packed
½ cup grated Parmesan cheese
2 tablespoons olive oil

In large pot of boiling water cook fettuccine until al dente (tender but firm). While pasta is cooking, prepare sauce.

Pesto Sauce: In food processor, combine garlic and basil; process until chopped. Add Parmesan and olive oil, process until smooth. Remove ½ cup of the pasta cooking liquid and add to sauce. You can substitute water for the pasta cooking liquid. Process until smooth.

Drain pasta and toss with pesto sauce. Sprinkle with pepper and Parmesan to taste.

Compare the Fat in One Serving of:

Fettuccine with Pesto Sauce	12 g
Most pesto sauce recipes	20+ g

Vegetable Lasagna

MAKES 8 SERVINGS

PER SERVING

332 calories
11 g fat
30 mg cholesterol
664 mg sodium

22 g protein
37 g carbohydrate

GOOD: fiber, iron
EXCELLENT: vitamin A,
vitamin C, niacin,
calcium

This is light and easy to make. It can be prepared a day or two in advance and refrigerated.

1 tablespoon vegetable oil
1 small onion, chopped
3 cloves garlic, minced
1 carrot, chopped
1 stalk celery, chopped
2 cups sliced mushrooms
1 16-ounce can whole tomatoes
1 8-ounce can tomato sauce
1 teaspoon dried basil
1 teaspoon dried oregano
Salt and freshly ground pepper
3 cups small broccoli florets
9 lasagna noodles
1 cup low-fat cottage cheese
3 cups shredded low-fat mozzarella cheese, about ¾ pound
⅓ cup grated Parmesan cheese

In large saucepan, heat oil over medium heat; add onion and cook until tender. Stir in garlic, carrot, celery, and mushrooms; cook, stirring often, for 5 minutes.

Add tomatoes, breaking up with fork. Stir in tomato sauce, basil, oregano; season with salt and pepper to taste. Simmer, uncovered, for 10 minutes or until thickened slightly. Let cool; stir in broccoli.

In large pot of boiling water, cook noodles until al dente (tender but firm); drain and rinse under cold water.

In lightly greased 13- × 9-inch baking dish, arrange 3 noodles evenly over bottom. Spread with one half of the vegetable mixture then half of the cottage cheese. Sprinkle with ⅓ of the mozzarella cheese.

Repeat noodle, vegetable mixture, cottage and mozzarella cheese layers once. Arrange remaining noodles over top; sprinkle with remaining mozzarella and Parmesan. Bake in 350°F oven for 35 to 45 minutes or until hot and bubbly.

Cabbage and Potato Pie

MAKES 4 SERVINGS

PER SERVING

246 calories
7 g fat
1 mg cholesterol
137 mg sodium

7 g protein
40 g carbohydrate

GOOD: vitamin A,
thiamin, niacin,
calcium
EXCELLENT: fiber,
vitamin C

Crinkly savoy cabbage, collard greens, kale, chard, or a combination of these in light cream sauce with mashed potato topping is a delicious vegetable dish.

1 pound savoy cabbage or 1 bunch collard greens
4 medium potatoes, peeled and quartered
1/4 cup skim milk
1 tablespoon soft margarine
Freshly ground pepper
Paprika

CREAM SAUCE

1 1/2 tablespoons soft margarine
1 medium onion, chopped
2 tablespoons all-purpose flour
1 cup skim milk
Salt, freshly ground pepper, and nutmeg

Separate and trim cabbage leaves or stems from collard leaves. In large pot of boiling water, cover and cook cabbage for 5 to 10 minutes, collards for 10 to 15 minutes, or until tender. Drain thoroughly; chop coarsely and set aside.

In saucepan of boiling water, cook potatoes until tender; drain. Mash potatoes along with milk, margarine, and pepper to taste.

Cream Sauce: Meanwhile, in small saucepan, melt margarine over medium heat; add onion and cook for 3 to 5 minutes or until tender. Stir in flour and mix well; cook, stirring, for 1 minute. Add milk and cook, stirring, for 3 to 5 minutes or until mixture comes to simmer and has thickened. Season with salt, pepper, and nutmeg to taste.

Mix sauce with cabbage; spoon into 4-cup baking dish. Cover evenly with mashed potatoes; sprinkle lightly with paprika. Bake in 350°F oven for 20 to 30 minutes or until heated through.

Gratin of Fall Vegetables

MAKES 8 SERVINGS

PER SERVING

129 calories
8 g fat
14 mg cholesterol
136 mg sodium

8 g protein
9 g carbohydrate

GOOD: fiber, vitamin A,
niacin, calcium
EXCELLENT: vitamin C

This cheese-topped vegetable casserole dish is a nice dish to serve as part of a meatless meal, or with roast chicken, turkey, or meats.

2 tablespoons vegetable oil
2 cups thin strips of small yellow turnip or rutabaga
1/2 cup water
1 sweet red pepper, cut in thin strips
3/4 cup thinly sliced onion
2 cups thinly sliced zucchini
1 cup sliced mushrooms (about 8)
4 medium tomatoes, cut in chunks
1/2 teaspoon dried oregano
Salt and freshly ground pepper
1 1/2 cups shredded low-fat mozzarella cheese
1 tablespoon grated Parmesan cheese

In large skillet or Dutch oven, heat oil over medium heat. Add turnip and cover and cook for 10 minutes or until tender, stirring occasionally. If necessary, add more water to prevent burning. Add red pepper and onions; cook, stirring, for 2 minutes.

Add zucchini and mushrooms; cook, stirring, for 3 minutes. Add tomatoes and increase heat to high; cook, stirring occasionally, 5 to 10 minutes or just until excess moisture has evaporated. Stir in oregano; season with salt and pepper to taste.

Spoon vegetable mixture into shallow heatproof baking dish; sprinkle evenly with mozzarella and Parmesan cheeses. Broil for 3 to 5 minutes or until cheese is melted and slightly browned. Or, prepared in advance, cover and refrigerate. Reheat in 350°F oven for 20 to 25 minutes or microwave at high (100%) power for 3 to 5 minutes or until heated through.

Mexican Rice and Bean Casserole

MAKES 6 SERVINGS, 1 CUP EACH

PER SERVING

263 calories
5 g fat
12 mg cholesterol
709 mg sodium

13 g protein
42 g carbohydrate

GOOD: vitamin A, thiamin, calcium
EXCELLENT: fiber, vitamin C, niacin, iron

This is a well-liked dish at our house. You may want to add a little less chili or cayenne if you have young children. Serve with a green vegetable, salad, and toast, tortillas, or pita bread.

1 teaspoon vegetable oil
½ cup water
1 large onion, chopped
2 cloves garlic, minced
1½ cups mushrooms, sliced (¼ pound)
2 sweet green peppers, chopped
¾ cup long-grain rice
3 cups canned red kidney beans, drained, about 2 16-ounce cans
1 16-ounce can whole peeled tomatoes
1 tablespoon chili powder
2 teaspoons ground cumin
¼ teaspoon cayenne pepper
1 cup shredded low-fat mozzarella cheese

In large skillet or Dutch oven, heat oil with water over medium heat. Add onion, garlic, mushrooms, and green peppers; simmer, stirring often, until onion is tender, about 10 minutes.

Add rice, beans, tomatoes, chili powder, cumin, and cayenne; cover and simmer for about 25 minutes or until rice is tender and most of the liquid is absorbed.

Transfer to baking dish and sprinkle with cheese. Bake in 350°F oven for 15 minutes or microwave at high (100%) power for 1 to 2 minutes or until cheese melts.

Vegetables

When my daughter asks what's for dinner, she can't understand why I often answer by mentioning only the meat course; to her the vegetables are as important and most enjoyable. I, too, love vegetables but often plan meals around the meat or fish because they usually take more time to prepare or cook. For healthy eating, vegetables should cover at least three-quarters of your dinner plate.

Vegetables are an important source of vitamins, minerals, carbohydrates, protein, and fiber. They are cholesterol-free and low in fat and calories.

Choose locally grown fresh vegetables that are in season for the best flavor and nutritive value. When out of season, frozen vegetables are often higher in nutritive value than fresh because imported vegetables lose nutrients during transportation and storage. For example, lettuce loses half its vitamin C in one week after it is picked. Canned vegetables are often higher in sodium than fresh or frozen.

Compare the Sodium Content of:

	Fresh	Canned	Frozen
Peas	5 mg	394 mg	147 mg
Green beans	4 mg	361 mg	19 mg

Cherry Tomatoes and Mushroom Sauté

MAKES 6 SERVINGS

PER SERVING

40 calories
2 g fat
0 mg cholesterol
24 mg sodium

1 g protein
5 g carbohydrate

GOOD: fiber
EXCELLENT: vitamin C

This dish is good any time of year, but especially in the winter when cherry tomatoes are usually less expensive and have better color and flavor than larger ones. Most fresh herbs can be used instead of dried.

1 tablespoon soft margarine
1 clove garlic, minced
½ pound medium mushrooms, halved
2 cups cherry tomatoes, stems removed
½ teaspoon dried oregano (or 1 tablespoon fresh)
½ teaspoon dried thyme (or 1 tablespoon fresh)
¼ cup chopped fresh parsley
Salt and freshly ground pepper

In large nonstick skillet, melt margarine over medium-high heat; cook garlic and mushrooms, shaking pan, for 3 minutes.

Add tomatoes, oregano, and thyme; cook for 3 to 5 minutes or until tomatoes are heated through and mushrooms are tender. (Can be prepared an hour or two in advance and reheated.) Sprinkle with parsley; season with salt and pepper to taste.

Skillet Zucchini with Chopped Tomatoes

MAKES 4 SERVINGS

PER SERVING

41 calories
1 g fat
0 mg cholesterol
18 mg sodium

1 g protein
8 g carbohydrate

GOOD: fiber
EXCELLENT: vitamin C

In the summer and fall when tomatoes are everywhere, this is the way I often prepare zucchini.

1 teaspoon soft margarine
2 small onions, chopped
4 small (6-inch) zucchini, thinly sliced
2 medium tomatoes, chopped
Freshly ground pepper

In large nonstick skillet, melt margarine over medium heat; add onions and cook, stirring, until softened. Add zucchini and cook for

2 minutes. Add tomatoes and cook for 3 to 5 minutes or until zucchini is tender-crisp. Season to taste with pepper.

Spaghetti Squash with Parsley and Garlic

MAKES 8 SERVINGS

PER SERVING

55 calories
2 g fat
0 mg cholesterol
41 mg sodium

1 g protein
9 g carbohydrate

GOOD: vitamin C

The spaghettilike strands of this unusual squash are very good tossed with garlic and parsley. Be sure to cut the squash crosswise or else you will cut the strands in half.

1 4-pound spaghetti squash
1 tablespoon margarine
3 cloves garlic, minced
1 cup coarsely chopped fresh parsley or grated zucchini
¼ cup low-fat plain yogurt (optional)
Freshly ground pepper

In large pot of boiling water, cook whole spaghetti squash until tender when pierced with skewer, about 30 minutes (some varieties of spaghetti squash may take longer).

In small skillet, melt margarine over medium-low heat; add garlic and cook until tender, about 1 minute.

Drain squash and cut in half crosswise. Scoop out seeds. Run tines of fork lengthwise over squash to loosen spaghettilike strands; scoop out strands into baking dish or serving bowl. Add garlic mixture, parsley, yogurt (if using), and pepper to taste; toss to mix. (Recipe can be prepared a day in advance and refrigerated. To serve, bring to room temperature, then reheat, covered, in 350°F oven for 35 minutes, or microwave on high for 8 to 10 minutes or until heated through.)

MICROWAVE METHOD: Pierce spaghetti squash in 10 to 15 places with a fork; place in microwave-safe dish and microwave at high (100%) power for 5 to 7 minutes per pound or until tender when pierced with a fork. Turn over halfway through cooking. Let stand 5 minutes.

VARIATION

For a very low-calorie meal serve spaghetti squash topped with vegetable mixture in lasagna recipe (page 134).

Note: Spaghetti squash can also be steamed. Cut squash in half crosswise; scoop out seeds. Steam for 15 to 20 minutes or until tender.

Squash

I love winter squash and most often serve it very simply—either in wedges still in its skin or mashed with a small amount of margarine and freshly ground pepper. If it is dry, add some orange or apple juice.

Preparation:
Cut squash in half and scoop out seeds and interior pulp.

To bake:
Place cut-side down on lightly greased baking sheet. Bake in 375°F oven 50 minutes for acorn squash, 70 minutes for butternut, at least 70 minutes for hubbard, or until flesh is tender when pierced with a fork.
Bake spaghetti squash whole. Prick skin with long tined fork in several places. Bake in 350°F oven for 50 to 90 minutes, depending on size. Squash is cooked when it is tender when pierced with a fork.

To steam:
Cut prepared squash into halves or quarters, hubbard or other large squash into chunks; peel if desired. Arrange on rack in steamer; add boiling water; cover and steam until tender, about 15 to 25 minutes depending on size of pieces. Serve as is or remove squash from skin and mash.

To microwave:
Place halves or quarters cut-side up on microwave-safe baking dish; cover with plastic wrap. Microwave on high (100%) power approximately 7 to 8 minutes per pound or until flesh is tender when pierced with a fork. (One whole acorn squash [about 1½ pounds], halved, will take 12 to 13 minutes, a 14-ounce butternut squash will take 7 minutes.)

Seasonings to add to mashed squash:
Nutmeg, cinnamon, maple syrup, brown sugar, minced fresh ginger, lemon juice, applesauce, fruit juice.

Baked Parsnips and Carrots

MAKES 4 SERVINGS

PER SERVING

119 calories
3 g fat
0 mg cholesterol
76 mg sodium

2 g protein
23 g carbohydrate

GOOD: vitamin C
EXCELLENT: fiber,
vitamin A

As a child, parsnips were one of the few foods I didn't like; now I love them. I'm not sure if it was because of the parsnips themselves or that they might have been overcooked. In any case, parsnips cooked around a roast, baked, or microwaved, are really sweet and delicious. Even my children like them this way.

2 parsnips
4 carrots
1 tablespoon soft margarine
Salt and freshly ground pepper
Pinch ground cumin (optional)
1 tablespoon water

Peel parsnips and carrots; cut in half crosswise, then cut lengthwise into strips. Place in baking dish and dot with margarine. Sprinkle with salt, pepper, and cumin (if using) to taste; add water.

Cover and bake in 375°F oven for 50 to 60 minutes or until vegetables are tender.

MICROWAVE METHOD: Place in a microwave-safe baking dish. Cover and microwave at high (100%) power for 12 to 15 minutes or until vegetables are tender.

Chinese-Style Vegetables

MAKES 6 SERVINGS

PER SERVING

71 calories
3 g fat
0 mg cholesterol
167 mg sodium

3 g protein
10 g carbohydrate

EXCELLENT: fiber,
vitamin A, vitamin C

Any seasonal vegetables can be added to this colorful stir-fry. Consider celery, onion, sweet peppers, mushrooms, green peas, beans, snow peas, tomatoes, asparagus, or Brussels sprouts. Instead of red or green cabbage, consider using bok choy or napa cabbage.

1 tablespoon vegetable oil
2 cups cauliflower florets
2 cups broccoli florets
4 medium carrots, sliced
½ cup chicken stock

¼ pound snow peas
1 teaspoon minced garlic
2 tablespoons minced fresh gingerroot
4 cups chopped red or green cabbage or bok choy (see Note)
1 teaspoon low-sodium soy sauce

In wok or large nonstick skillet, heat oil over medium heat. Add cauliflower, broccoli, and carrots; stir-fry for 3 minutes. Add chicken stock; cover and steam for 2 minutes.

Add snow peas; stir-fry for 1 minute. Add garlic, gingerroot, and cabbage; stir-fry for 1 minute. Stir in soy sauce.

Note: Bok choy is the Cantonese word for cabbage. We also call it Chinese cabbage. Its mild flavor is a pleasing addition to a stir-fry, soup, or salad. Napa cabbage is a crinkly-leafed lettuce also good in stir-frys.

Fresh Gingerroot

I love the flavor fresh ginger gives to cooked dishes and always try to have it on hand. It is far superior to ground ginger. Gingerroot is usually available in the fresh-produce section in supermarkets and at Oriental grocery stores.

To store: Will keep in the refrigerator for 2 to 3 weeks, or wrap tightly in plastic wrap and freeze for up to 4 weeks.

To use: I usually peel the skin from the portion of gingerroot I plan to use with a sharp knife or vegetable peeler, then either chop or finely grate it. I use fresh gingerroot most often in stir-frys such as Szechuan Orange-Ginger Chicken (page 111), and with vegetables, such as Broccoli with Ginger and Lemon (page 144).

Ground Ginger

To substitute ground ginger in recipes calling for gingerroot: Use ground ginger only if you can't find gingerroot. Use about ½ teaspoon ground ginger in most recipes in this book. Taste, then add another ½ teaspoon if desired.

Use ground ginger where called for in baked recipes such as cookies.

Peas with Scallions

MAKES 6 SERVINGS, ABOUT ½ CUP EACH

PER SERVING (½ cup)

68 calories
2 g fat
0 mg cholesterol
89 mg sodium

4 g protein
10 g carbohydrate

GOOD: vitamin A, fiber
EXCELLENT: vitamin C

Scallions or any other member of the onion family and green peas are a nice flavor combination. I use the white part of scallions, or chopped Spanish or regular cooking onions. Tiny pearl onions are lovely if you have the time it takes to peel them.

2 tablespoons soft margarine
1 cup chopped scallions (white parts) or Spanish or cooking onion
3 cups fresh or frozen peas
Freshly ground pepper

In nonstick skillet, melt margarine over medium heat; add scallions and cook, stirring often, until tender, about 5 minutes.

Meanwhile, blanch peas in boiling water; drain and add to skillet. Sprinkle with pepper to taste and mix gently.

Broccoli with Ginger and Lemon

MAKES 6 SERVINGS

PER SERVING

43 calories
2 g fat
0 mg cholesterol
10 mg sodium

2 g protein
5 g carbohydrate

GOOD: fiber, vitamin A
EXCELLENT: vitamin C

Broccoli, an excellent source of vitamin C and a good source of Vitamin A and fiber, is delightful with fresh gingerroot. However, using garlic instead of ginger is equally good.

1 1¼-pound bunch broccoli
1 tablespoon vegetable oil or soft margarine
2 teaspoons chopped fresh gingerroot
2 tablespoons lemon juice
Freshly ground pepper

Trim broccoli stalks (peel if tough) and cut into ½-inch thick pieces. Separate top into florets. In large pot of boiling water, cook broccoli for 3 to 5 minutes or until tender-crisp when pierced with knife; drain.

Meanwhile, in small skillet, heat oil or margarine over medium-low heat; cook gingerroot for 2 minutes. Add lemon juice.

Transfer broccoli to warmed serving dish; pour lemon-juice mixture over. Sprinkle with pepper to taste and mix lightly.

Green Beans with Sautéed Mushrooms

MAKES 4 SERVINGS

PER SERVING

57 calories
3 g fat
0 mg cholesterol
11 mg sodium

2 g protein
6 g carbohydrate

GOOD: fiber, vitamin C

Mushrooms and herbs dress up green beans and add extra flavor. If you want to be really fancy, use wild mushrooms.

3/4 pound green beans
1 tablespoon margarine
1 clove garlic, minced
2 teaspoons chopped fresh basil (or 1/2 teaspoon dried)
1/4 teaspoon dried crumbled rosemary
8 medium mushrooms, sliced
Dash hot pepper sauce

In saucepan of boiling water, cook beans for 6 to 8 minutes or until tender-crisp; drain.

Meanwhile in small saucepan or microwave-safe dish, melt margarine, add garlic, basil, rosemary, mushrooms, and hot pepper sauce; cook over medium heat for 3 to 4 minutes, or cover and microwave at high (100%) power for 1 minute, or until mushrooms are tender.

Transfer beans to warm serving dish; pour mushroom mixture over and toss to mix.

Make-Ahead Broccoli or Green Beans

If you are entertaining, you might want to partially cook a green vegetable in advance. I find this a big help when serving a first course at a dinner party. It's hard to judge how long it will take everyone to eat the first course, let alone get to the table. If you put the broccoli on to cook before everyone sits down, it'll be overcooked. If you wait until after the first course, it takes too long.

Cook prepared green vegetable in boiling water until tender-crisp when pierced with knife. Immediately drain and plunge into large bowl of ice water. Drain and wrap in paper towels; refrigerate for up to 1 day.

To serve: Blanch vegetable in large pot of boiling water; drain thoroughly. Toss with margarine and lemon juice or other seasonings.

Note: Don't add lemon juice to a green vegetable until just before serving. The acid will cause it to turn yellowish.

Brussels Sprouts with Peppers and Potatoes

MAKES 6 SERVINGS

PER SERVING

106 calories
2 g fat
0 mg cholesterol
69 mg sodium

4 g protein
20 g carbohydrate

GOOD: fiber
EXCELLENT: vitamin C

Wonderful with turkey or roast chicken, this is a tasty, colorful vegetable dish to serve for Sunday or Thanksgiving dinner.

1 tablespoon soft margarine or vegetable oil
1 large onion, chopped
1 large potato, cut in small cubes
1 bay leaf
1 pound Brussels sprouts, halved if large
1 sweet red pepper, cut in ½-inch pieces
¼ cup vegetable or chicken stock
Freshly ground pepper
2 tablespoons chopped fresh parsley or scallions

In large nonstick skillet, melt margarine over medium heat; cook onion, potato, and bay leaf, stirring often, for 2 to 3 minutes or until onion is softened.

Add Brussels sprouts, red pepper, and stock; cover and cook for 8 to 10 minutes or until sprouts and potatoes are tender (add water if necessary to prevent scorching).

Season with pepper to taste. Serve sprinkled with parsley or scallions.

About Brussels Sprouts

Look for small, compact, firm, bright-green Brussels sprouts.

Prepare by trimming outer leaves and base. Cut shallow "X" in base for even cooking. Boil, steam, stir-fry, or microwave. Cook until just tender-crisp to retain their bright-green color.

Carrots and Leeks with Parsley

MAKES 6 SERVINGS

PER SERVING

74 calories
2 g fat
0 mg cholesterol
71 mg sodium

2 g protein
14 g carbohydrate

GOOD: vitamin C, fiber
EXCELLENT: vitamin A

Choose tender, young carrots to combine with delicate-flavored leeks. Chopped fresh dill, thyme, or basil is a lovely addition to this dish.

1 pound carrots (6 medium)
4 medium leeks
2 teaspoons water (for microwave method)
1 tablespoon soft margarine
¼ cup chopped fresh parsley
Salt and freshly ground pepper

Scrape carrots and cut diagonally into ¼-inch-thick slices. Clean leeks, discarding tough green parts. Slice white and tender green parts in half lengthwise; cut crosswise into ½-inch-thick slices.

Place carrots in steamer over boiling water; cover and steam for 5 to 8 minutes or nearly tender-crisp. Add leeks and steam another 5 minutes. Transfer to warmed serving dish; toss with margarine, parsley, salt and pepper.

MICROWAVE METHOD: In microwave-safe dish, combine carrots and water; cover with lid or vented plastic wrap and microwave at high (100%) power for 5 minutes. Stir in leeks; dot with margarine. Cover and microwave at high (100%) power for 3 to 5 minutes or until vegetables are tender. Stir in parsley; season with salt and pepper to taste.

Leeks

To clean leeks: Trim base and tough green leaves from leeks, leaving tender green and white part.

If you want to use leeks whole, cut lengthwise in half part way down leek; otherwise cut in half lengthwise. Rinse under cold running water, spreading leaves apart.

To bake leeks: Place leeks on lightly oiled foil, dot with a small amount of high-polyunsaturated margarine (see page 253) and pepper. Wrap in foil. Bake in 350°F oven for 25 minutes or until tender.

Skillet Greens with Ginger and Celery

MAKES 5 SERVINGS

PER SERVING

59 calories
3 g fat
0 mg cholesterol
86 mg sodium*

2 g protein
8 g carbohydrate

GOOD: fiber
EXCELLENT: vitamin A,
vitamin C

*Nutrient analysis is based
on 1 cup of each of the
vegetables listed. The
sodium is mainly from the
Swiss chard.

Cabbage, kale, and collards belong to the cruciferous family of vegetables. It's now thought that these vegetables may help to reduce the risk of cancers of the colon, stomach, and esophagus. Kale, Swiss chard, spinach, and cabbage are all delicious cooked this way, either on their own or in a combination. Some tougher greens, such as collard or beet greens, should first be blanched. Rice vinegar is particularly good but any white vinegar can be used.

> 2 tablespoons cider, rice, or white vinegar
> 2 tablespoons water
> 2 teaspoons cornstarch
> 1 teaspoon granulated sugar
> 1 tablespoon vegetable oil
> 1 large onion, chopped
> 2 cups sliced celery
> 4 cups thinly sliced kale, Swiss chard, spinach, or cabbage
> 1 tablespoon grated fresh gingerroot

In small dish, mix together vinegar, water, cornstarch, and sugar; set aside.

In large wok or nonstick skillet, heat oil over medium-high heat. Add onion and stir-fry for 1 minute. Add celery, greens and gingerroot; stir-fry for 1 minute. Add about 2 tablespoons water; cover and steam for 3 minutes or until greens are wilted and celery is tender-crisp.

Pour in vinegar mixture and stir-fry for 1 minute or until liquid comes to boil. Serve immediately.

Mushroom-Stuffed Zucchini Cups

MAKES 4 SERVINGS

This is a delicious vegetable dish for a special dinner. It can be prepared early in the day then reheated in the oven or microwave just before serving.

> 2 medium zucchini (about 8 to 10 inches in length)

PER SERVING

45 calories
2 g fat
1 mg cholesterol
44 mg sodium

2 g protein
6 g carbohydrate

GOOD: vitamin C, fiber

2 teaspoons margarine
1 cup finely chopped mushrooms
1 tablespoon minced onion or shallots
1 tablespoon minced fresh parsley
Salt and freshly ground pepper
1 tablespoon grated Parmesan cheese

Trim ends from zucchini; cut crosswise into 1-inch-thick pieces. Steam zucchini for about 5 minutes or until tender-crisp; let cool. Scoop out small hollow from one end of each piece; set aside.

In nonstick skillet, melt margarine over medium-high heat; cook mushrooms and onion or shallots, stirring, for 2 minutes or until onion is tender. Stir in parsley; season with salt and pepper to taste. Spoon mushroom mixture into zucchini cavities. Arrange in micro-wave-safe dish or baking dish. Sprinkle with Parmesan cheese.

Just before serving, microwave at high (100%) power for 1 to 2 minutes or bake in 350°F oven for 15 to 20 minutes or until heated through.

Middle-Eastern Eggplant Baked with Yogurt and Fresh Mint

MAKES 6 SERVINGS

PER SERVING

116 calories
7 g fat
2 mg cholesterol
121 mg sodium

3 g protein
10 g carbohydrate

GOOD: fiber

This is one of the tastiest and easiest ways to prepare eggplant. It's very good with lamb. You can also serve it with pork, beef, or chicken or as part of a buffet or meatless dinner.

3 tablespoons vegetable oil
2 tablespoons water
1 large onion, sliced
1 medium eggplant, unpeeled (1¼ pound)
1 cup low-fat plain yogurt
3 tablespoons chopped fresh mint and/or parsley
2 cloves garlic, minced
¼ teaspoon salt
Freshly ground pepper
Paprika

(continued)

In large nonstick skillet, heat 1 teaspoon of the oil and water over medium heat; cook onion, stirring, for 5 minutes or until softened. Remove onion and set aside.

Cut eggplant into ¼-inch thick slices. Brush remaining oil over eggplant slices. In skillet over medium heat, cook eggplant (in batches) turning once, until tender, about 10 minutes (or arrange in a single layer on baking sheet and bake in 400°F oven for 15 minutes or until tender and soft).

In ungreased shallow baking dish, arrange overlapping slices of eggplant alternating with onion.

In small bowl, stir together yogurt, fresh mint or parsley, garlic, salt, and pepper to taste; drizzle over eggplant slices. Sprinkle liberally with paprika. Bake in 350°F oven until hot and bubbly, 10 to 15 minutes.

VARIATION

When tomatoes are in season, add slices of tomato between eggplant slices and onion in baking dish. Sprinkle top with grated low-fat mozzarella cheese.

Stir-Fry Ratatouille

MAKES 6 SERVINGS

PER SERVING

107 calories
7 g fat
0 mg cholesterol
12 mg sodium

2 g protein
11 g carbohydrate

GOOD: fiber, niacin
EXCELLENT: vitamin C

This version of the colorful Mediterranean vegetable dish is lower in oil and quicker to make than most and is good hot or cold. It's a colorful fall dish to serve with rice and cold meat or grilled lamb chops; for a meatless meal, cover with grated cheese and place under broiler until cheese melts and is golden brown. The vegetables are cooked in oil to soften and develop flavor. It's important to use as little oil as possible. If the vegetables stick to the pan, or to prevent scorching, add water, a spoonful at a time, and cook until water evaporates.

2 tablespoons vegetable oil
1 medium onion, sliced
2 cloves garlic, minced

8 medium mushrooms, halved
1 small sweet yellow or red pepper, cubed
2 cups cubed (½-inch pieces) unpeeled eggplant
1 small zucchini, sliced
2 tomatoes, cut in wedges
½ teaspoon dried thyme
½ teaspoon dried basil
Salt and freshly ground pepper

In large nonstick skillet, heat half of oil over medium-high heat; add onion, garlic, mushroom, and sweet pepper, and stir-fry until tender, about 4 minutes. With slotted spoon remove to side dish and set aside.

Heat remaining oil in skillet; add eggplant and zucchini; stir-fry for 4 minutes or until tender. Return mushroom mixture to pan, add tomatoes, thyme, and basil; cover and simmer for 5 minutes. Add salt and pepper to taste.

Steamed Fresh Vegetables

MAKES 4 SERVINGS

PER SERVING

121 calories
3 g fat
0 mg cholesterol
59 mg sodium

3 g protein
22 g carbohydrate

GOOD: niacin
EXCELLENT: fiber, vitamin A, vitamin C

It's easy to add interest and flavor to a dinner by serving a combination of 4 colorful vegetables. It takes the same amount of time to peel two carrots and two parsnips as it does to peel four carrots. It's also a great way to use up the four mushrooms or half a stalk of broccoli lurking in the back of your refrigerator. Other vegetables to substitute or add: celery, fennel, sweet red or green pepper, snow peas, cauliflower, zucchini, cabbage, and Brussels sprouts.

2 medium carrots, peeled and sliced
2 medium parsnips, peeled and sliced
1 stalk broccoli, cut in florets
8 mushrooms
1 tablespoon soft margarine
Salt and freshly ground pepper

Steam carrots and parsnips for 3 to 5 minutes or until tender-crisp. Add broccoli and mushrooms; steam for 3 minutes or until broccoli is bright green. Transfer to warm serving dish and add margarine. Sprinkle lightly with salt and pepper to taste; toss to mix.

MICROWAVE METHOD: In microwave-safe dish, combine carrots, parsnips, broccoli, and mushrooms. Add 1 tablespoon water. Dot with margarine; sprinkle with pepper to taste. Cover with lid or vented plastic wrap; microwave at high power for 6 minutes or until vegetables are tender; rotate dish once or twice during cooking. Add salt to taste.

Steamed Fennel with Zucchini, Carrots, and Scallions

The mild licorice flavor of fennel makes a pleasing addition to zucchini and carrots.

Cut about 6 scallions in half lengthwise then cut into 2-inch lengths. Steam scallions and 2 cups each julienne (thin strips) carrots, fennel, and zucchini for 6 to 8 minutes or until tender-crisp.

Transfer to warm serving platter and toss with a small amount of margarine, salt, and freshly ground pepper to taste.

Turnip and Apple Purée

MAKES 6 SERVINGS

Apple adds a mellow, sweet flavor to yellow turnip or rutabaga. For an equally delicious variation, use pear instead of apple. The recipe can be prepared up to a day in advance, but omit the yogurt and add when reheating.

1 small turnip (about 1¼ pounds), peeled and cubed
1 large apple, peeled, cored, and cut in chunks
¼ cup low-fat plain yogurt
1 tablespoon margarine

PER SERVING

54 calories
2 g fat
1 mg cholesterol
68 mg sodium

1 g protein
9 g carbohydrate

GOOD: fiber, vitamin C

Pinch nutmeg
Salt and freshly ground pepper

Steam turnip for 15 to 20 minutes or until nearly tender. Add apple and cook for 5 to 10 minutes or until turnip and apple are tender. Drain well.

In food processor or blender, purée turnip mixture until smooth (or mash or put through food mill). Add yogurt, margarine, and nutmeg; season with salt and pepper to taste and process just until combined. Reheat in saucepan over medium-low heat or in microwave at medium (50%) power until heated through.

Tomatoes Broiled with Goat Cheese and Basil

MAKES 6 SERVINGS

This simple dish is one of my favorites for entertaining. It goes well with any meat or poultry or as part of a buffet or meatless meal. It tastes best when made in the summer or fall when tomatoes are juicy and full of flavor. A soft or cream goat cheese, or chèvre, has a distinctive flavor that is lovely with tomatoes. If not available, use fresh mozzarella instead.

(continued)

Compare Fresh vs. Processed Foods for Sodium Content

Fresh Food	Milligrams Sodium	Processed Food	Milligrams Sodium
Tomatoes, 2 medium	20	Canned (1 cup)	683
		Tomato juice (1 cup)	931
		Ketchup (1 tablespoon)	177
Pork chop (3 ounces)	61	Ham, lean (3 ounces)	1319
Beef, round steak (3 ounces)	45	Canned beef and vegetable stew (1 cup)	1064
Beets, sliced, boiled (1 cup)	88	Beets, sliced, canned (1 cup)	493
Potatoes, boiled (1)	5	Scalloped potatoes (prepared from a dry mix)	883
Oatmeal, regular or quick cooking, cooked (½ cup)	1	Oatmeal, premix, ready to serve (1 1-ounce pouch)	323

PER SERVING

58	calories
3	g fat
13	mg cholesterol
173	mg sodium

3	g protein
5	g carbohydrate

GOOD: fiber, vitamin A
EXCELLENT: vitamin C

4 medium tomatoes
3 ounces soft goat cheese (chèvre)
Freshly ground pepper
3 tablespoons chopped fresh basil

Slice each tomato into about 4 thick slices. Arrange in single layer in shallow baking dish or microwave-safe dish.

Thinly slice goat cheese; arrange over tomatoes. Sprinkle with pepper to taste, then basil. Broil for 2 to 3 minutes or microwave at high (100%) power for 2 minutes or until cheese melts.

Fettuccine with Basil and Parsley

MAKES 4 SERVINGS

PER SERVING

237	calories
4	g fat
0	mg cholesterol
28	mg sodium

7	g protein
43	g carbohydrate

GOOD: fiber

Serve this as a side dish with any meats or as part of a meatless meal. Keep a pot of fresh parsley on the windowsill or a bunch in a plastic bag in the refrigerator to give a fresh flavor to this dish. Use any other fresh herbs you have, such as sage, rosemary, or thyme (start with 1 tablespoon and add more to taste), before adding dried.

¼ pound fettuccine or any pasta
1 tablespoon soft margarine
1 clove garlic, minced
⅓ cup chopped fresh parsley
¼ cup chopped fresh basil (or 1 teaspoon dried)
Freshly ground pepper

In large pot of boiling water, cook noodles according to package directions or until al dente (tender but firm). Drain in colander.

Add margarine and garlic to pot; cook, stirring, for 1 minute over medium heat. Add hot noodles, parsley, basil, and pepper to taste; toss to mix. Serve hot.

VARIATION

Add one large tomato, chopped, along with herbs. Sprinkle each serving with grated Parmesan cheese. Make with capellini or vermicelli noodles and serve as a first course.

Bulgur Pilaf with Apricots and Raisins

MAKES 4 SERVINGS

PER SERVING

230 calories
  3 g fat
  0 mg cholesterol
395 mg sodium

  8 g protein
 44 g carbohydrate

GOOD: iron
EXCELLENT: niacin,
fiber

Bulgur, or cracked wheat, is the rice of the Mediterranean. It is available in some supermarkets and most health food stores. Its mild nutty flavor and slightly crunchy texture are a nice change from regular rice. And, it is a good source of fiber.

2 teaspoons margarine
1 large onion, chopped
1 cup bulgur or cracked wheat
¼ cup raisins
¼ cup diced dried apricot
2 cups chicken stock, boiling
¼ cup chopped fresh parsley (optional)
Salt and freshly ground pepper

In nonstick skillet, melt margarine over medium heat; cook onion, stirring, until softened. Stir in bulgur and cook, stirring, for 1 minute. Stir in raisins, apricot, and stock; cover and simmer over low heat for 15 minutes or until liquid is absorbed. Stir in parsley (if using); season with salt and pepper to taste.

Compare the Following per Cup Cooked:

	Grams Fat	Milligrams Cholesterol	Milligrams Sodium	Grams Fiber	Grams Protein	Grams Carbohy-drate	Calories
Bulgur or cracked wheat	1	0	2	4	6	41	191
Rice, parboiled (converted)	0	0	5	0.5	4	41	186
Rice, regular white	0	0	4	0.6	4	50	223
Rice, brown	1	0	6	2	5	50	232
Macaroni	0.5	0	1	1	5	31	150
Spaghetti	0.5	0	1	1	5	31	150
Rice, wild	0.4	0	4	NA	8	40	188
Rice, enriched, instant (no added salt)	0	0	0	1	3	38	171

New Potatoes with Herbs

MAKES 4 SERVINGS

PER SERVING*

109 calories
1 g fat
0 mg cholesterol
5 mg sodium

2 g protein
23 g carbohydrate

EXCELLENT: vitamin C

*including oil

Small new potatoes, boiled in their skins, are delicious. Instead of butter, top with chopped fresh herbs and a dash of lemon juice and oil. These go well with any meats, poultry, or fish.

> 1 pound tiny new potatoes (about 20)
> 1 tablespoon chopped fresh basil or thyme
> 1 tablespoon chopped chives
> 1 teaspoon lemon juice
> 1 teaspoon olive or vegetable oil (optional)
> Freshly ground pepper

In saucepan, boil unpeeled potatoes until tender, about 15 minutes; drain. Add basil, chives, lemon juice, oil (if using), and pepper to taste. Mix lightly and serve.

Garlic-Parsley Potatoes

MAKES 4 SERVINGS

Boil 1 pound tiny new potatoes, red-skinned potatoes, or any you have on hand until tender. Peel only if skins are old and tough, because the skins add flavor, fiber, and vitamins.

In small saucepan or microwave dish combine 2 teaspoons margarine or oil and 2 cloves minced garlic, and cook over medium heat, stirring, for 1 minute or microwave on medium (50%) power for 30 seconds.

Drain potatoes and cut in half or quarters if large; transfer to warm serving dish. Toss with garlic mixture and ¼ cup chopped fresh parsley.

VARIATION

Instead of potatoes use green beans, carrots, cauliflower, broccoli, or peas.

Compare 1 Tablespoon of These Potato Toppings:

Starchy foods or complex carbohydrates, such as whole-wheat breads, pastas, rice, and potatoes, are not high in fat or calories. They are a good source of B vitamins, iron, and trace minerals. It's what we add to these starchy foods that increases the fat content in our diet.

	Grams Fat	Calories
Yogurt	1 or less	2 or less
Sour cream (14% butterfat)	3	28
Butter or margarine	11	100

Quick Lentils with Onion and Celery

MAKES 4 SERVINGS

PER SERVING

144 calories
  3 g fat
  0 mg cholesterol
 51 mg sodium

  8 g protein
 23 g carbohydrate

GOOD: vitamin C, iron
EXCELLENT: fiber

Keep a can of cooked lentils or a package of dried red lentils on your shelf and you can have a quick vegetable dish in minutes.

1 tablespoon soft margarine or vegetable oil
2 medium onions, chopped
2 stalks celery, chopped
1 clove garlic, minced
1 19-ounce can lentils, drained (or 2 cups cooked)
Pinch dried oregano
Salt and freshly ground pepper
½ cup chopped fresh parsley

In skillet, heat margarine over medium-high heat; cook onions, celery, and garlic, stirring, for 3 minutes or until onion is tender. Add lentils and oregano; cook until heated through. Season with salt and pepper to taste; sprinkle with parsley.

How to Cook Dried Lentils

Lentils are a good source of iron and an excellent source of fiber and vegetable protein. Serve with complementary cereal protein such as bread or rice. One cup of dried lentils will yield about 2 to 2½ cups cooked lentils.

Rinse and drain dried lentils. In saucepan, combine lentils with three times the amount of water (add a quartered onion and bay leaf if desired). Bring to a boil; reduce heat and simmer, covered, for 10 to 45 minutes depending on type, or until tender; drain. Use in salads, casseroles, soups, or as a vegetable.

Types of Lentils
Red lentils are used in most soups and cook in 10 to 15 minutes.

Green or brown whole lentils retain their shape when cooked and take about 45 minutes to cook.

Barley and Mushroom Pilaf

MAKES 8 SERVINGS, ⅔ CUP EACH

PER SERVING

122 calories
2 g fat
0 mg cholesterol
295 mg sodium

5 g protein
21 g carbohydrate

GOOD: fiber
EXCELLENT: niacin

I like to serve this as an alternative to rice or potatoes. Sometimes I vary it by adding chopped almonds, chopped celery or scallions, chopped fresh dill, thyme, or basil. It's nice for a buffet; it can be prepared a day in advance and refrigerated. Reheat, covered, in 350°F oven for 30 minutes.

1 tablespoon soft margarine
1 medium onion, chopped
¾ pound mushrooms, sliced
1 cup pot barley (see Note)
3 cups chicken stock, hot
½ cup chopped fresh parsley
Freshly ground pepper

In nonstick skillet, melt margarine over medium heat; add onion and cook for about 2 minutes or until softened. Add mushrooms and cook, stirring occasionally, for 5 minutes.

Transfer mixture to 11- × 7-inch baking dish; add barley and chicken stock. Bake, covered, in 350°F oven for 1 hour; uncover and bake for 10 minutes longer (or bake in 325°F oven for 1½ hours). Stir in parsley and pepper to taste.

Note: Pot barley is higher in fiber and more nutritious than pearl barley, which has been polished. They take the same length of time to cook. Both can be used instead of rice or pasta, in soups, and in casseroles.

VARIATION

RICE AND MUSHROOM PILAF: Substitute 1½ cups parboiled (converted) rice or brown rice for the barley. Stir rice into mushroom mixture. Add hot stock, then simmer covered 20 minutes for parboiled rice, 40 minutes for brown rice or transfer to baking dish. Bake, covered, in 350°F oven, 30 minutes for parboiled, 45 to 50 minutes for brown rice or until liquid has been absorbed. Makes 8 cups.

Cooking Rice

To cook white, parboiled, brown, or short- or long-grain rice:
Rinse under cold water. For each cup of rice bring 2 cups water or stock to a boil. Stir in rice; reduce heat, cover and simmer for 20+ minutes for white, 45 minutes for brown or until water is absorbed and rice is tender. One cup of raw rice yields about 3 cups when cooked.

To cook instant rice:
Follow package directions for cooking.

To cook wild rice:
Rinse under running water. Place in a saucepan. For each cup of rice add 4 cups cold water; bring to a boil. Cover and boil for 40 minutes or until grains are firm-tender but not mushy or split; drain.

Kinds of Rice

White rice is most common; during processing the bran is removed. It is either short- or long-grain.

Short-grain cooked rice is more sticky; long-grain rice is more firm and separate after cooking.

Parboiled rice is a white rice that has been processed so that when cooked, the grains are firm and separate. It is more nutritious than white rice because the thiamin is retained during processing. One manufacturer's brand name for parboiled rice is "converted" rice.

Brown rice is the most nutritious because it contains the bran and germ. It's higher in fiber and B vitamins than other rice.

Instant or precooked rice is white rice that has been cooked, then dehydrated. It cooks the fastest but is the least nutritious.

Wild rice is not really a rice but we use it as a rice. It has a wonderful nutty flavor and chewy texture. It is expensive and is often served mixed with cooked white or brown rice.

Sauces and Accompaniments

Sauces are like jewelry: they add the finishing touch to a meal, can dress it up, and pull it all together. Many traditional sauces contain large amounts of saturated fat, cholesterol, and calories from the butter, cream, and egg yolks used.

TO REDUCE FAT AND CHOLESTEROL IN SAUCES

- Use skim or 1% milk for whole milk.
- Use yogurt or milk instead of cream.
- Use recommended oil or margarine instead of butter and use as little as possible.
- Use low-fat cheese or part-skim instead of high-fat cheese.
- Use flour or cornstarch to thicken instead of egg yolk.
- Use thinner sauces or reduced sauces instead of thick sauces.
- Use meat drippings (au jus) instead of fatty gravies.
- Use a different kind of sauce (cranberry sauce, applesauce, or a relish) instead of gravy.
- Use the sauce recipes in this book.

Fresh Tomato Sauce

One of my favorite meals in August and September is a fresh tomato sauce made with plum tomatoes and fresh herbs served over pasta. Sometimes I add some cooked Italian sausage. I don't follow a recipe and the result is slightly different every time.

Cook a few pounds of small plum tomatoes (chopped) in a spoonful or two of olive oil (sometimes I add a chopped onion and some garlic) until they are soft, nearly smooth, thick, and of a saucelike consistency. This should take about 30 minutes. Add a handful of chopped fresh basil, or a pinch of dried rosemary or oregano, and you will have a wonderful Italian tomato sauce to toss with pasta. Top with freshly grated Parmesan cheese.

Note: The skin and seeds of tomatoes are high in fiber. I only peel tomatoes if the skin is very tough. When making a sauce using the small plum tomatoes, peeling isn't necessary.

The easiest way to peel tomatoes is to put them in a pot or bowl and cover with boiling water; let stand for about 30 seconds, then drain. The skin can easily be removed using a knife.

Cheese Sauce

MAKES ABOUT 1½ CUPS

PER SERVING (¼ cup)

97 calories
6 g fat
12 mg cholesterol
135 mg sodium

6 g protein
4 g carbohydrate

GOOD: Calcium

Cheese sauce is a traditional favorite to serve over cauliflower, broccoli, or other steamed vegetables and pasta. Because it adds extra fat but is a source of protein, it's a good choice to serve with a meatless meal. If serving as part of a meatless meal, you could add a little extra low-fat cheese for more protein. Using skim milk and a low-fat or part-skim cheese keeps the saturated fat content at a minimum.

1½ tablespoons soft margarine
2 tablespoons all-purpose flour
1 cup skim milk
1 cup shredded low-fat mozzarella cheese
Cayenne pepper

In saucepan, melt margarine over medium-low heat. Stir in flour and mix well; cook for 1 minute.

Stir in milk and cook over medium heat, stirring, 3 to 5 minutes, until mixture comes to a low boil and has thickened. Add cheese and stir until melted. Season with cayenne to taste.

Compare One Serving of Cheese Sauce Made with:

	Grams Fat	Calories
Skim milk and part-skim cheese	6	97
2% milk and part-skim cheese	7	103
Whole milk and Cheddar cheese	10	134

VARIATIONS

FRESH DILL CREAM SAUCE: Prepare cheese sauce recipe omitting grated cheese. Instead add ⅓ cup (not packed) chopped fresh dill, ¼ teaspoon salt, ¼ teaspoon dried mustard, and freshly ground pepper to taste. Serve with salmon, sole, or other fish either whole or in fillets or steaks. It's also very good with cauliflower.

Fresh dill makes this sauce delicious. If unavailable, use ⅓ cup chopped fresh parsley and 1 teaspoon dried dill. Other fresh herbs such as basil are also good but the amounts will vary. Add a tablespoon at a time and taste.

CREAM SAUCE: Prepare cheese sauce recipe, omitting grated cheese.

Yogurt Béarnaise Sauce

MAKES ABOUT 1¼ CUPS, ENOUGH FOR 12 PEOPLE
(1 TABLESPOON EACH)

In this version of a béarnaise sauce, the classic accompaniment to steak, I use yogurt instead of butter and half the usual number of egg yolks—so I call it a halfway healthy sauce. It's also delicious with grilled chicken, turkey, lamb, or fish. To serve with fish or seafood, substitute dill for tarragon. To serve with lamb or chicken, substitute basil for tarragon.

(continued)

PER SERVING
(1 tablespoon)

26 calories
1 g fat
47 mg cholesterol
16 mg sodium

2 g protein
2 g carbohydrate

NUTRITION NOTE

Instead of salt, keep a mixture of herbs handy and use to season meats, poultry, soups, salads, or salad dressings.

One pleasing combination is 1 teaspoon each of dried thyme, sage, and rosemary mixed with 1½ teaspoon each of dried marjoram and savory.

4 teaspoons chopped shallots or onions
¼ cup dry white wine
1 small clove garlic, crushed
1 tablespoon chopped fresh tarragon (or 1¼ teaspoon dried)
1 cup 2% plain yogurt (see Note)
2 egg yolks
1 teaspoon cornstarch
¼ teaspoon granulated sugar
Salt, cayenne, and freshly ground pepper

In small saucepan, combine shallots, wine, garlic, and tarragon; bring to boil over medium heat. Boil until liquid is reduced to 1 tablespoon.

In top of nonaluminum double boiler or saucepan, beat together yogurt, egg yolks, cornstarch, and sugar; add wine mixture.

Cook over simmering water, stirring often, until sauce has thickened, about 20 minutes. Remove from heat and season to taste with salt, cayenne, and pepper. Serve warm.

Sauce can be prepared in advance and refrigerated for up to 1 week. Reheat over hot water or at low (10%) power in microwave.

Note: For best results use a 2% or richer yogurt; a skim-milk yogurt isn't as good.

Compare the Nutritional Content in 1 Tablespoon of:

	Fat	Cholesterol	Calories
Yogurt Béarnaise Sauce	1 g	47 mg	26
Regular béarnaise sauce	12 g	98 mg	117

Cooking Beets

Beets can be steamed, baked, or microwaved as well as boiled. Don't peel before cooking beets for they will "bleed" too much. Boiling and steaming take about the same time. At least 30 minutes for small to medium young beets, about 60 minutes or longer for large, mature beets. Baking takes at least 10 to 15 minutes longer. Large old beets take twice as long to cook as young beets.

To microwave 1 ½ pounds medium to small beets: Place beets in microwave-safe dish; add ¼ cup water. Cover with lid or vented plastic wrap and microwave on high (100%) power for 12 to 15 minutes or until tender.

Beets Vinaigrette

MAKES 6 SERVINGS, ½ CUP EACH

Slice or julienne 1 ½ pounds cold cooked beets and toss with Mustard-Garlic Vinaigrette (page 83).

If desired add chopped onions, chives, or parsley. A beautiful addition to salad plates or appetizer salads. Use in late-summer and fall menus.

Old-Fashioned Pickled Beets

MAKES ABOUT 4 CUPS

PER SERVING (¼ cup)

11 calories
 0 g fat
 0 mg cholesterol
16 mg sodium

 0 g protein
 3 g carbohydrate

These are extremely easy to make, especially if you have any leftover cooked beets. They are a colorful addition to appetizer trays, salad plates, buffets, and potluck dinners and are good with hot or cold meats.

  9 medium beets (or 1 ½ pounds trimmed baby beets)
  1 cup water
  1 cup cider or white vinegar
  3 tablespoons granulated sugar

(continued)

Compare the Sodium Content of:

Old-Fashioned Pickled Beets (¼ cup)	16 mg
Dill pickle, 1 (4-inches)	1,942 mg

The dietary recommendation is that we limit our sodium intake to 3,000 milligrams per day. Pickles, especially dill pickles, can be very high in sodium; instead choose homemade pickled beets.

Trim beets leaving at least 1-inch stems attached. Place in saucepan and cover with warm water; bring to boil and simmer for 40 minutes or until tender.

Drain and rinse under cold running water. Using fingers, slip off skins. Quarter or cut into thick slices and place in clean 4-cup jar.

In saucepan, combine water, vinegar, and sugar; heat until sugar dissolves. Pour over beets; cover and let cool. Refrigerate for up to 2 months.

Sterilizing and Sealing Jars for Preserves and Relishes

Use Mason-type home-canning jars or glass jars with tight-fitting lids. Assemble the number of jars required, plus one extra in case there is a little more preserve than expected.

Wash jars in hot soapy water; rinse and set upright on a metal tray or sturdy baking sheet along with metal tongs, a heatproof measure or ladle, and a wide-mouthed metal funnel.

About 20 minutes before the preserve is ready, heat prepared equipment on tray in 225°F oven for 15 minutes. Leave all equipment in turned-off oven until needed.

Place lids and screw bands in small saucepan; cover with boiling water and boil for 5 minutes just before sealing jars or follow manufacturer's instructions.

Using ladle or measuring cup, pour preserve through funnel into jars, leaving ¼ inch headspace. Seal immediately. Wipe cooled, sealed jars and label. Store in a cool dark place for up to 1 year.

TO SEAL WITH PARAFFIN WAX

Melt paraffin wax in an old double boiler over simmering water or in a microwave-safe container with pouring spout using medium (50%) power. Pour thin layer of paraffin over preserve; tilt and rotate jar to extend seal to rim. Let cool and apply second thin layer in similar manner.

Red Pepper Jelly

MAKES ABOUT 6 CUPS

PER SERVING
(1 tablespoon)

40 calories
 0 g fat
 0 mg cholesterol
 2 mg sodium

 0 g protein
10 g carbohydrate

One year I make this with red peppers, the next, I use green. It is extremely quick and easy to make, is delicious with roast pork or chicken, and is a nice hostess gift. Use this jelly instead of gravy and rich sauces. Most store-bought condiments have a high salt content, this doesn't.

5 cups granulated sugar
2 cups finely chopped or puréed sweet red or green peppers (3 medium peppers)
1½ cups white vinegar
1 bottle (170 milliliters) liquid pectin

In large saucepan, combine sugar, red peppers, and vinegar; stir and bring to full boil. Boil over medium heat for 15 minutes, skimming off foam. Remove from heat; blend in pectin and stir for 2 minutes.

Pour into sterilized jars, leaving ¼ inch headspace; seal with paraffin wax. (See directions on pages 166–167.) Cover with lids. Store in cool, dry place.

Fresh-Tasting Cucumber Relish

MAKES ABOUT 8 CUPS

PER SERVING
(1 tablespoon)

19 calories
0 g fat
0 mg cholesterol
28 mg sodium

0 g protein
5 g carbohydrate

This recipe makes the best relish I've ever tasted. Serve it with cold meats, chops, or hamburgers.

4 cups coarsely shredded, peeled cucumbers (about 3½ large cucumbers) (see Note)
2 cups chopped onions
1 sweet red pepper, chopped
Half bunch celery, chopped
2½ cups packed brown sugar
1½ teaspoons salt
2⅓ cups white vinegar
6 tablespoons all-purpose flour
½ teaspoon ground turmeric
½ teaspoon dry mustard

In large heavy saucepan, combine cucumbers, onions, red pepper, celery, sugar, salt, and 1½ cups of the vinegar. Bring to boil over medium-high heat and boil for 15 minutes.

Meanwhile, in small bowl, blend together flour, turmeric, mustard, and remaining vinegar until smooth; whisk into cucumber mixture. Boil for 15 minutes (reduce heat but maintain a boil), stirring and skimming off any foam. Be careful mixture doesn't burn.

Ladle into sterilized jars, leaving ¼-inch headspace. Immediately cover with sterilized lids and seal tightly (See directions on pages 166–167.) Will keep up to a year unrefrigerated.

Note: If cucumbers have large seeds, remove and discard before shredding.

Compare the Sodium Content of 1 Tablespoon of:

Fresh-Tasting Cucumber Relish	28 mg
Sweet relish, store-bought	61 mg
Sour relish, store-bought	117 mg

Homemade Ketchup

MAKES ABOUT 1 CUP

PER SERVING
(1 tablespoon)

22 calories
0 g fat
0 mg cholesterol
9 mg sodium

0.5 g protein
5 g carbohydrate

This tastes delicious, is a snap to make, and is much lower in sodium than commercial ketchup.

1 6-ounce can tomato paste
¼ cup packed brown sugar
¼ cup water
2 tablespoons cider vinegar
¼ teaspoon dry mustard
¼ teaspoon ground cinnamon
Pinch cloves
Pinch allspice

In jar or bowl, combine tomato paste, sugar, water, vinegar, mustard, cinnamon, cloves, and allspice; mix well. Cover and store in refrigerator for up to 1 month.

Compare Sodium Content in 1 Tablespoon of:

Homemade Ketchup	9 mg
Commercial ketchup	170 mg

Fresh Mint Sauce

MAKES ABOUT ½ CUP

PER SERVING
(1 tablespoon)

21 calories
0 g fat
0 mg cholesterol
1 mg sodium

0 g protein
6 g carbohydrate

Make this accompaniment to roast lamb in the summer when fresh mint is everywhere because it grows like a weed. Since I'm a lazy gardener, I just keep a pot of it near the back door.

3 tablespoons granulated sugar
⅓ cup cider vinegar
¼ cup water
1½ teaspoon cornstarch
½ cup firmly packed fresh mint leaves, finely chopped

(continued)

In small saucepan, combine sugar, vinegar, water, and cornstarch; bring to boil over medium heat, stirring constantly. Stir in mint; simmer for 3 minutes.

Transfer to sauce boat and let stand for 30 minutes to develop flavors. Refrigerate any leftovers (up to 2 months).

Desserts and Baked Goods

When I take the time to bake or make a dessert I want it to taste really delicious. Cookies may have to be a little higher in fat than I would like but there is no sense making low-fat cookies that nobody eats. You can make some adjustments to a recipe to make it more nutritious, such as using whole-wheat flour instead of all-purpose and keeping sugar to a minimum. Most homemade cookies, as long as you use a recommended margarine or oil, are probably going to be lower in saturated fat than commercial cookies.

Too many rich desserts can add a huge amount of saturated fat and calories to your diet. There are desserts, however, that taste wonderful and are also low in fat. Instead of trying to make a low-fat chocolate mousse, try a fresh strawberry mousse; instead of an apple pie make an apple crisp. Imitation nondairy creams and toppings could be worse for you, as they usually contain saturated fats (palm and coconut oils). Fresh fruits in season are one of the best desserts for any type of meal.

Recipe Modification for Baked Goods

It is critical to understand the purpose of an ingredient before you change it.

- Flour forms the network of a baked product. In most recipes, to increase the fiber, you can substitute one-half the amount of all-purpose flour with a less refined flour, e.g., whole-wheat.

- Leavening agents are sodium-based (except yeast), but this ingredient can't easily be modified or the baked goods won't rise.
- Shortening, such as lard, and other fats add tenderness, crispness, lightness, and volume. All sources of animal fat, plus coconut and palm oil, and hydrogenated fats, should be avoided and replaced with polyunsaturated products (see the list of recommended margarines and vegetable oils on pages 253–255). Instead of butter or a margarine that is high in hydrogenated fats, choose a margarine that has twice as much polyunsaturated fats; instead of an oil containing palm or coconut oil, choose sunflower, safflower, or canola oil.
- Sugar and other sweeteners add flavor, color, tenderness, and crispness and can sometimes be reduced without affecting the quality of a product. Flavors that give the illusion of sweetness (without adding calories) are cinnamon, nutmeg, and vanilla.
- Liquids act as solvents for other ingredients as well as activating chemical reactions. Low-fat liquids that can sometimes be substituted are water, fruit juice, skim milk, or buttermilk.
- Eggs form the network of baked goods, adding flavor, color, and moisture. To reduce cholesterol, you can often substitute two egg whites for one whole egg.
- Salt adds flavor and acts as a catalyst that controls chemical reactions. However, there is no need to add salt in baked goods that call for margarine as margarine already contains salt.

Cranberry-Orange Muffins

MAKES 12 MEDIUM MUFFINS

These moist, high-fiber muffins are the best way I know to use up leftover cranberry sauce. It's even worth buying or making cranberry sauce just to use in these muffins.

> ¾ cup bran
> 1 cup whole-wheat flour

PER SERVING (1 muffin)

156 calories
  5 g fat
 23 mg cholesterol
126 mg sodium

  2 g protein
 27 g carbohydrate

GOOD: fiber

½ cup granulated sugar
1½ teaspoons ground cinnamon
1 teaspoon baking powder
1 teaspoon baking soda
1 cup whole cranberry sauce
1 egg
½ cup buttermilk or low-fat plain yogurt
¼ cup vegetable oil
1 teaspoon grated orange rind

In bowl, combine bran, flour, sugar, cinnamon, baking powder, and baking soda; mix well. Add cranberry sauce, egg, buttermilk or yogurt, vegetable oil, and orange rind; stir just until combined.

Spoon batter into paper-lined or nonstick medium-size muffin tins. Bake in 400°F oven for 25 minutes or until firm to the touch. Remove from oven and let stand 2 minutes before removing muffins from tin.

VARIATIONS

APPLE-RAISIN: Instead of cranberry, use 1 cup applesauce plus ½ cup raisins.

BANANA-DATE: Instead of cranberry, use 1 cup mashed banana and ½ cup chopped dates.

ZUCCHINI: Instead of cranberry, use 1 cup grated unpeeled zucchini and ½ cup raisins.

Oat Bran Banana-Raisin Muffins

MAKES 12 MEDIUM MUFFINS

Oat bran is available in the cereal section in most supermarkets. It is an excellent source of the kind of fiber that is currently thought to help lower blood cholesterol; wheat bran doesn't have the same cholesterol-lowering effect.

(continued)

PER SERVING (1 muffin)

165 calories
5 g fat
23 mg cholesterol
102 mg sodium

3 g protein
29 g carbohydrate

GOOD: fiber

1 egg, lightly beaten
1/4 cup vegetable oil
1/2 cup granulated sugar
1 cup mashed bananas
1 teaspoon vanilla
1 cup whole-wheat flour
1 teaspoon baking soda
1 teaspoon baking powder
3/4 cup oat bran
1/2 cup raisins

In bowl, combine egg, oil, sugar, bananas, and vanilla; mix well. In another bowl, mix together flour, baking soda, baking powder, oat bran, and raisins; stir into egg mixture, mixing only until combined.

Spoon into 12 nonstick or paper-lined medium-size muffin tins, filling each about 2/3 full. Bake in 400°F oven for 20 to 25 minutes or until firm to the touch. Remove from oven and let stand 2 minutes before removing muffins from tin.

Buttermilk, Bran, and Blueberry Muffins

MAKES ABOUT 20 LARGE MUFFINS

These are delicious and healthy low-fat, high-fiber muffins.

PER SERVING (1 muffin)

160 calories
5 g fat
31 mg cholesterol
111 mg sodium

5 g protein
29 g carbohydrate

GOOD: niacin, iron
EXCELLENT: fiber

3 cups bran
2 cups whole-wheat flour
1/2 cup granulated sugar
1 tablespoon baking powder
1 teaspoon baking soda
2 eggs, beaten
2 cups buttermilk (see Note)
1/3 cup vegetable oil
1/2 cup molasses
1 cup fresh or frozen blueberries

In large bowl, mix together bran, flour, sugar, baking powder, and baking soda. In another bowl, combine eggs, buttermilk, oil, and molasses; pour into bran mixture and stir just enough to moisten, being careful not to overmix. Fold in blueberries.

Spoon into nonstick or paper-lined large muffin tins filling almost to top. Bake in 375°F oven for about 25 minutes or until firm to the touch. Remove from oven and let stand for 2 minutes before removing muffins from tin.

Note: Instead of buttermilk, you can substitute soured milk. To sour milk, combine 2 cups milk with 2 tablespoons white vinegar.

Oatmeal Carrot Muffins

MAKES 12 LARGE MUFFINS

This fabulous muffin recipe is as good tasting as it is for you.

PER SERVING (1 muffin)

176 calories
5 g fat
23 mg cholesterol
307 mg sodium

4 g protein
30 g carbohydrate

GOOD: fiber

1 cup buttermilk
1 cup quick-cooking rolled oats
½ cup grated carrots
¼ cup packed brown sugar
¼ cup margarine, melted
1 egg, slightly beaten
1 teaspoon grated orange rind
1 cup all-purpose flour
¼ cup granulated sugar
1 tablespoon baking powder
1 teaspoon salt
½ teaspoon baking soda
¾ cup raisins

In large bowl, pour buttermilk over oats; stir to mix. Cover and let stand for 2 hours or refrigerate overnight.

Mix together carrots, brown sugar, margarine, egg, and orange rind; stir into oat mixture. Sift together flour, granulated sugar, baking powder, salt, and baking soda; stir in raisins. Stir into batter just until moistened.

(continued)

Spoon into nonstick or paper-lined large muffin tins filling almost to top. Bake in 400°F oven for 20 to 25 minutes or until firm to the touch. Let stand for 2 minutes before removing from tins.

Applesauce-Raisin Squares

MAKES 25 1½-INCH SQUARES

PER SERVING (1 square)

88 calories
3 g fat
11 mg cholesterol
10 mg sodium

2 g protein
14 g carbohydrate

Cinnamon and lemon add extra flavor to these moist, cakelike squares.

1 egg
¼ cup vegetable oil
½ cup low-fat plain yogurt
¾ cup packed brown sugar
1 cup unsweetened applesauce
1 teaspoon vanilla
1 teaspoon grated lemon rind
½ cup raisins
1 cup whole-wheat flour
½ cup bran
1 teaspoon baking powder
2 teaspoons ground cinnamon
1 teaspoon ground ginger
¼ teaspoon ground nutmeg
⅓ cup sliced almonds

In large mixing bowl, beat egg; add oil, yogurt, brown sugar, applesauce, vanilla, and lemon rind; mix well.

In another bowl, stir together raisins, flour, bran, baking powder, cinnamon, ginger, and nutmeg; add to wet ingredients and mix only until combined.

Turn into lightly greased 8-inch square cake pan. Lightly press almonds into top of batter. Bake in 350°F oven for 45 minutes or until tester inserted in center comes out clean. (Squares will be moist.) Let cool, then cut into squares.

Oatmeal-Apricot Cookies

MAKES ABOUT 50 COOKIES

PER SERVING (1 cookie)

52 calories
2 g fat
6 mg cholesterol
25 mg sodium

1 g protein
1 g carbohydrate

I test how good cookies are by how long they stay around my house. These passed with flying colors because they were all gone in a few hours. They are much lower in fat and higher in fiber than most cookies.

⅓ cup margarine
1 cup packed brown sugar
1 egg
½ cup 2% milk
1 teaspoon vanilla
1 cup whole-wheat flour
1 teaspoon baking powder
½ teaspoon baking soda
½ teaspoon ground cinnamon
1¼ cups rolled oats
¼ cup wheat germ
1 cup chopped dried apricots (or dates, raisins, or a combination)

In large mixing bowl, combine margarine, sugar, and egg; beat well. Beat in milk and vanilla. Add flour, baking powder, baking soda, cinnamon, rolled oats, wheat germ, and raisins; mix well.

Drop batter a small spoonful at a time onto nonstick baking sheet. Bake in 375°F oven for 12 to 15 minutes or until golden. Remove from oven and let stand a minute or two before removing from baking sheet to a rack to cool.

Easy Oat Bran and Date Cookies

MAKES ABOUT 3 DOZEN COOKIES

These easy-to-make, crisp cookies are a favorite in our house. Oat bran is available in the cereal section of most supermarkets. An excellent source of soluble fiber, it helps to reduce blood cholesterol.

(continued)

PER SERVING
(1 cookie)*

---

97 calories
4 g fat
8 mg cholesterol
64 mg sodium

---

1 g protein
14 g carbohydrate

*made with coconut

²⁄₃ cup soft margarine
1 cup packed brown sugar
1 egg, slightly beaten
1 tablespoon water
1 cup whole-wheat flour
1 cup oat bran
¼ cup wheat germ
1 teaspoon baking soda
1 teaspoon baking powder
1 cup chopped dates or raisins
½ cup chopped nuts, chocolate chips, or coconut (optional)

In large bowl, cream margarine, brown sugar, egg, and water together thoroughly. Add flour, oat bran, wheat germ, baking soda, and baking powder; mix well. Stir in dates or raisins, and nuts (if using).

Drop batter by spoonfuls onto lightly greased baking sheets; flatten slightly with floured fork. Bake in 350°F oven for 15 minutes or until light golden. Remove from oven and let stand a minute or two. Then transfer to a rack to cool.

Multigrain Date Quickbread

MAKES 1 LOAF, ABOUT 20 SLICES

PER SERVING (1 slice)

81 calories
1 g fat
1 mg cholesterol
82 mg sodium

---

2 g protein
18 g carbohydrate

GOOD: fiber

Serve this dark, flavorful bread for lunch with Tarragon Chicken Salad (page 64) or Pasta and Fresh Vegetable Salad (page 80) and sliced tomatoes.

1 cup boiling water
1 cup dates or raisins
1 teaspoon baking soda
¾ cup bran
1 cup whole-wheat flour or graham flour
1 cup rolled oats
⅓ cup granulated sugar
1 teaspoon baking powder
¼ teaspoon salt
1 cup 2% milk

Grease and flour a 9- × 5-inch loaf pan.

In large bowl, pour boiling water over dates or raisins; add soda and let stand for 5 minutes.

Add natural bran, flour, rolled oats, sugar, baking powder, salt, and milk; mix until combined. Pour into pan. Bake in 350°F oven for 70 to 80 minutes or until toothpick inserted in center comes out clean.

Whole-Wheat Zucchini Bread

MAKES 2 LOAVES, ABOUT 13 SLICES EACH

PER SERVING (1 slice)

152 calories
  4 g fat
 21 mg cholesterol
100 mg sodium

  3 g protein
 27 g carbohydrate

This version of zucchini bread is lower in fat and cholesterol than most, yet it is moist and full of flavor. If you are on a low-cholesterol diet, you can reduce the cholesterol to zero by substituting 4 egg whites for the 2 eggs.

1½ cups all-purpose flour
1½ cups whole-wheat flour
1 tablespoon ground cinnamon
1 teaspoon ground nutmeg
1 teaspoon baking soda
1 teaspoon baking powder
½ teaspoon salt
¾ cup raisins
2 eggs
⅓ cup vegetable oil
¾ cup low-fat plain yogurt
¼ cup milk
1 cup packed brown sugar
2 teaspoons vanilla
2 cups finely shredded unpeeled zucchini

In bowl, combine all-purpose and whole-wheat flours, cinnamon, nutmeg, baking soda, baking powder, salt, and raisins.

In large bowl, beat eggs until foamy; beat in oil, yogurt, milk, sugar, and vanilla. Stir in zucchini. Add flour mixture and stir until combined.

Pour batter into 2 well-greased 8- × 4-inch loaf pans. Bake in

350°F oven for 55 minutes or until toothpick inserted in center comes out clean. Remove from pan and let cool thoroughly before slicing.

Five-Grain Soda Bread

MAKES 1 LOAF, ABOUT 16 SLICES

PER SERVING (1 slice)

128 calories
3 g fat
1 mg cholesterol
185 mg sodium

4 g protein
22 g carbohydrate

GOOD: fiber

This is a quick and easy bread to make. It's particularly good served hot with brunch or with bean dishes, such as Bean Casserole with Tomato and Spinach (page 129). If you don't have all of these flours, use a combination of what you have to make a total of 3¼ cups and add ¾ cup rolled oats.

1 cup all-purpose flour
¾ cup whole-wheat flour
¾ cup rye flour
¾ cup graham flour
¾ cup rolled oats
2 tablespoons granulated sugar
1 tablespoon baking powder
1 teaspoon baking soda
½ teaspoon salt
3 tablespoons soft margarine or vegetable oil
¾ cup raisins (optional)
1¾ cups buttermilk, or soured milk (page 175)

In bowl, combine all-purpose, whole-wheat, rye, and graham flours, rolled oats, sugar, baking powder, baking soda, and salt; cut in margarine until well mixed. Stir in raisins (if using), add buttermilk, and stir to make soft dough.

Turn out onto lightly floured surface and knead about 10 times or until smooth. Place on greased baking sheet; flatten into circle about 2½ inches thick. Cut large "X" about ¼ inch deep on top.

Bake in 350°F oven for 1 hour or until toothpick inserted in center comes out clean.

Whole-Wheat Oatmeal Bread

MAKES 2 LOAVES, ABOUT 16 SLICES EACH

PER SERVING (1 slice)

83	calories
1.5	g fat
1	mg cholesterol
40	mg sodium
3	g protein
15	g carbohydrate

Whole-wheat bread has three times the fiber of white bread, more protein, and much more flavor.

1 cup 2% milk
⅓ cup packed brown sugar
2 tablespoons vegetable oil
½ teaspoon salt
1 teaspoon granulated sugar
1 cup warm water (approximately 110°F)
1 package active dry yeast (or 1 tablespoon)
4 cups (approximately) whole-wheat flour
1 cup rolled oats
¼ cup wheat germ (optional)

TOPPING
1 egg white
1 tablespoon 2% milk
1 teaspoon dill seeds
1 teaspoon celery seeds
2 tablespoons rolled oats

In saucepan (or large bowl in microwave), heat milk until hot; stir in brown sugar, oil, and salt until blended and sugar has dissolved. Let cool to lukewarm.

In small bowl, dissolve granulated sugar in warm water; sprinkle yeast over top and let stand for 10 minutes or until foamy.

In large bowl, combine milk mixture and yeast mixture. Using electric mixer or by hand, gradually beat in 3 cups of the flour; beat for 2 to 3 minutes or until smooth.

Gradually mix in rolled oats and wheat germ (if using); add enough of the remaining flour to make medium-stiff dough. Turn out onto lightly floured surface and knead until smooth and elastic, about 10 minutes. (If dough is sticky, knead in more flour.)

Place dough in lightly greased bowl, turning to grease all sides. Cover bowl with greased plastic wrap. Let rise in warm place until doubled in bulk, about 1 hour.

Punch down dough and turn out onto lightly floured surface.

Divide in half, forming each half into smooth ball. Cover and let rest for 10 minutes.

Shape each half into round or rectangular shape; place rectangular shapes in 2 greased 8- × 4-inch loaf pans; place round shapes on baking sheet. Cover with plastic bag or greased waxed paper; let rise until doubled in bulk, about 1 hour.

Topping: In small bowl, mix egg white with milk; brush over top of dough. Combine dill seeds, celery seeds, and rolled oats; sprinkle over dough.

Bake in 400°F oven for 15 minutes; reduce heat to 350°F and bake for 20 to 25 minutes longer or until crusts are brown and loaves sound hollow when tapped on bottom. Remove from pans and let cool on racks.

VARIATION

FOOD PROCESSOR METHOD: Halve recipe, except use the same amount of yeast (1 package or 1 tablespoon). Dissolve granulated sugar and yeast as directed.

In food processor fitted with metal or dough blade, combine flour, rolled oats, wheat germ (if using), brown sugar, and salt; process to combine. Stir oil into dissolved yeast mixture; add to flour mixture and process for 5 seconds.

With machine running, gradually add cold milk; process until dough forms ball, about 45 seconds. If dough is too dry, add more water 1 tablespoon at a time. If too sticky, add more flour a little at a time and process with off-on turns. Transfer dough to greased bowl and follow above recipe.

Flatbread Crackers

MAKES 24 SERVINGS,
ABOUT 5 PIECES EACH

Arrange this crisp, thin bread, or crackers, in a wicker basket and serve with salads or soups, or break into small pieces and use instead of chips for dipping.

PER SERVING (5 pieces)

96 calories
4.5 g fat
 1 mg cholesterol
98 mg sodium

 3 g protein
12 g carbohydrate

½ cup sesame seeds
½ cup cracked wheat
1 cup all-purpose flour
1 cup whole-wheat flour
1 tablespoon granulated sugar
½ teaspoon salt
½ teaspoon baking soda
⅓ cup soft margarine
¾ cup buttermilk

TOPPING

1 egg white
1 tablespoon water
2 tablespoons poppyseeds

In bowl, combine sesame seeds, cracked wheat, all-purpose and whole-wheat flours, sugar, salt, and baking soda; cut in margarine. Add buttermilk; mix well.

Shape into 6 balls about the size of a lemon; roll out on lightly floured surface into circles less than ⅛ inch thick (as thin as you can). Using spatula, transfer to ungreased baking sheet.

Topping: Combine egg white and water; brush over top of circles. Sprinkle with poppyseeds. Bake in 400°F oven for 10 minutes or until golden brown.

Let cool on wire rack until crisp. Break in smaller pieces and store in airtight container.

Basic Crêpes

MAKES 8 (8-INCH) CRÊPES

This all-purpose crêpe batter is low in cholesterol and fat. If you're on a low-cholesterol diet, use 2 whites instead of a whole egg. Prepare a batch of crêpes when you have time; freeze them and you'll be able to make a main course such as Curried Chicken Crêpes (page 104) or a luscious dessert of Peach Crêpes with Easy Grand Marnier Sauce (page 191) at a moment's notice.

PER SERVING*

39 calories
0.5 g fat
1 mg cholesterol
20 mg sodium

2 g protein
7 g carbohydrate

*plain crêpe

PER SERVING*

44 calories
0.5 g fat
1 mg cholesterol
20 mg sodium

2 g protein
8 g carbohydrate

*dessert crêpe

½ cup all-purpose flour
Pinch salt
2 egg whites, lightly beaten
⅓ cup 2% milk
⅓ cup water
½ teaspoon soft margarine

In bowl, combine flour and salt. Make a well in center and add egg whites. While whisking, gradually add milk and water, whisking until mixture is smooth.

Heat small nonstick skillet or crêpe pan (6 to 8 inches) over medium-high heat. Add margarine and brush over bottom of pan. Add 1 to 2 tablespoons of batter and swirl to cover bottom of pan. You should have just enough batter to lightly coat bottom of pan; pour off any excess. Shake pan and cook until edges begin to curl and crêpe no longer sticks to pan. Turn crêpe and cook for a few seconds or until golden. Remove from pan and set aside. Repeat with remaining batter. You shouldn't need to add any more margarine.

Crêpes can be made in advance; stack between waxed paper and refrigerate for 1 day or freeze up to 1 month.

VARIATION

DESSERT CRÊPES: For dessert crêpes, add 2 teaspoons granulated sugar, and ½ teaspoon each grated orange and lemon rind to batter.

Lemon Roll with Berries or Fresh Fruit

MAKES 8 SERVINGS

Serve this light lemon-filled cake roll with whatever fruit is in season—orange and kiwi slices are nice in winter, strawberries in spring, blueberries in summer, and peaches or grapes in the fall. For maximum flavor be sure to serve the fruit at room temperature, not straight from the refrigerator.

PER SERVING

198 calories
  2 g fat
 34 mg cholesterol
 95 mg sodium

  4 g protein
 42 g carbohydrate

GOOD: vitamin C, fiber

LEMON FILLING

3 tablespoons cornstarch
⅓ cup granulated sugar
1 teaspoon grated lemon rind
⅓ cup lemon juice
¾ cup water
1 egg yolk
1 tablespoon margarine

CAKE

5 egg whites
⅛ teaspoon salt
⅛ teaspoon cream of tartar
½ cup granulated sugar
½ cup sifted cake flour
2 teaspoons lemon juice
½ teaspoon vanilla
¼ teaspoon almond extract
3 tablespoons confectioners' sugar

2 oranges, peeled and sliced
2 kiwi, peeled and sliced
     or
4 cups strawberries or blueberries

Lemon Filling: In small saucepan, combine cornstarch with sugar; whisk in lemon rind, juice, and water. Bring to boil over medium heat, stirring constantly, and cook for 2 minutes or until thickened and smooth. Blend a little of the hot mixture into egg yolk; stir yolk mixture into saucepan. Cook over low heat, stirring constantly, for 2 minutes. Remove from heat and stir in margarine. Let cool, stirring frequently to prevent skin from forming on top.

Cake: Line 15- × 10-inch jelly-roll pan or baking sheet with foil; thoroughly grease and flour foil.

In large bowl, beat egg whites, salt, and cream of tartar just until mixture mounds on spoon (not quite to soft peak stage). Using spatula, fold in granulated sugar, a large spoonful at a time. Sift half of the flour over egg white–mixture and fold in gently; repeat with remaining flour. Fold in lemon juice, vanilla, and almond extract.

Spread in prepared pan; bake in 300°F oven for 25 minutes or until firm to the touch. (Cake will be light in color.)

Sift half of confectioners' sugar over cake; cover with tea towel then inverted baking sheet. Turn cake over and carefully remove jelly-roll pan and foil. Trim any crusty edges. While cake is hot, roll up in towel, starting at long side, jelly-roll fashion; let cool. (Cake and filling can be prepared to this point, covered, and refrigerated for up to 1 day.)

Unroll cake and spread evenly with lemon filling. Roll up cake using towel to help roll. Sift remaining confectioners' sugar over top. Place seam-side down on serving platter. Just before serving arrange slices of fresh orange and kiwi around lemon roll.

Blueberry Cream Flan

MAKES 12 SERVINGS

PER SERVING

232 calories
6 g fat
25 mg cholesterol
89 mg sodium

5 g protein
40 g carbohydrate

No one will ever guess that this cheesecake-type dessert is made with yogurt.

1½ cups all-purpose flour
½ cup granulated sugar
1½ teaspoons baking powder
⅓ cup soft margarine
2 egg whites
1 teaspoon vanilla
3 cups blueberries, fresh or frozen (not thawed)

TOPPING

2 tablespoons all-purpose flour
2 cups low-fat plain yogurt
1 egg, lightly beaten
⅔ cup granulated sugar
2 teaspoons grated lemon or orange rind
1 teaspoon vanilla

In food processor or mixing bowl, combine flour, sugar, baking powder, margarine, egg whites, and vanilla; mix well. Press into bottom of 10-inch springform, flan, or square cake pan; sprinkle with blueberries.

Topping: In bowl, sprinkle flour over yogurt. Add egg, sugar, rind, and vanilla; mix until smooth. Pour over berries.

Bake in 350°F oven for 60 to 70 minutes or until golden. Serve warm or cold.

Streusel Plum Cake

MAKES 10 SERVINGS

PER SERVING (1 piece)

288 calories
8 g fat
56 mg cholesterol
109 mg sodium

4 g protein
50 g carbohydrate

This is a lovely cake to serve for a special Sunday-night dinner or for dessert when you have guests in for bridge or after the movies. I like it because it isn't too sweet, yet it's moist and full of flavor. The glaze is optional—it only takes a minute to prepare and makes the cake look fancy, yet adds only a few more calories.

¼ cup margarine
¾ cup granulated sugar
2 eggs, separated
1½ cups all-purpose flour
1 teaspoon baking powder
½ cup 2% milk
2 16-ounce cans plums, drained (or 2 cups halved, pitted ripe plums)

STREUSEL TOPPING

½ cup packed brown sugar
1 tablespoon soft margarine
1 teaspoon ground cinnamon

GLAZE (OPTIONAL)

¼ cup confectioners' sugar
1 teaspoon 2% milk
¼ teaspoon vanilla

Grease 9-inch square cake pan (see Note), or use greased springform or flan pan.

In large bowl, cream together margarine, sugar, and egg yolks until fluffy. Combine flour and baking powder; beat into egg mixture alternately with milk. Beat egg whites until stiff but not dry; fold into batter. Turn into prepared pan. Halve and pit plums and arrange over top.

Streusel topping: In small bowl, combine brown sugar, margarine, and cinnamon; mix well and sprinkle over fruit.

Bake in 350°F oven for 35 to 45 minutes or until top is golden and toothpick inserted into cake comes out clean.

Glaze: Combine confectioners' sugar, milk, and vanilla; mix well. Drizzle over cool cake.

Note: I sometimes use a 10-inch cake pan because I like a thinner cake. However, a 9- or 8-inch pan also works well but will take a longer cooking time.
Cooking times: 8-inch pan—50 minutes
9- or 10-inch pan—35 to 45 minutes

VARIATIONS

PEACH STREUSEL CAKE: Instead of plums use 2 fresh peaches, sliced into wedges, or 1 16-ounce can sliced peaches, thoroughly drained.

APPLE STREUSEL CAKE: Instead of plums use 2 apples, sliced into thin wedges. (If apples are unpeeled the fiber content is higher.)

PEAR STREUSEL CAKE: Instead of plums use 2 pears, sliced into wedges, or 1 16-ounce can sliced pears, thoroughly drained.

Portable Picnic Dessert

Take a container of sliced strawberries sprinkled with a small amount of sugar, a container of plain yogurt, and a small jar of brown sugar to picnic. Also pack some clear plastic glasses and spoons. Spoon strawberries into glasses, top with yogurt, and sprinkle with brown sugar.

Strawberry Mousse

MAKES 6 SERVINGS.

This is a wonderful dinner-party dessert. It's light yet full of flavor, can be prepared in advance, and is easy to make.

1 envelope unflavored gelatin
¼ cup orange juice
3 cups fresh strawberries
¼ cup confectioners' sugar
⅓ cup whipping cream (optional)
4 egg whites
¼ cup granulated sugar

Fresh strawberries, hulled

In small microwave-safe dish or saucepan, sprinkle gelatin over orange juice; let stand for 5 minutes to soften. Microwave at medium (50%) power for 30 seconds, or warm over low heat until gelatin has dissolved.

Meanwhile, hull strawberries and place in food processor or blender; add confectioners' sugar and process just until puréed (you should have about 1½ cups). Transfer to mixing bowl and stir in gelatin mixture. Refrigerate until mixture is consistency of raw egg whites.

Whip cream (if using) and set aside. In large bowl, beat egg whites until soft peaks form; gradually add granulated sugar, beating until stiff peaks form. Whisk about ¼ of the beaten egg whites into strawberry mixture.

Fold strawberry mixture along with whipped cream into remaining beaten egg whites. Pour into 6-cup glass serving bowl or individual sherbet or stemmed glasses; refrigerate for at least 4 hours or up to 2 days. Garnish with fresh strawberries.   *(continued)*

Compare One Serving of Strawberry Mousse Made with:

	Grams Fat	Milligrams Cholesterol	Calories
No whipping cream	0	0	90
⅓ cup whipping cream	4	15	128
1 cup whipping cream	13	44	206

VARIATION

STRAWBERRY MOUSSE CAKE: Prepare Strawberry Mousse (page 189). Cut a sponge cake or a small angel food cake into 2 layers.

Place one layer on serving platter. Spread one-third of strawberry mousse over cake. (If mousse is too firm to spread, let stand at room temperature to soften slightly.) Cover with second cake layer. Spread remaining mousse over top and sides of cake. Refrigerate for up to 8 hours.

Just before serving, arrange fresh strawberries around or over top of cake. Makes 8 servings.

Hot Apricot Soufflé

MAKES 4 SERVINGS

PER SERVING

91 calories
0 g fat
0 mg cholesterol
52 mg sodium

4 g protein
20 g carbohydrate

GOOD: vitamin A

This light dessert is surprisingly easy to make—and no one will guess that it's low in calories and fat. Try to buy the apricots that are canned in a light or a low-sugar syrup.

1 16-ounce can apricot halves, unpeeled
½ teaspoon grated lemon rind
1 teaspoon lemon juice
2 tablespoons granulated sugar
4 egg whites
¼ teaspoon cream of tartar
1 teaspoon cornstarch

Drain apricots; place between paper towels and pat dry. In food processor, blender, or food mill, purée apricots, lemon rind, lemon juice, and sugar.

In large bowl, beat egg whites and cream of tartar until stiff peaks form; sift cornstarch over whites and fold in. Add about ¼ of the beaten whites to apricot mixture and pulse 4 times or mix just until combined. Add apricot mixture to remaining beaten whites and fold together.

Pour into ungreased 8-cup soufflé dish. Bake in 350°F oven for 30 to 35 minutes or until puffed and golden brown. Serve immediately.

Peach Crêpes with Easy Grand Marnier Sauce

MAKES 8 CRÊPES, 4 LARGE OR 8 SMALL SERVINGS

PER SERVING (1 crêpe)

97 calories
1 g fat
2 mg cholesterol
30 mg sodium

3 g protein
20 g carbohydrate

GOOD: vitamin C

This dessert is a favorite any time of year but is particularly good in peach season. For a fancy dessert, it is surprisingly low in calories.

½ cup low-fat plain yogurt
1 tablespoon maple syrup or honey
3 fresh peaches, peeled and sliced
8 Dessert Crêpes (page 184)

GRAND MARNIER SAUCE

¾ cup orange juice
1 tablespoon cornstarch
3 tablespoons Grand Marnier or other orange liqueur or Drambuie

Sliced peaches, blueberries, or other fresh berries

Grand Marnier Sauce: In saucepan, combine orange juice with cornstarch; whisk until smooth. Cook over medium heat, stirring constantly, until mixture thickens and comes to boil; simmer for 2 minutes. Remove from heat and stir in liqueur.

In bowl, combine yogurt with syrup or honey; stir until smooth. Add peaches and mix lightly.

Wrap crêpes in paper towels and heat in microwave at high (100%) power for 30 seconds. Or heat in 350°F oven for 5 to 10 minutes or until warm.

Spoon some peach mixture onto each crêpe; roll up and place on individual plates. Drizzle with warm sauce and garnish with fresh fruit.

VARIATIONS

JIFFY PEACH DESSERT: Sweeten yogurt with maple syrup and spoon over sliced peaches.

PEACHES AND BLUEBERRIES WITH GRAND MARNIER SAUCE: Spoon Easy Grand Marnier Sauce over sliced peaches and blueberries.

BANANAS AND KIWI WITH EASY GRAND MARNIER SAUCE: Spoon
Easy Grand Marnier Sauce over sliced bananas and kiwi.

Apricot Yogurt Parfaits

MAKES 4 SERVINGS

PER SERVING

140 calories
  1 g fat
  4 mg cholesterol
 49 mg sodium

  5 g protein
 25 g carbohydrate

GOOD: vitamin A,
vitamin C, fiber

Enjoy this rich-tasting, easy-to-make dessert without any pangs of
guilt—it's healthy and low-calorie.

1 16-ounce can apricot halves, unpeeled
1 envelope unflavored gelatin
2 tablespoons lemon juice
2 tablespoons apricot brandy
1 cup low-fat plain yogurt
1 cup fresh apricot slices, kiwi slices, or berries

Yogurt and brown sugar or mint leaves

Drain apricots, pouring ¼ cup of the juice into saucepan or
microwave-safe dish. Sprinkle gelatin over juice and let stand for
5 minutes to soften. Warm over low heat or microwave at medium
(50%) power for 30 seconds or until gelatin has dissolved.

In food processor or blender, purée apricots; add lemon juice,
brandy, yogurt, and gelatin mixture and process for 30 seconds or
until combined.

Pour into parfait or stemmed glasses, or champagne flutes. Cover
and refrigerate until set, at least 1 hour or overnight.

Just before serving, arrange fresh fruit on top. Garnish each with
small spoonful of yogurt and sprinkling of brown sugar or mint leaf.

Iced Raspberry Mousse

MAKES 6 SERVINGS

This make-ahead dessert looks very pretty served in small ramekins
or a soufflé dish. You can also chill it in a mold, unmold and

PER SERVING

169 calories
1 g fat
2 mg cholesterol
49 mg sodium

6 g protein
37 g carbohydrate

GOOD: vitamin C
EXCELLENT: fiber

surround with fresh fruit, then garnish with mint leaves and flowers. Don't strain the raspberry purée mixtures. Raspberries, including the seeds, are an excellent source of fiber.

> 2 envelopes unflavored gelatin
> ½ cup water
> 1 10-ounce package frozen raspberries in light syrup or 2 cups
>   puréed raspberries
> ¾ cup low-fat plain yogurt
> ½ teaspoon grated orange rind
> 3 egg whites
> ½ cup granulated sugar
>
> Fresh raspberries, mint leaves, and flowers

In saucepan or microwave-safe dish, sprinkle gelatin over water; let stand for 5 minutes to soften. Heat over low heat or microwave at medium (50%) power for 50 seconds or until gelatin has dissolved.

In food processor or blender, purée raspberries (if using unsweetened, add about ¼ cup sugar). Transfer to bowl and stir in gelatin mixture, yogurt, and orange rind. Refrigerate until mixture begins to set or is consistency of raw egg whites.

In large bowl, beat egg whites until soft peaks form. Gradually add sugar, beating until stiff peaks form. Whisk about ¼ of beaten whites into raspberry mixture; fold in remaining whites.

Spoon into serving bowl or divide among prepared dishes as directed in soufflé variation. Divide among prepared dishes. Cover and refrigerate for at least 1 hour before serving. Garnish with raspberries, fresh mint, and flowers.

VARIATION

TO SERVE AS A SOUFFLÉ: Cut 8 pieces of waxed paper 4 inches wide and slightly longer than circumference of ¾-cup ramekins or soufflé dishes, or demitasse or espresso coffee cups. (Or cut 1 strip for 4-cup soufflé dish.) Fold in half lengthwise. Using string, tie each strip around outside of dish so 1 inch extends above rim. Divide raspberry mousse mixture among prepared dishes and refrigerate for at least 1 hour before serving.

Sherbets, Sorbets, Ices

Whether you call them sherbets, sorbets, or ices, a light refreshing frozen mixture of fresh fruit is the dessert I order most often in restaurants. The desserts are extremely easy to make, especially if you have an ice-cream maker. For a special dinner, serve a combination of sherbets plus fresh berries. Here is a selection to make year-round.

FREEZING AND SERVING INSTRUCTIONS FOR SORBETS

Freeze in ice-cream maker following manufacturer's instructions. Alternatively, transfer to metal pan or bowl and freeze until barely firm. Then either process in food processor or beat with electric mixer until smooth. Transfer to freezer container and freeze until firm.

To Serve: Remove from freezer 15 to 30 minutes before serving or until mixture is soft enough to scoop. Serve on dessert plates surrounded with fresh berries or in sherbet glasses, each garnished with its own fruit or fresh mint leaf.

SORBET, FRESH FRUIT, AND FRUIT SAUCE COMBINATIONS

There are countless variations of sorbet (sherbets), fresh fruit, and sauces you can use.

CONSIDER: Kiwi Sorbet (page 196); fresh sliced kiwi and peaches, and Raspberry Sauce (page 197); Whole-Berry Blueberry Sorbet (page 195); fresh blueberries and Blueberry Wine Sauce (page 204); Pineapple-Orange Sorbet (page 196); sliced oranges, and Blueberry Wine Sauce (page 204) or Raspberry Sauce (page 197); Rhubarb-Strawberry Sorbet (page 195); blackberries or blueberries (or any other berry), and Raspberry Sauce (page 197).

Rhubarb-Strawberry Sorbet

MAKES 8 SERVINGS, ½ CUP EACH

PER SERVING

109 calories
  0 g fat
  0 mg cholesterol
  2 mg sodium

0.5 g protein
28 g carbohydrate

EXCELLENT: vitamin C

1½ cups sliced fresh rhubarb
1 cup granulated sugar
1½ cups water
2 cups fresh strawberries
1 tablespoon lemon juice
1 teaspoon grated orange rind or 2 tablespoons orange liqueur
  such as Grand Marnier or Cointreau

In saucepan, combine rhubarb, sugar, and half of the water; simmer, covered, until rhubarb is very tender. Purée in food processor; transfer to bowl.

In food processor, purée strawberries; stir into rhubarb mixture. Add lemon juice, orange rind, and remaining water.

Freeze according to instructions on page 194.

Whole-Berry Blueberry Sorbet

MAKES 6 SERVINGS, ½ CUP EACH

PER SERVING

106 calories
  0 g fat
  0 mg cholesterol
  1 mg sodium

0.5 g protein
27 g carbohydrate

EXCELLENT: vitamin C

2 cups blueberries (fresh or frozen)
½ cup granulated sugar
½ cup water
1 cup orange juice
1 tablespoon lemon juice

In saucepan, combine blueberries, sugar, water, and orange and lemon juices; simmer for 10 minutes. Chill then freeze according to instructions on page 194.

VARIATION

FROZEN BLUEBERRY SNOW: Prepare Whole-Berry Blueberry Sherbet. When mixture is cold, process in food processor with 1 egg white until frothy and light in color.

Raspberry Sorbet

MAKES 4 SERVINGS

In food processor purée 1 package 10-ounce frozen sweetened raspberries, thawed. Add ½ cup water and 1½ teaspoons lemon juice. Freeze according to instructions on page 194.

Kiwi Sorbet

MAKES 10 SERVINGS, ½ CUP EACH

PER SERVING

141 calories
0.5 g fat
0 mg cholesterol
6 mg sodium

1 g protein
36 g carbohydrate

GOOD: fiber
EXCELLENT: vitamin C

12 kiwi
1 cup granulated sugar
1 cup water
1 tablespoon lemon juice

Using sharp knife, peel kiwi; purée in food processor or pass through food mill and place in bowl.

In saucepan, bring sugar, water, and lemon juice to boil, stirring occasionally until sugar has dissolved. Add to kiwi and mix well.

Freeze according to instructions on page 194.

Pineapple-Orange Sorbet

MAKES 10 SERVINGS, ½ CUP EACH

PER SERVING

93 calories
0 g fat
0 mg cholesterol
1 mg sodium

1 g protein
24 g carbohydrate

EXCELLENT: vitamin C

½ cup water
½ cup granulated sugar
1 pineapple or 1 20-ounce can crushed pineapple
2 cups orange juice
2 teaspoons grated orange rind
1 tablespoon lemon or lime juice

In saucepan, combine water and sugar; simmer until sugar dissolves. Peel pineapple and cut into quarters; purée quarters or undrained pineapple in food processor.

In bowl, combine sugar syrup, orange juice, pineapple, orange rind, and lemon juice. Freeze according to instructions on this page.

Strawberry Meringue Tarts with Raspberry Sauce

MAKES 6 SERVINGS

PER SERVING

213 calories
1 g fat
0 mg cholesterol
27 mg sodium

3 g protein
52 g carbohydrate

EXCELLENT: fiber, vitamin C

Individual meringue shells filled with fresh fruit sherbet, covered with juicy berries or sliced fruit and a drizzling of fruit sauce, make a delicious and glamorous dessert that is also light and refreshing.

MERINGUE SHELLS

3 egg whites, at room temperature
Pinch cream of tartar
⅔ cup granulated sugar
½ teaspoon vanilla

FILLING

2 cups Rhubarb-Strawberry Sorbet (page 195) or Frozen Strawberry Yogurt (page 228)
2 cups sliced fresh strawberries or other fruit

RASPBERRY SAUCE

1 10-ounce package frozen unsweetened raspberries
1 tablespoon (approximately) honey or confectioners' sugar

Meringue Shells: In bowl, beat egg whites with cream of tartar until soft peaks form. Gradually add sugar a tablespoon at a time, beating until stiff peaks form. Beat in vanilla.

Spoon meringue onto foil-lined baking sheet in six 4- to 5-inch rounds. Using spoon, shape into nests. Bake in 250°F oven for 2 hours or until meringues are crisp but not browned and can be removed from foil. If foil sticks, continue baking. Cool, then store in airtight container up to 2 days; freeze for longer storage.

Raspberry Sauce: In food processor, blender, or food mill, purée raspberries. Stir in honey or sugar, adding more to taste. Cover and refrigerate for up to 2 days.

To serve: Spoon sherbet into meringue shells; spoon fresh fruit over. Pass sauce separately.

VARIATION

STRAWBERRY SAUCE: Make Raspberry Sauce but substitute fresh or frozen strawberries for raspberries. If sweetened, omit honey or sugar.

Strawberry Meringue Parfait

If you have extra meringue, make this wonderful, easy dessert. Break meringue into pieces and mix with Frozen Strawberry Yogurt (page 228). Spoon into parfait glasses and drizzle with Strawberry Sauce recipe (above). Garnish with fresh berries if in season—either strawberry, raspberry, blueberry, or blackberry.

Rhubarb Stewed with Apple and Strawberries

MAKES 8 SERVINGS, ⅔ CUP EACH

PER SERVING

85 calories
0.5 g fat
1 mg cholesterol
14 mg sodium

2 g protein
20 g carbohydrates

GOOD: fiber
EXCELLENT: vitamin C

Combine spring rhubarb with apple and orange, then add some dried fruit such as raisins or apricots during cooking. Or after cooking, add any other fresh fruit such as kiwi, grapes, bananas, or strawberries.

1 orange
1 pound fresh or frozen rhubarb
1 large apple
1 cup water
¼ cup (approximately) granulated sugar
2 cups fresh strawberries (optional)

½ cup low-fat plain yogurt
2 tablespoons packed brown sugar

Grate rind and squeeze juice from orange. Cut rhubarb into 1-inch lengths. Peel, core, and thinly slice apple.

In saucepan, combine orange rind and juice, rhubarb, apple, water, and sugar; cover and bring to boil. Reduce heat and simmer for 10 minutes or until fruit is tender, stirring occasionally. Remove from heat and stir in strawberries. Add more sugar to taste. Serve warm or at room temperature. Top each serving with a spoonful of yogurt and sprinkle with brown sugar.

Apple and Raspberry Crisp

MAKES 8 SERVINGS

PER SERVING

219 calories
7 g fat
0 mg cholesterol
77 mg sodium

2 g protein
39 g carbohydrate

GOOD: vitamin C
EXCELLENT: fiber

Combining 2 fruits, such as apple and raspberry, in a crisp adds more flavor and color to the crisp than if you use 1 fruit. Depending on the sweetness of the apples you might want to add more sugar. This recipe uses the minimum amount of fat—less than half of a standard crisp recipe—while extra flavor is gained through fruits and cinnamon. Oatmeal adds fiber and flavor. Fruit crisps have less fat than fruit pies. For example, see the comparison of Sunday Chicken Dinner menus (page 213).

6 cups sliced peeled apples, about 1½ pounds
1 10-ounce package frozen unsweetened raspberries (1½ cups, fresh)
⅓ cup granulated sugar
2 tablespoons all-purpose flour
2 teaspoons ground cinnamon

TOPPING

1 cup quick-cooking rolled oats
¼ cup packed brown sugar
1 teaspoon ground cinnamon
¼ cup soft margarine

(continued)

In 8 cup baking dish, combine apples and raspberries (thawed or frozen). In small bowl, combine sugar, flour, and cinnamon; add to fruit and toss to mix.

Topping: Combine rolled oats, sugar, and cinnamon. With pastry blender or 2 knives, cut in margarine until crumbly. Sprinkle over top of fruit mixture.

Bake in 350°F oven for 55 minutes or microwave at high (100%) power for 15 minutes or until mixture is bubbling and fruit is barely tender. Serve warm or cold.

VARIATIONS

APPLE-CRANBERRY CRISP: Prepare Apple and Raspberry Crisp, substituting 1 cup fresh cranberries for raspberries and increase granulated sugar to ⅔ cup.

APPLE, PEAR, AND APRICOT CRISP: Prepare Apple and Raspberry Crisp using 4 cups sliced peeled apples, 2 cups sliced peeled pears and ½ cup coarsely chopped dried apricots.

MAPLE YOGURT SAUCE FOR FRUIT CRISPS: Combine ½ cup plain yogurt with 2 teaspoons maple syrup and mix well. Drizzle over individual servings of fruit crisp.

Berries with Orange-Honey Yogurt

MAKES 4 SERVINGS

Any kind of fresh fruit is wonderful with this tasty, easy-to-make sauce. Choose the fruits depending on the season. This looks nice served in stemmed glasses.

PER SERVING

126 calories
3 g fat
4 mg cholesterol
43 mg sodium

5 g protein
24 g carbohydrate

GOOD: fiber
EXCELLENT: vitamin C

4 cups strawberries or combination of berries

ORANGE-HONEY YOGURT

1 cup low-fat plain yogurt
1 teaspoon grated orange rind
1 tablespoon orange juice

Compare the Following Sunday-Night Chicken Dinners

A few easy choices can make a big difference in the amount of fat and cholesterol in our diet.

Dinner 1: 18% of Calories from Fat	*Grams Fat*	*Milligrams Cholesterol*	*Milligrams Sodium*	*Calories*
Roast chicken (no skin) breast (3 ounces)	3	73	64	142
Cranberry sauce	0	0	7	38
Baked potato	0	0	7	118
with sour cream and yogurt	2	3	8	16
(1 tablespoon light of each)				
Baked squash	1	0	1	38
Steamed broccoli	0	0	10	26
Apple and Raspberry Crisp (1 serving)	7	0	77	219
(page 199)				
TOTALS	12	76	174	597

Dinner 2: 44% of Calories from Fat				
Roast chicken (with skin) (4 ounces	18	100	93	287
dark meat)				
Gravy	3	1	249	34
Mashed potatoes	0	0	10	182
with butter and milk	8	21	80	70
Baked squash (with 1 teaspoon butter)	5	0	41	74
Steamed broccoli (with 1 teaspoon butter)	4	11	51	62
Apple pie (⅙ of 9-inch, 2-crust pie)	18	11	478	406
TOTALS	56	144	1,002	1,027

   2 tablespoons honey
   ½ teaspoon vanilla or almond extract

   Fresh mint leaves, thin strips of orange rind, or 1 tablespoon
     toasted sliced or slivered almonds

   Orange-Honey Yogurt: In bowl, combine yogurt, orange rind, orange juice, honey, and vanilla; mix well.
   Wash berries and hull; slice if large.
   Either mix fruit with sauce, cover, and refrigerate for 1 hour or, alternatively, at serving time spoon fruit into individual bowls or stemmed glasses and pour sauce over. Garnish each serving with fresh mint leaves, orange rind, or almonds.

(continued)

FRUITS TO COMBINE WITH OR SUBSTITUTE FOR BERRIES

Winter: sliced oranges, bananas, kiwi, pineapple, cantaloupe, or honeydew melon

Spring: strawberries, or stewed rhubarb

Summer: raspberries, blackberries, or blueberries

Fall: peaches, plums, or grapes

SUGGESTED BERRY OR FRUIT COMBINATIONS

grapes and melon;
melon and blueberries;
blackberries and sliced peaches;
raspberries and blueberries,
strawberries and kiwi;
bananas and kiwi or sliced oranges.

Winter Fruit Compote with Figs and Apricots

MAKES 8 SERVINGS

PER SERVING

148 calories
1 g fat
0 mg cholesterol
6 mg sodium

2 g protein
38 g carbohydrate

EXCELLENT: fiber, vitamin C

Figs, apricots, and prunes spiked with rum are a delicious base for an easy compote. Add the fresh fruits suggested here or any you have on hand such as pineapple or kiwi. You can substitute orange juice for the rum, if desired. For a stronger rum flavor add it to the cooled mixture.

¾ cup dried figs (about 5 ounces)
¾ cup dried apricots (about 5 ounces)
¾ cup dried prunes (about 5 ounces)
½ cup rum
1½ cups orange juice
2 cups seedless green grapes
1 cup purple or red grapes, halved and seeded, or seedless red grapes

1 11-ounce can mandarin oranges, undrained
1 grapefruit, peeled and sectioned

In saucepan, combine dried figs, apricots, prunes, rum, and orange juice; cover and bring to boil. Simmer for 10 minutes; remove from heat and let stand for 20 minutes or until fruit is plump and tender. Let cool.

In serving dish, combine fig mixture, green and purple grapes, mandarin oranges, and grapefruit. Serve immediately or cover and refrigerate up to 3 days.

Oranges in Grand Marnier

MAKES 6 SERVINGS

PER SERVING

196 calories
  0 g fat
  0 mg cholesterol
 11 mg sodium

  1 g protein
 45 g carbohydrate

GOOD: fiber
EXCELLENT: vitamin C

This very elegant dessert is one of my favorites. It's a good choice in February and March when navel oranges are so sweet and juicy. Serve with cake or wafer-thin cookies.

6 oranges
½ cup granulated sugar
1 cup water
¼ cup corn syrup
2 tablespoons lemon juice
¼ cup (approximately) Grand Marnier or Triple Sec liqueur

Using zester or vegetable peeler, peel thin strips of orange rind from 2 of the oranges, being careful not to include any white part. Cut into wispy thin strips and place in saucepan. Pour in enough cold water to cover and bring to boil (this removes bitter flavor); drain and set aside.

Using sharp knife, cut peel, including any white pith and membrane, from oranges. Cut oranges into round slices and place in glass bowl or in overlapping slices on platter.

In saucepan, combine sugar, water, and corn syrup; bring to boil, stirring only until sugar has dissolved. Add strips of orange rind; simmer, uncovered, for 25 minutes or until syrup is slightly thickened. Remove from heat; stir in lemon juice and liqueur. Let cool, then pour over oranges.

Refrigerate for 2 to 8 hours, turning oranges once or twice. Taste and add more liqueur if desired.

Fresh Pineapple Slices with Rum

MAKES 6 SERVINGS

PER SERVING

87 calories
0 g fat
0 mg cholesterol
3 mg sodium

0 g protein
18 g carbohydrate

EXCELLENT: vitamin C

Juicy, sweet, fresh pineapple spiked with a touch of rum is a quick and easy dessert. For a special occasion, cut pineapple carefully so you can present it in quarters garnished with strawberries, purple grapes, kiwi, or other fresh fruits. Serve with a crisp cookie.

1 pineapple
3 tablespoons packed brown sugar
3 tablespoons rum, preferably dark

Sliced kiwi fruit, orange segments, grapes, or strawberries

Cut top and bottom from pineapple. Cut down sides to remove peel and eyes. Cut pineapple into quarters. If core is tough or pithy, remove. Slice quarters into cubes.

In bowl, toss pineapple with brown sugar and rum; cover and let stand for 30 minutes or refrigerate up to 3 hours.

Serve in frosted sherbet or wine glasses and garnish with fresh fruit.

Blueberry Wine Sauce

MAKES 2 CUPS, ABOUT 6 SERVINGS

Rich with blueberries, this easy-to-make sauce is delicious over ice cream, sherbets, or angel-food cake.

½ cup granulated sugar
1 tablespoon cornstarch

PER SERVING (⅓ cup)

69 calories
0 g fat
0 mg cholesterol
3 mg sodium

0 g protein
18 g carbohydrate

1 cup dry white wine
1 tablespoon lemon juice
1½ cups blueberries (fresh or frozen)

In small saucepan, stir together sugar and cornstarch; stir in wine and lemon juice. Cook, stirring constantly, over medium heat until mixture thickens, clears, and comes to boil.

Stir in blueberries and simmer, stirring, for 1 minute or until at least half of the berries burst. Let cool and refrigerate.

Fresh Peaches with Banana Cream Whip

MAKES 4 SERVINGS

PER SERVING

82 calories
0 g fat
0 mg cholesterol
13 mg sodium

1 g protein
20 g carbohydrate

GOOD: fiber, vitamin C

For a quick, low-calorie, family dessert, serve this on sliced peaches, berries or other fruits or instead of whipped cream. It's best to make it about an hour or less before serving because it will darken upon standing.

BANANA CREAM

1 egg white
1 large banana, mashed
1 tablespoon confectioners' sugar
1 teaspoon lemon juice
2 cups sliced fresh peaches

In small bowl, beat egg white until foamy. Add banana, confectioners' sugar, and lemon juice; beat until mixture forms stiff peaks. Spoon peaches into individual dishes; top with Banana Cream.

Buttermilk Apple Cake

MAKES 12 SERVINGS

PER SERVING*

192 calories
5 g fat
1 mg cholesterol
168 mg sodium

4 g protein
35 g carbohydrate

GOOD: fiber

*including coconut

This coffeecake-type cake stays moist and is great for brunch, with fruit desserts, or packed lunches. I don't peel the apples because the skin adds fiber.

¼ cup soft margarine
⅔ cup packed brown sugar
1½ cups buttermilk
1 cup all-purpose flour
1 cup whole-wheat flour
1 teaspoon baking powder
1 teaspoon baking soda
1 tablespoon ground cinnamon
½ teaspoon salt
2 medium apples, cored and finely chopped (about 2½ cups)

TOPPING
¼ cup packed brown sugar
2 teaspoons ground cinnamon
2 tablespoons chopped nuts or ¼ cup coconut (optional)

Lightly grease and flour 8- or 9-inch square cake pan or Bundt pan.

In large bowl, beat together margarine and sugar until combined; beat in buttermilk. Add all-purpose and whole-wheat flour, baking powder, baking soda, cinnamon, salt, and apples; mix until combined. Spread batter evenly in pan.

Topping: Combine sugar, cinnamon, and nuts or coconut (if using); sprinkle over batter. Bake in 350°F oven for 40 to 45 minutes or until toothpick inserted in center comes out clean. Let cool in pan.

Menus

AFTER BRIDGE SNACK

ITALIAN TOMATO BRUSCHETTA *(page 37)*
BLUEBERRY CREAM FLAN *(page 186)*

AFTER THE BALL GAME SUPPER

BEEF AND PASTA CASSEROLE FOR A CROWD *(page 97)*
TOSSED SEASONAL GREENS *(page 71)*
FRENCH BREAD
ICED RASPBERRY MOUSSE *(page 192)*

ALFRESCO SUMMER SUPPER

CHILLED CUCUMBER-CHIVE SOUP *(page 53)*
PASTA AND FRESH VEGETABLE SALAD *(page 80)*
SLICED COLD CHICKEN BREAST, NO SKIN
WHOLE-WHEAT ROLLS
SLICED PEACHES AND BLUEBERRIES
MILK

BEFORE THE CONCERT LIGHT SUPPER

FETTUCCINE AND MUSSEL SALAD *(page 81)*
SLICED TOMATOES WITH FRESH BASIL
FLATBREAD CRACKERS *(page 182)*
FRESH STRAWBERRIES

BEFORE THE THEATER LIGHT SUPPER

FETTUCCINE WITH PESTO SAUCE *(page 133)*
TOMATOES BROILED WITH GOAT CHEESE AND BASIL *(page 153)*
MULTIGRAIN DATE QUICKBREAD *(page 178)*
STRAWBERRIES WITH ALMONDS AND AMARETTO

BUFFET DINNER FOR 16

SPINACH-ONION DIP WITH FRESH VEGETABLES *(page 33)*
SPICED MEATBALLS WITH CORIANDER DIPPING SAUCE *(page 39)*
CHICKEN AND SHRIMP CREOLE *(page 109)*
TOSSED SEASONAL GREENS *(page 71)*
HOT FRENCH BREAD
ORANGES IN GRAND MARNIER *(page 203)*
STRAWBERRY MOUSSE *(page 189)*

COCKTAIL PARTY

SHRIMP MOUSSE WITH DILL *(page 35)*
BROCCOLI AND MUSHROOM DIP WITH FRESH VEGETABLES *(page 34)*
SPICED MEATBALLS WITH CORIANDER DIPPING SAUCE *(page 39)*
CURRIED CHICKEN CROUSTADES *(page 44)*

DINNER PARTY FOR EIGHT

SHRIMP MOUSSE WITH DILL *(page 35)*
ZUCCHINI AND WATERCRESS VICHYSSOISE *(page 57)*
MAKE-AHEAD PAELLA *(page 112)*
SPINACH SALAD WITH SESAME SEED DRESSING *(page 73)*
FRUIT SORBETS WITH FRESH FRUIT AND RASPBERRY SAUCE
  (page 194)

EARLY AUGUST DINNER

TOSSED SEASONAL GREENS *(page 71)*
ROTINI WITH FRESH TOMATO, BASIL, AND PARMESAN *(page 131)*
BLUEBERRY CREAM FLAN *(page 186)*

EASY FRIDAY-NIGHT SEAFOOD DINNER FOR FOUR

MUSHROOM BISQUE WITH TARRAGON *(page 51)*
FETTUCCINE WITH MUSSELS, LEEKS, AND TOMATOES *(page 123)*
FRENCH BREAD
FRESH PINEAPPLE SLICES WITH RUM *(page 204)*, OR BERRIES
    WITH ORANGE-HONEY YOGURT *(page 200)*

EASY JULY SUPPER

FETTUCCINE WITH PESTO SAUCE *(page 133)*
SLICED CUCUMBERS WITH CHIVES AND YOGURT (OMIT BASIL)
    (page 69)
RAW BABY CARROTS
WHOLE-WHEAT PITA BREAD
STRAWBERRIES WITH ORANGE-HONEY YOGURT *(page 200)*

EASY SUMMER DINNER

ROTINI WITH FRESH TOMATOES, BASIL, AND PARMESAN *(page 131)*
TOSSED SEASONAL GREENS WITH RANCH-STYLE BUTTERMILK
    DRESSING *(page 84)*
HOT BREAD
FRESH BLUEBERRIES WITH ORANGE-HONEY YOGURT *(page 200)*

FALL FRIDAY-NIGHT DINNER

HARVEST PUMPKIN AND ZUCCHINI SOUP *(page 56)*
BARLEY, GREEN PEPPER, AND TOMATO CASSEROLE *(page 132)*
TOSSED SEASONAL GREENS *(page 71)*
BUTTERMILK APPLE CAKE *(page 206)*

FATHER'S DAY BARBECUE DINNER

GINGER-GARLIC MARINATED FLANK STEAK *(page 93)*
YOGURT BÉARNAISE SAUCE *(page 163)*
NEW POTATOES WITH HERBS *(page 156)*
ASPARAGUS
STRAWBERRY MOUSSE *(page 189)* OR
BERRIES WITH ORANGE-HONEY YOGURT *(page 200)*
APPLESAUCE-RAISIN SQUARES *(page 176)*

FISH BARBECUE DINNER

SWORDFISH STEAKS WITH LIME AND CORIANDER *(page 126)*
PEAS WITH SCALLIONS *(page 144)*
NEW POTATOES WITH HERBS *(page 156)*
PEACHES AND BLUEBERRIES WITH EASY GRAND MARNIER SAUCE
   (page 191)

FRIDAY NIGHT DINNER PARTY

SPINACH SALAD WITH SESAME SEED DRESSING *(page 73)*
GRILLED BUTTERFLIED LEG OF LAMB WITH LEMON AND GARLIC
   (page 98)
BULGUR PILAF WITH APRICOTS AND RAISINS *(page 155)*
BAKED PARSNIPS AND CARROTS *(page 142)*
FRESH PINEAPPLE SLICES WITH RUM *(page 204)* OR
FRESH STRAWBERRIES

GREY CUP BUFFET

GINGER-GARLIC MARINATED FLANK STEAK, COLD *(page 93)*
TOSSED SEASONAL GREENS *(page 71)*
WHOLE-WHEAT OATMEAL BREAD *(page 181)*
STREUSEL PLUM CAKE *(page 187)*
APRICOT YOGURT PARFAITS *(page 192)*

HARVEST-DINNER PARTY

FRESH BEET SOUP WITH YOGURT *(page 58)*
ROASTED RED PEPPER, CHÈVRE, AND ARUGULA SALAD *(page 68)*
LAMB TENDERLOINS WITH ROSEMARY AND PEPPERCORNS *(page 99)*
MUSHROOM-STUFFED ZUCCHINI CUPS *(page 148)*
SPAGHETTI SQUASH WITH PARSLEY AND GARLIC *(page 140)*
PEACH CRÊPES WITH EASY GRAND MARNIER SAUCE *(page 191)*

HORS D'OEUVRE DINNER PARTY

MUSSELS ON THE HALF SHELL *(page 38)*
CURRIED CHICKEN CROUSTADES *(page 44)*
SPICED MEATBALLS WITH CORIANDER DIPPING SAUCE *(page 39)*

MUSHROOM-STUFFED ZUCCHINI CUPS *(page 148)*
MARINATED SPICED CARROTS *(page 41)*
MARINATED MUSHROOMS AND ARTICHOKES *(page 40)*
STRAWBERRY MERINGUE TARTS WITH RASPBERRY SAUCE *(page 197)*

LADIES' BUFFET LUNCH

SHELL PASTA SALAD WITH SALMON AND GREEN BEANS *(page 79)* OR
CURRIED CHICKEN CRÊPES WITH YOGURT AND CHUTNEY *(page 104)*
SLICED CUCUMBERS WITH CHIVES, YOGURT, AND BASIL *(page 69)*
WHOLE-WHEAT ZUCCHINI BREAD *(page 179)*
LEMON ROLL WITH BERRIES OR FRESH FRUIT *(page 184)*

MAKE-AHEAD DINNER PARTY

SPICED MEATBALLS WITH CORIANDER DIPPING SAUCE *(page 39)*
TOSSED SEASONAL GREENS *(page 71)*
CURRIED CHICKEN AND TOMATO CASSEROLE *(page 106)*
BULGUR PILAF WITH APRICOTS AND RAISINS *(page 155)*
SLICED CUCUMBERS WITH CHIVES, YOGURT, AND BASIL *(page 69)*
ORANGES IN GRAND MARNIER *(page 203)*
EASY OAT BRAN AND DATE COOKIES *(page 177)*

MAKE-AHEAD WINTER LUNCH OR LATE-NIGHT DINNER

PARSLEY-ONION DIP WITH FRESH VEGETABLES *(page 33)*
MUSSEL, CLAM, AND FISH CHOWDER *(page 49)*
FIVE-GRAIN SODA BREAD *(page 180)*
WINTER FRUIT COMPOTE WITH FIGS AND APRICOTS *(page 202)*

MEATLESS BUFFET DINNER

SALMON SPREAD WITH CAPERS *(page 32)*
MARINATED MUSHROOMS *(page 40)*
VEGETABLE LASAGNA *(page 134)*
TOSSED SEASONAL GREENS *(page 71)*
STRAWBERRY MOUSSE *(page 189)*
FRESH PINEAPPLE SLICES WITH RUM *(page 204)*
OATMEAL-APRICOT COOKIES *(page 177)*

OCTOBER DINNER

HARVEST PUMPKIN AND ZUCCHINI SOUP *(page 56)*
FISH FILLETS WITH BASIL AND LEMON *(page 118)*
MICROWAVE CARROTS AND LEEKS *(page 147)*
NEW POTATOES WITH HERBS *(page 150)*
STREUSEL PLUM CAKE *(page 187)*

PICNIC AT THE BEACH OR ON THE BOAT

SLICED ROAST BEEF
ITALIAN RICE AND MOZZARELLA SALAD WITH VEGETABLES *(page 70)*
OLD-FASHIONED PICKLED BEETS *(page 165)*
WHOLE-WHEAT BUNS
NECTARINES
EASY OAT BRAN AND DATE COOKIES *(page 177)*

SEPTEMBER DINNER PARTY

WARM VEGETABLE SALAD *(page 43)*
BROCHETTE OF PORK WITH LEMON AND HERB MARINADE *(page 100)*
BARLEY AND MUSHROOM PILAF *(page 158)*
TOMATOES BROILED WITH GOAT'S CHEESE AND BASIL *(page 153)*
LEMON ROLL WITH FRESH FRUIT *(page 184)*

SPRING BARBECUE

GRILLED TURKEY SCALLOPINI WITH HERBS AND GARLIC *(page 113)*
ASPARAGUS
WILD RICE AND MUSHROOMS
SPINACH SALAD WITH SESAME SEED DRESSING *(page 73)*
RHUBARB-STRAWBERRY SORBET *(page 195)*

SUMMER BARBECUE

GRILLED TANDOORI CHICKEN *(page 103)*
NEW POTATOES WITH HERBS *(page 156)*
SLICED TOMATOES WITH BASIL
WHOLE-BERRY BLUEBERRY SORBET *(page 195)*
MICROWAVE OATMEAL SQUARES *(page 228)*

SUNDAY FAMILY DINNER

TARRAGON ROASTED CHICKEN *(page 107)*
CRANBERRY SAUCE
GREEN BEANS WITH SAUTÉED MUSHROOMS *(page 145)*
POTATOES
BERRIES WITH ORANGE-HONEY YOGURT *(page 200)* OR
APPLE AND RASPBERRY CRISP *(page 199)*

SUNDAY CHICKEN DINNER

ROAST CHICKEN (NO SKIN)
CRANBERRY SAUCE
BAKED POTATO
BAKED SQUASH
STEAMED BROCCOLI
APPLE AND RASPBERRY CRISP *(page 199)*

SUNDAY OR HOLIDAY BUFFET LUNCH

TARRAGON CHICKEN SALAD *(page 64)*
CURRIED VERMICELLI NOODLE SALAD *(page 77)*
SPINACH SALAD WITH SESAME SEED DRESSING *(page 73)*
FIVE-GRAIN SODA BREAD *(page 180)*
STRAWBERRY MOUSSE CAKE *(page 190)*

THANKSGIVING DINNER MENU

TARRAGON-ROASTED CHICKEN *(page 107)*
BRUSSELS SPROUTS WITH PEPPERS AND POTATOES *(page 146)*
TURNIP AND APPLE PURÉE *(page 152)*
PEAR STREUSEL CAKE *(page 188)*
WHOLE-BERRY BLUEBERRY SORBET *(page 195)*

THIRTY-MINUTE SUMMER BARBECUE

GRILLED TURKEY SCALLOPINI WITH HERBS AND GARLIC *(page 113)*
CORN ON THE COB
FRENCH BREAD
SLICED TOMATOES
STRAWBERRIES WITH RASPBERRY SAUCE *(page 197)*

WINTER MEATLESS DINNER

CABBAGE AND POTATO PIE *(page 135)*
BAKED PARSNIPS AND CARROTS *(page 142)*
WHOLE-WHEAT BUNS WITH LOW-FAT MOZZARELLA CHEESE
FRESH FRUIT COMPOTE
MILK

WINTER SUNDAY DINNER MENU

TARRAGON-ROASTED CHICKEN *(page 107)*
CRANBERRY SAUCE
GARLIC-PARSLEY POTATOES *(page 156)*
PEAR STREUSEL CAKE *(page 188)*

Life-style

Feeding Your Family

One of the primary responsibilities of parents is to see that their children are well fed and develop good eating habits. Sometimes this can take all your wits and patience, but it is worth every bit of thought and effort. The sooner children develop good eating habits the healthier they'll be, and the more likely it will be that they'll continue eating well throughout life.

Now that our three children are teenagers, we get a great deal of pleasure from trying new foods together, eating out at ethnic restaurants, and having a nice dinner in the dining room as often as everyone can be home. But this wasn't always the case: I can remember the children screaming with 2-year-old rage because I wouldn't give them a cookie 20 minutes before dinner; or as 5-year-olds refusing homemade soup but loving it out of a can; or saying "Yuck" to what I thought was delicious homemade stew.

Unhealthy eating can cause behavior problems, lack of concentration, and drowsiness in children. Poor nutrition can be the result of skipping breakfast and eating too many fast foods; too few fruits, vegetables, and whole-grain breads and cereals; and too much sugar and fat. It means a lack of necessary nutrients and fiber, as well as too many calories.

DIETARY RECOMMENDATIONS AND CHILDREN

Dietary recommendations are designed for healthy adults. Most school-age children can also follow the recommendations, keeping in mind that it's most important to eat a balanced diet, choosing foods from the four food groups: milk and milk products; breads and cereals; fruits and vegetables; meats and alternates. Children don't need to limit their fat, sodium, and cholesterol content to the same extent as adults. They can choose 2% or whole milk and eat more eggs. They should, however, follow the other suggestions in the book for healthy eating. Families with a history of heart disease may want to consult their doctor to see if a more restrictive diet is necessary for their children.

Young babies to the age of one year should be on whole milk if not on breast milk or formula. Babies shouldn't be given high-fiber foods. Consult your doctor for further dietary advice.

The unbalanced meals shown below are ones that many children might enjoy. They are fine for energy (calories), protein, and carbohydrates but are lacking in milk, whole grain cereals, fruits, and vegetables. Children who follow this eating pattern are not getting enough vitamins, minerals, and fiber.

Unbalanced, Less-Healthy Meals	*Balanced, Healthy Meals*
Breakfast	*Breakfast*
Cereal, high in sugar, low in fiber	Bran flakes
Milk	Milk
Toast and jam	Orange
	Toast and peanut butter
Lunch	*Lunch*
Hot dog, or jam or bologna sandwich on white bread	Tuna fish sandwich on whole-wheat bread
1 small bag potato chips	Raw carrots
4 chocolate cookies	2 oatmeal cookies
Soft drink	Milk
Dinner	*Dinner*
Fried chicken	Roast chicken
French fries	Baked potato
Roll	Green beans
Strawberry Jell-O	Cantaloupe (or any fresh fruit)
Milk	Milk

DEVELOPING GOOD EATING HABITS IN YOUR FAMILY

1. If you prepare good-tasting nutritious foods and don't let children snack too close to meal times, the rest is up to them. Don't nag, don't tell them that it is good for them or that other children around the world are starving—they couldn't care less. Make mealtimes enjoyable.
2. If you don't have potato chips, candy, or soft drinks in the house, you won't have to argue with your kids about whether or not they can have some. Healthy, nutritious food doesn't take long to prepare and young children like simple food best. What is faster for snacks than a banana, apple, carrot, or yogurt?
3. Children will learn most from the example you set. If you don't like a certain food, there is a pretty good chance your child won't either. If you snack on potato chips just before dinner, so will your child.
4. If kids don't like a particular food or dish, try to figure out why. Young children usually don't like hot, spicy food, mixtures of foods, sauces, or unfamiliar foods. Don't give up on new foods and don't make a fuss. Eventually they will be curious and want to try them. Sometimes young children will say they don't like a food because they are angry at you and they know this will upset you. Don't let a child's poor eating habits be an attention-getter.

For more information on feeding children you can refer to these two excellent books:

Lagace, Louise-Lambert. *Feeding Your Child.* Don Mills, Ontario, Canada: Stoddart Publishing, 1986.

Satter, Ellyn. *Child of Mine: Feeding with Love and Good Sense.* Palo Alto, Calif.: Bull Publishing, 1983.

FEEDING YOUR TEENAGER

The main challenge to feeding teenage boys is keeping enough food in the house. I concentrate on stocking wholesome foods rather than junk foods. I keep a large bowl of fruit out on the counter and they usually grab a banana or apple because they are there.

With teenage girls, eating problems are more complex and eating disorders such as anorexia nervosa are becoming distressingly prevalent. If you are worried about your daughter in this respect, don't hesitate to seek outside help from health professionals specializing in the field.

Iron and calcium deficiencies are common among teenagers, especially if they don't eat red meat or drink milk. Milk and milk products are the best sources of calcium. Most meats and meat alternates are good sources of iron. Many of the recipes in this book are high in calcium and/or iron. For example pizza is often a good source of calcium.

Here are some recipes with particular appeal to teenagers, which they may enjoy preparing. All of the recipes in this section are quick and easy to prepare and have been chosen with kids' preferences in mind. (See also menu and recipes for beginner cooks, pages 226–228.)

Mexican Beef Tacos or Tostadas

MAKES 6 SERVINGS, 2 TACOS EACH

PER SERVING*

295 calories
14 g fat
39 mg cholesterol
742 mg sodium

19 g protein
24 g carbohydrate

GOOD: vitamin C, iron, fiber
EXCELLENT: niacin

*made with 1 tablespoon cheese

A tostada is a flat tortilla with toppings. A taco is a folded tortilla filled with a variety of foods such as grated cheese, shredded lettuce, and meat sauce. Use this meat sauce as a basis for either and let each person top or fill his or her own taco or tostada.

1 pound lean ground beef
1 medium onion, chopped
1 clove garlic, minced
⅓ cup tomato paste
⅔ cup water
2 teaspoons chili powder
1 teaspoon dried oregano
½ teaspoon ground cumin
¼ teaspoon dried hot pepper flakes
Salt and freshly ground pepper
16 6-inch corn tortillas (tacos or tostadas)

TOPPINGS

Shredded lettuce

Chopped tomato
Chopped sweet green pepper
Bottled or homemade taco sauce (below) or Tomato Salsa Sauce
   (page 126)
Yogurt or light sour cream
Grated part-skim mozzarella

In large skillet, cook beef over medium heat until brown; pour off fat. Add onion and garlic; cook until tender. Stir in tomato paste, water, chili powder, oregano, cumin, and dried hot pepper flakes. Simmer for 5 to 10 minutes. Taste and add salt, pepper, and hot pepper flakes to taste. (If mixture becomes dry, add a little water.) Spoon into serving dish.

Toppings: Place bowls of various toppings on table. Serve packaged crisp tortillas cold, or warm in 300°F oven for 5 minutes. Soft tortillas are usually fried in hot oil, but to keep fat content down, crisp them in a 400°F oven for 10 minutes instead.

To make tacos or tostadas, let each person spoon some meat mixture into tortilla then top with cheese, lettuce, and other toppings of their choice.

Keep the fat down by avoiding high-fat toppings. Avocado, or guacamole, is a popular taco topping, but avocado is extremely high in fat: One raw avocado has about 30 grams of fat, nearly half the daily requirement of a small woman.

Instead of bottled taco sauce, you can make your own by adding chopped fresh hot peppers or hot pepper sauce and dried hot pepper flakes to homemade tomato sauce. Alternatively, to keep the salt at a minimum, use Tomato Salsa (page 126) and add hot chilis to taste.

Vegetable Taco Sauce

MAKES 3½ CUPS, ENOUGH FOR 12 TACOS,
ALONG WITH OTHER TOPPINGS

Kidney beans make a tasty and nutritious change from meat in a taco or tostada filling. Add other seasonal vegetables, such as

PER SERVING
(1 taco)

116 calories
3 g fat
0 mg cholesterol
469 mg sodium

4 g protein
19 g carbohydrate

GOOD: vitamin C
EXCELLENT: fiber,
vitamin A, niacin

chopped zucchini, broccoli, sweet peppers, or corn, that you might have on hand. Use the same toppings and procedure as in Mexican Beef Tacos or Tostadas (page 219).

2 teaspoons vegetable oil
2 medium onions, chopped
1 clove garlic, minced
2 carrots, minced
2 tomatoes, chopped
1 19-ounce can red kidney beans, drained
1 green chili (canned or fresh), chopped (optional)
2 teaspoons chili powder
1 teaspoon ground cumin
¼ teaspoon dried hot pepper flakes, crushed
Salt and freshly ground pepper

In large nonstick skillet or saucepan, heat oil over medium heat; add onions, garlic, and carrots and cook for 5 minutes or until tender, stirring often. Add tomatoes, beans, green chili (if using), chili powder, cumin, and dried hot pepper flakes. Season to taste with salt, pepper, and more hot pepper flakes, if desired.

Simmer, uncovered, for 15 to 20 minutes or until sauce is thickened and flavors blended.

VARIATION

Instead of taco shells serve Vegetable Taco Sauce over toasted whole-wheat bread or hamburger buns.

Compare Two Pieces of:

	Grams Fat	Milligrams Cholesterol	Milligrams Sodium	Calories
Mushroom, Broccoli, and Onion Pizza	16	42	658	424
Regular homemade pizza (made with regular mozzarella, pepperoni, anchovies, green olives)	29	73	1,343	541

Mushroom, Broccoli, and Onion Pizza

MAKES 4 SERVINGS, 2 PIECES EACH

PER SERVING (2 pieces)

424 calories
 16 g fat
 42 mg cholesterol
658 mg sodium

 25 g protein
 46 g carbohydrate

GOOD: riboflavin,
vitamin A, iron
EXCELLENT: fiber,
vitamin C, thiamin,
niacin, calcium

Keep some homemade or store-bought pizza dough rounds in your freezer so you can easily make your own fast food. Depending on the toppings you choose, your pizzas can be nutritious as well as delicious. If you choose vegetables such as broccoli, onion, sweet peppers, tomatoes, zucchini, mushrooms, and reduced-fat cheese for toppings, your pizza will be a good source of calcium, vitamins A and C, and fiber.

If, instead, you choose anchovies, olives, pepperoni, and regular mozzarella cheese, you will double the fat and sodium. The pizza will still be a good source of calcium but it will be low in fiber and vitamins.

If your children don't like broccoli, don't assume they won't like it on pizza. They might be receptive to it in this way.

> 1 12-inch round pizza dough
> ½ cup tomato sauce
> 1 teaspoon dried oregano (or 2 tablespoons fresh)
> ½ teaspoon dried basil (or 1 tablespoon fresh)
> 10 mushrooms, sliced
> 3 cups small broccoli florets
> 1 small onion, thinly sliced
> ½ sweet red and/or yellow pepper, chopped
> 2½ cups shredded low-fat mozzarella cheese
> Pinch dried hot pepper flakes

Place pizza dough on baking sheet. Combine tomato sauce, oregano, and basil; mix well and spread over pizza dough. Arrange mushrooms, broccoli, onion, and red pepper on top. Sprinkle with cheese and dried hot pepper flakes (if using). Bake in 475°F oven for 12 minutes or until cheese is bubbling. Cut into 8 pieces.

Feeding a Family on the Run

Today every family has a busy schedule. Mothers who work outside the home and single parents are particularly hard-pressed to find the time and energy to make meals. Once you get in the habit, though, you'll find it is not difficult to make a delicious and healthy meal for four in 30 minutes, if you have the ingredients in the house. Here are some tips for mealtimes in busy households:

- If getting a meal on the table is a problem, discuss meal planning with the whole family and try to divide up the jobs, from shopping to putting groceries away to cooking and cleaning up. Younger family members like to help and they can set the table, peel carrots, wash lettuce—don't worry about the mess, they eventually get tidier.

  Don't give up if you meet some resistance. In our house, every year—sometimes every month—we come up with new ways to divide the jobs. We have just started a system in which each person makes dinner one night a week. Even if it only lasts for two weeks it's worth it to me.

- Cook extra on the weekends: Double whatever you make on Saturday and Sunday and eat it again during the week. Many of the recipes in the book are suitable for reheating or can be eaten cold throughout the week: Easy Oven Beef and Vegetable Stew (page 95); Split Pea, Bean, and Barley Soup (page 60); Chunky Vegetable-Bean Soup (page 52); Mexican Rice and Bean Casserole (page 137); Beef and Pasta Casserole for a Crowd (page 97); Pasta and Fresh Vegetable Salad (page 80). Or, cook a number of vegetables and a large roast, chicken, or turkey on Sunday, then on Monday have it cold and reheat the vegetables. On Tuesday use the meat in a casserole or soup.

- Do a little meal preparation before you go out in the morning; for example, chop up meat and maybe a vegetable for a stir-fry (page 93), or get a chicken out of the freezer and leave a note or make arrangements for someone else in the family to put it in the oven at a certain time.

- Hire someone to do some cooking as an alternative to fast foods, eating out, and using many prepared foods. If you are constantly eating meals at fast-food chains or using prepared and convenience foods (which are usually high in fat and sodium and low in fiber), examine the reasons why and consider alternatives.

It might not be any more expensive to hire someone to do some cooking for you: a student, a cleaning lady, your own child, or your housekeeper. This person could help you on a regular basis either daily, weekly, or monthly—or just occasionally. Consider spending an evening cooking with the fill-in chef and show him or her how to make a few of your favorite dishes, or prepare some of the recipes in this book. When I'm really under the gun for work, I hire someone to make huge quantities of All-Purpose Quick Spaghetti Sauce (below) and freeze it in 2- or 4-cup containers. I then use it as a base for chili, tacos, casseroles, and lasagna, as well as spaghetti.

All-Purpose Quick Spaghetti Sauce

MAKES 6 SERVINGS, 6 CUPS TOTAL

PER SERVING (1 cup)*

195 calories
  9 g fat
 38 mg cholesterol
280 mg sodium

 17 g protein
 14 g carbohydrate

GOOD: fiber, vitamin A
EXCELLENT: vitamin C, niacin, iron

*Made with canned whole tomatoes. If made with water instead of tomatoes, sodium is 61 mg per serving.

I make this sauce in large amounts then freeze it in 2-cup containers. You can double or triple this recipe. Sometimes I add chopped carrot, green pepper, celery, or mushrooms. My kids like it best over spaghetti noodles sprinkled with Parmesan cheese. It's also good as a base for lasagna, tacos, chili, or casseroles.

1 pound ground beef
2 medium onions, chopped
1 large clove garlic, minced
1 6-ounce can tomato paste
1 28-ounce can whole tomatoes (or 2 cups water)
1 teaspoon dried oregano
1 teaspoon dried basil
½ teaspoon dried thyme
¼ teaspoon freshly ground pepper

In large heavy skillet, cook beef over medium heat until no longer pink, breaking up with spoon. Pour off fat. Stir in onion and garlic; cook until softened. Stir in tomato paste, tomatoes (breaking up with back of spoon), oregano, basil, thyme, and pepper.

(continued)

Bring to boil, reduce heat, and simmer for 10 minutes; thin with water if desired. Taste and adjust seasonings if necessary.

Last-Minute Pasta Casserole

MAKES 4 SERVINGS

PER SERVING

247 calories
5 g fat
21 mg cholesterol
187 mg sodium

14 g protein
37 g carbohydrates

GOOD: fiber, iron
EXCELLENT: vitamin C, niacin

This is another of my kids' favorites. If there are any leftovers, my son John heats them up in the microwave for breakfast or snacks. It's a good dish for small children who don't like to chew meat. I never seem to make this exactly the same way twice, and I add what vegetables I have on hand: fresh tomatoes and zucchini in the summer, celery and carrots in the winter. Add fresh basil if you have it.

> 4 ounces macaroni (1 cup) or shell pasta
> 2 cups All-Purpose Quick Spaghetti Sauce (page 223)
> 1 small sweet green or yellow pepper, chopped
> 4 large mushrooms, sliced
> 1 cup kernel corn or green peas
> 2 tablespoons grated Parmesan cheese

In large pot of boiling water, cook macaroni until al dente (tender but firm); drain.

Meanwhile, in flameproof casserole or heavy saucepan over medium heat, combine Spaghetti Sauce, sweet pepper, mushrooms, and corn or peas; simmer for 5 minutes. Stir in hot cooked pasta; sprinkle each serving with Parmesan cheese.

Stocking the Basics

Sometimes we eat out at food chains or order in because we don't have the ingredients in the house to make a fast meal. There are a few simple tips for always having the makings of a fast, healthy meal at home.

Keep your kitchen stocked with staple foods, such as whole-wheat pastas, cereals, rice, tomato paste, canned beans, tuna, salmon, peanut butter, and low-fat yogurt. Keep whole-wheat pita bread, muffins, peas, corn, and juice in your freezer, along with chicken and fish fillets.

Vegetables such as cabbage, cauliflower, turnip, cucumber, and carrots, and reduced-fat cheeses and eggs will keep for three to four weeks in the refrigerator.

Below are a few recipes for which you can keep the ingredients on your shelf or in the freezer. Even when the refrigerator looks bare you'll still be able to make these nutritious dishes.

Linguine with Salmon and Chives (page 122)
Fish Fillets with Basil and Lemon (page 118)
Fish Fillets with Herbed Crumbs (page 117)
Barbecued Lemon Chicken (page 104)
Herb-Breaded Chicken (page 229)
Bean Casserole with Tomatoes and Spinach (page 129)
Mexican Rice and Bean Casserole (page 137)

Penne with Herbed Tomato-Tuna Sauce

MAKES 4 SERVINGS

PER SERVING

328 calories
4 g fat
22 mg cholesterol
502 mg sodium

23 g protein
49 g carbohydrate

GOOD: fiber, iron
EXCELLENT: vitamin C, niacin

You'll probably have all the ingredients for this popular economical family dish right in your own cupboard. My kids gobble it up and, at first, didn't know if it was tuna or chicken in the sauce.

1 tablespoon soft margarine or olive oil
1 small onion, chopped
1 clove garlic, minced
1 14-ounce can whole tomatoes
1/2 cup chicken stock
1 teaspoon dried basil (or 2 tablespoons chopped fresh)
1/2 teaspoon dried rosemary (or 2 teaspoons fresh)
1 6 1/2-ounce can tuna, packed in water, drained
Salt and freshly ground pepper
1/3 cup chopped fresh parsley (optional)
1/2 pound penne or macaroni (about 3 cups dried pasta)

(continued)

In heavy saucepan, heat oil over medium heat; cook onion and garlic for 5 minutes or until tender, stirring occasionally.

Add tomatoes and break up using back of spoon. Stir in chicken stock, basil, and rosemary; simmer, uncovered, for 10 minutes. Stir in tuna and simmer for 5 minutes. Season with salt and pepper to taste; add parsley (if using).

Meanwhile, in large pot of boiling water, cook penne until al dente (tender but firm); drain. Toss with tomato mixture and serve immediately.

The Beginner Cook

Often we get tied up at work and can't get home or are just too tired at the end of a day to make a meal. Instead of ordering in a pizza, here are some suggestions for meals that teenagers or a beginning cook can make for themselves or for the family.

- Hamburger, raw carrots, milk, apple or pear
- Scrambled eggs, peas, salad, toast, milk, sherbet, cookies
- Roast chicken, baked potatoes, any frozen vegetables (or fresh if they know how to prepare and cook them), salad, milk, fresh or canned fruit (light or low-sugar syrup)

One of the most difficult tasks for young cooks is to have everything ready at once. It's a good idea to choose a menu with one or two cold dishes, or foods for which timing isn't critical. Try this one.

Hamburgers
Oven-Baked French Fries (page 227)
Red and Green Cabbage Slaw (page 227)
Frozen Strawberry Yogurt (page 228)
Microwave Oatmeal Squares (page 228)

Oven-Baked French Fries

MAKES 4 SERVINGS

PER SERVING

179 calories
  3 g fat
  0 mg cholesterol
 11 mg sodium

  3 g protein
 35 g carbohydrate

GOOD: fiber, niacin, iron
EXCELLENT: vitamin C

These good-tasting french fries are much healthier and easier to make than the ones that you deep-fry in fat.

4 medium potatoes (1½ pound)
1 tablespoon vegetable oil
Paprika
Grated Parmesan cheese (optional)

Wash potatoes but don't peel; slice into ½-inch thick strips. Toss potatoes with oil in a bowl until coated; sprinkle with paprika. Spread on baking sheet and bake in 475°F oven for 25 to 30 minutes, or until golden, turning occasionally.

Toss with Parmesan (if using).

Red and Green Cabbage Slaw

MAKES 6 SERVINGS

PER SERVING

 49 calories
  4 g fat
  6 mg cholesterol
105 mg sodium

  1 g protein
  4 g carbohydrate

GOOD: fiber
EXCELLENT: vitamin C

This colorful, easy-to-make salad goes well with hamburgers, toasted cheese sandwiches, and many summer barbecue menus. If red cabbage is hard to find, use only green cabbage and add one or two shredded carrots. Chopped sweet red or green pepper, celery, zucchini, onion, apple, or raisins are nice additions.

2 cups shredded green cabbage
1 cup shredded red cabbage
¼ cup chopped scallion or red onion
¼ cup light mayonnaise
¼ cup low-fat plain yogurt
¼ cup chopped fresh parsley
Salt and freshly ground pepper

In salad bowl, combine green and red cabbage, scallion or onion, mayonnaise, yogurt, parsley, and salt and pepper to taste. Mix well, cover, and refrigerate for up to 4 hours.

Microwave Oatmeal Squares

PER SERVING (1 square)

71 calories
4 g fat
0 mg cholesterol
32 mg sodium

1 g protein
8 g carbohydrate

These are very easy and the fastest squares I know how to make. Use any crumbs left in the pan with yogurt as a topping over fruit.

½ cup margarine
½ teaspoon almond or vanilla extract
½ cup packed brown sugar
2 cups rolled oats

In 8-inch square glass or microwave-safe dish, microwave margarine at high power for 40 to 60 seconds or until melted. Stir in extract and sugar; mix well. Stir in rolled oats; mix well.

Firmly press mixture into pan. Microwave at high power for 5 minutes. Let cool and cut into 25 squares.

TO BAKE IN CONVENTIONAL OVEN: Melt margarine, combine with extract and sugar, then add oats; mix well. Press into pan; bake in 350°F oven for 15 minutes or until bubbling and golden brown.

Frozen Strawberry Yogurt

MAKES 5 SERVINGS, ½ CUP EACH

PER SERVING

81 calories
1 g fat
3 mg cholesterol
35 mg sodium

3 g protein
17 g carbohydrate

EXCELLENT: vitamin C

Creamy and full of flavor, this frozen dessert is a refreshing finale to any meal and a favorite of my daughter Susie. In strawberry season serve with fresh berries and a crisp cookie.

2 cups fresh strawberries or 1 10-ounce package frozen, thawed
1 cup low-fat plain yogurt
⅓ cup confectioners' sugar
1 tablespoon lemon juice

In food processor or blender, purée strawberries; you should have about 1⅓ cups. Add yogurt, sugar, and lemon juice; process for 1 second or until mixed.

Pour into pan or ice cream machine and freeze according to instructions on page 194.

Fast Food at Home

Instead of ordering in a pizza or takeout chicken, here are a few tasty and healthy alternatives.

Herb-Breaded Chicken

MAKES 4 SERVINGS

PER SERVING

162 calories
3 g fat
70 mg cholesterol
240 mg sodium

26 g protein
6 g carbohydrate

My son John likes to make this when it is his turn to cook dinner. I try to keep chicken breasts and a jar of these seasoned bread crumbs in my freezer so I can make this in a jiffy. Don't worry if you don't have all the herbs, just use a little more of the ones you have. I also use these crumbs on pork tenderloin, fish fillets, and broiled tomato halves.

1½ slices whole-wheat bread
¼ teaspoon dried basil
¼ teaspoon dried thyme
¼ teaspoon dried oregano
¼ teaspoon dried tarragon
¼ teaspoon paprika
¼ teaspoon salt
Freshly ground pepper
1 pound boneless skinless chicken breasts (about 4 breast pieces)
    or 2 pounds bone-in chicken breasts (see Note)

In food processor or blender, process bread to make crumbs. Add basil, thyme, oregano, tarragon, paprika, salt, and pepper to taste; process to mix.

Rinse chicken under cold running water; shake off water. Transfer crumb mixture to plastic bag; add chicken a few pieces at a time and shake to coat.

Place chicken in single layer in microwave-safe dish or on baking sheet. Bake in 400°F oven for 18 to 20 minutes for boneless breasts, 40 minutes for bone-in, or until no longer pink inside.

(continued)

MICROWAVE METHOD: Microwave, uncovered, at high power for 5 minutes for boneless, 9 minutes for bone-in; let stand for 1 minute.

Note: When using bone-in chicken breasts, double the amount of bread and herbs.

Compare These Three Chicken Dinners *(per serving):*

1. A Homemade Chicken Dinner for Four (20% of Calories from Fat):	Grams Fat	Milligrams Cholesterol	Milligrams Sodium	Calories
Herb-Breaded Chicken (page 229)	3	70	240	162
Rice (½ cup)	0	0	5	80
Peas with Scallions (page 144)	2	0	89	68
Sliced tomato (½)	0	0	5	12
Milk, 2% (8 ounces)	5	19	129	128
TOTALS	10	89	468	450
TOTALS with 2 pieces of chicken	13	159	708	612

2. Kentucky Fried Chicken Dinner (47% of Calories from Fat)*				
1 piece side breast per person (3 ounces)	17	96	654	276
French fries, 1 serving (approximately 3 ounces)	13	2	81	268
Coleslaw (approximately 3 ounces)	6	4	171	105
Milk, 2% (8 ounces)	5	19	129	128
TOTALS	41	121	1,035	777
TOTALS with 2 pieces of chicken	58	217	1,689	1,053

3. Swanson Fried Chicken Breast Dinner (43% of Calories from Fat)**				
10¾-ounce portion (chicken, potatoes, corn)	32	80	1,425	650
Milk, 2% (8 ounces)	5	19	129	128
TOTALS	37	99	1,554	778

*Six pieces of Kentucky Nuggets have about the same amount of fat (19 grams) as one piece of Kentucky Fried breast meat.

**This is a smaller portion than the above two dinners. Frozen dinners vary considerably in their content; read the labels carefully.

Frozen Hamburger Patties

MAKES 20 PATTIES

PER SERVING (1 patty)

169 calories
10 g fat
59 mg cholesterol
54 mg sodium

17 g protein
1 g carbohydrate

GOOD: iron
EXCELLENT: niacin

Until I was assigned a magazine article on using frozen hamburger patties, I didn't realize what a convenience it would be to have these on hand. It doesn't take long to make hamburger patties, and they are much easier to use than a block of frozen meat. Lean ground pork or lamb also make tasty patties, and they can be combined with beef to make patties.

4 pounds lean ground beef
3 medium onions, finely chopped
1 sweet green pepper, finely chopped (optional)
1 egg
1 teaspoon dry mustard
1 teaspoon Worcestershire sauce
½ teaspoon freshly ground pepper
Dash hot pepper sauce

In large bowl, combine beef, onions, green pepper (if using), egg, mustard, Worcestershire sauce, pepper, and hot pepper sauce; with spoon or hands, mix just until combined.

Using ice-cream scoop or hands, divide mixture into 20 portions; shape each portion into round patty. Place patties on baking sheets and freeze until solid, 4 to 5 hours. Stack patties with foil or paper plates between them. Package in freezer bags and store up to 4 months in freezer.

To broil, place frozen patties on grill 3 to 4 inches from broiler. Broil for about 5 minutes on each side or until browned and to desired doneness.

Middle-Eastern Burgers

MAKES 4 SERVINGS

For a nice change, try beef or lamb patties in whole-wheat pita bread pockets topped with garlicky Greek Tzatziki Sauce, which is so delicious any extra can be used as a dip with pita bread.

PER SERVING

357	calories
13	g fat
63	mg cholesterol
436	mg sodium

28	g protein
36	g carbohydrate

GOOD: fiber, vitamin C, thiamin, riboflavin, calcium, iron
EXCELLENT: niacin

4 hamburger patties (about 3 ounces each)
4 6-inch whole-wheat pita rounds
Shredded lettuce

QUICK TZATZIKI SAUCE

1 cup low-fat plain yogurt
½ English cucumber, peeled and finely chopped
1 large clove garlic, minced

Quick Tzatziki Sauce: In small bowl, combine yogurt, cucumber, and garlic; mix well.

Broil hamburger patties to desired doneness. Cut slice off each pita bread about 1 inch from edge; pull apart to form opening. Heat pitas in oven or microwave until warm. Place hot hamburger patty and shredded lettuce inside pita; spoon about ¼ cup Tzatziki Sauce over each hamburger.

VARIATION

BEST TZATZIKI SAUCE: If you have time to make Tzatziki Sauce in advance, use this method for a longer lasting thicker sauce. Line a sieve with cheesecloth or muslin; add yogurt and let drain for 2 to 4 hours. Place chopped cucumber in a colander and sprinkle with ¼ teaspoon salt, let stand for 30 minutes, then rinse under cold water and pat dry. Combine drained yogurt, cucumber, and garlic; mix well. Cover and refrigerate up to 2 days.

Eating Out and Traveling

Recent studies have shown that life-style is the important factor in determining how healthily you eat. Men and women who travel and eat out frequently are much more likely to have a high-fat diet than those who don't travel.

If you only eat out for special occasions or once a month, enjoy your meal and order what you want. If, however, you eat out often it's important to make nutritious menu choices. Too often we eat more than we would at home, more high-fat foods, and not enough fruits and vegetables.

Compare These Hamburger Dinners

The most notable difference between home-cooked and fast-food hamburgers is their sodium content. The extra fat and calories in a McDonald's meal come from the fries and shake. If you eat at a fast-food burger chain, omit the fries, choose skim or 2% milk, and make a salad from the salad bar using only a small amount of dressing.

Home-Cooked Hamburger Dinner	*Grams Fat*	*Milligrams Cholesterol*	*Milligrams Sodium*	*Calories*
Hamburger (lean ground beef, 23% fat maximum), broiled, 3½ to 4 ounces, includes bun	18	66	102	404
Pickle relish (1 tablespoon)	0	0	107	21
Lettuce, onions, tomatoes	0	0	3	8
Raw carrot (1)	0	0	25	31
Milk, 2% (8 ounces)	5	19	129	128
TOTAL	23	85	366	592

McDonald's Hamburger Dinner				
Quarter Pounder	24	81	718	427
Small french fries	12	9	109	220
Vanilla shake (10.2 ounces)	8	31	201	352
TOTAL	44	121	1,028	999
TOTAL with 2% milk (no shake)	41	99	956	775
TOTAL with Big Mac instead of Quarter Pounder	52	101	1,289	918

TAKEOUT AND FAST FOODS

Grabbing a quick bite on the way home from work or ordering in a pizza is part of today's life-style. Since these foods are often high in fat and sodium but adequate in protein, the other foods or meals you eat at home should be low in fat and high in vitamins and fiber. If your dieting daughter eats lunch at fast-food chains and often has a hamburger for lunch, she can balance it out with homemade soup, raw vegetables, bread, and an apple for dinner. The following table offers some excellent suggestions for making a fast-food meal more nutritious.

A Takeout Guide

Takeout	Nutritional Considerations	Nutrient Boosters
Chicken	· choose barbecued, baked, or broiled · remove the skin, hold the sauce/gravy, forget the fries · low in vitamins A and C, iron, and fiber	· add a whole-wheat bun, glass of skim or 2% milk, and a salad · choose a baked potato for added nutrients and fiber, hold the butter and sour cream, and eat the skin
Chinese	· high in salt and MSG · choose stir-fried dishes, include a vegetable dish and steamed rice · low in calcium and vitamin C	· boost vitamin C—include a dish with broccoli or Chinese greens · add milk to your meal or try a tofu stir-fry; you can even catch up on your calcium later in the day
Pizza	· order a cheese and vegetable pizza, leave off the ham, bacon, and pepperoni—these are high in fat and salt · lots of calcium here, but low in vitamins A and C, iron, and fiber	· start with a spinach/orange salad and finish with some fruit for added fiber and vitamins · some pizza parlors offer a whole-wheat crust—ask when you order
Tacos	· high in fat · low in vitamins A and C, and calcium	· have a glass of skim or 2% milk, and fruit for dessert · try a bean or chicken taco for less fat and lots of iron; bean tacos also provide fiber
Souvlaki	· cubed lamb or pork in a pita bread with tomatoes and yogurt/garlic sauce · low in vitamins A and C, and fiber	· extra tomatoes boost the vitamin A and C · for added fiber and calcium, choose whole-wheat pita bread and a glass of skim or 2% milk
Hamburgers	· choose broiled or barbecued hamburgers · hold the mayo, sauce, and fries · usually low in vitamins A and C, calcium, and fiber	· stay away from the condiments and choose lots of lettuce and tomatoes for added vitamins A and C · choose a salad for added fiber · ask for a whole-wheat bun, for added fiber · add a glass of skim or 2% milk to your meal for calcium and/or have a cheeseburger—you'll boost your calcium even more

Chart produced by Public Health Nutritionists in Metropolitan Toronto and regions of Peel and York.

Healthy Meals (21% Calories from Fat) vs. Less Healthy Meals (55% of Calories from Fat)

Healthy Breakfast	Fat	Cholesterol	Calories	Less Healthy Breakfast	Fat	Cholesterol	Calories
Orange or fresh fruit	trace	0	62	Croissant or danish	12	13	235
Whole-grain cereal	trace	0	95	Fried eggs (2) and bacon (2 slices)	18	567	241
Yogurt or skim milk	trace	5	90	Coffee with cream	3	9	28

Healthy Lunch				Less Healthy Lunch			
Spinach salad (1 Tbsp regular or 2 Tbsp low-fat dressing)	7	0	93	Cream of mushroom soup made with whole milk (1 cup)	14	21	215
Pasta with tomato-based sauce and Parmesan cheese	11	8	368	Quiche (⅛ of 8-inch diameter)	48	285	600
Raspberry sorbet	0	0	109	Chocolate pudding (½ cup)	10	trace	191

Healthy Dinner				Less Healthy Dinner			
Consommé with vegetables	3	32	91	House pâté	5	28	59
Broiled fish or chicken breast, nonfat sauce (4 ounces)	4	73	148	12-ounce steak	36	256	752
Rice (½ cup) or potato, no butter and not fried	trace	0	101	Potato with 2 tsp butter or french fries (10)	8	7	158
Asparagus or green beans	trace	0	15	Tossed salad	trace	0	11
with lemon and 1 teaspoon margarine	4	0	33	with 2 tablespoons Thousand Island dressing	12	8	128
Fresh strawberries (1 cup)	trace	0	47	Strawberry cheesecake	8	0	222
TOTAL	29	118	1,252		174	1,194	2,840

TIPS FOR HEALTHY RESTAURANT EATING

- Choose a restaurant where you can make nutritious choices such as salads, soups, vegetables, and fruits. Some restaurants mark low-fat and low-cholesterol dishes on the menu.
- Have a glass of water as soon as you are seated in order to control your urge to eat, as well as to ensure you get enough fluids.
- Avoid buffets and all-you-can-eat specials if you tend to overeat.
- Order salad dressings and sauces on the side and add only a small amount.
- If you eat the breads and rolls, pass on the butter. Don't fill up on crackers and pretzels.
- Avoid gravies and sauces made with cream and butter.
- Avoid fried, sautéed, and deep-fried foods; instead, choose broiled, poached, baked, roasted, or boiled dishes.
- Trim all visible fat from meat, skin from poultry.
- Choose chicken or fish; avoid duck and goose.
- Choose baked potato over french fries. Avoid butter and go easy on the sour cream, or choose yogurt instead. Ask for extra vegetables and small portions of meat.
- If you have dessert, order fresh fruit or sherbet; avoid pastries and whipped-cream desserts.
- Don't feel you have to eat everything on your plate because you are paying for it. Some restaurant portions are very large and can easily be shared.
- Avoid nondairy creamer, which is high in saturated fat; for coffee or tea choose milk instead.
- If a restaurant or hotel room-service menu doesn't offer many healthy choices, make a special request. They are in the business to please; if enough people ask for nutritious dishes, they might change their menus.
- In Chinese restaurants ask for dishes without MSG (monosodium glutamate) to reduce your sodium intake.

Cooking for One

When I lived by myself I would come home from work, open the refrigerator, and start to eat. Unless I invited someone for dinner, I lived on cheese and crackers, scrambled eggs, sandwiches, soups, raw vegetables, and fruit. This diet can be nutritious but it does become boring. Because sometimes I didn't even bother to put the food on a plate but would snack on the run, I ate more than I needed and gained weight. Finding the motivation to cook and learning how to shop for one are the two key problems confronting people who live alone.

It's difficult to discuss cooking for one or two in a few pages because people's eating patterns vary widely. A single twenty-two-year-old male's nutritional requirements and eating preferences will be different from those of a seventy-year-old widow. Following the Guide to Good Eating (page 249) and eating foods from the four main food groups each day is an easy way to ensure that everyone eats healthily.

TIPS FOR SHOPPING AND COOKING FOR ONE

- Shop at a store where you can buy small portions and everything isn't prepackaged.
- When possible, buy only what you can use. It's more economical to buy a small can and use it all than to buy a larger size and throw half away.
- When you can't buy a small portion of a vegetable, think up different ways to use it. For example, use broccoli in a salad, soup, omelet, stir-fry, over pasta, with cheese, or just simply boiled.
- The microwave oven is an advantage not only for speed, but it means you don't have to warm up a large oven to cook or reheat a small portion. A toaster oven is also great for reheating small portions.
- If you eat out often at lunch, make it your main meal of the day; you will only need to prepare a light meal in the evening.
- Because you don't have to buy large amounts, you can treat yourself to special foods and more expensive foods, such as an out-of-season vegetable, a pint of strawberries, or a salmon steak.

- Many of the recipes (such as the pasta dishes) in this book are for four servings. You can easily halve them and either freeze one portion or refrigerate the leftovers and use the next day.

NUTRITION FOR SENIORS

Many people who live alone are also older and have some special nutritional needs. Nutritional recommendations are particularly important for the elderly, whose energy or calorie needs are often less but whose nutrient needs are not. This means the foods older people eat should be high in nutrients and there isn't much room for empty-calorie foods, such as sweets and alcohol. Most communities have Meals-on-Wheels programs for elderly people who have trouble shopping and preparing food for themselves. Make sure the elderly people you care about aren't making do with tea and toast.

- Fatigue and apathy can be the result of poor nutrition, especially too little protein and iron.
- Complex carbohydrates and fiber-rich foods such as fruits, vegetables, and whole-grain breads and cereals should be emphasized.
- Some medications, either prescription or over-the-counter drugs and laxatives, can cause vitamin and mineral deficiencies. Consult your doctor about whether you need a vitamin-mineral supplement.
- As you get older your taste buds and thirst signals aren't as strong. It's important to drink six to eight glasses of fluids and not to oversalt foods.

RECIPES FOR SOLO DINERS

Two recipes for solo diners—for Sole with Tomatoes (page 240) and Stir-Fry for One (page 239)—are simple and quick. The trick is always to keep such basic ingredients as tomato paste, oil, lemon juice, and seasonings in your cupboards so that you can prepare delicious meals on short notice.

Stir-Fry for One

MAKES 1 SERVING

PER SERVING*

292 calories
13 g fat
70 mg cholesterol
259 mg sodium

31 g protein
15 g carbohydrate

GOOD: iron
EXCELLENT: vitamin C, fiber, niacin, vitamin A

*with chicken

Stir-fries are a quick and easy meal for 1 or 2 people and an excellent way to use up a piece of broccoli or half a red pepper lurking in the refrigerator—add a few more vegetables and the stir-fry can easily be stretched to make an extra serving. Don't be put off by the long list of ingredients—the stir-fry only takes a minute or 2 to put together and tastes delicious. Serve over hot rice or noodles.

¼ pound boneless chicken, beef, or pork
1 teaspoon cornstarch
1 tablespoon sherry or white wine
1 stalk broccoli or celery, or ½ sweet pepper
2 tablespoons vegetable oil
1 clove garlic, minced
1 teaspoon minced fresh gingerroot

SEASONING SAUCE

1 tablespoon water
1 tablespoon sherry or white wine
½ teaspoon cornstarch
½ teaspoon low-sodium soy sauce

Cut meat into very thin strips about 2 inches long. In bowl, mix cornstarch and sherry; stir in meat and let stand for 10 minutes or up to 2 hours. Cut vegetables into thin strips or florets. In small bowl, combine seasoning sauce ingredients and mix well.

In wok or nonstick skillet, heat oil over high heat. Add garlic, ginger, and meat; stir-fry for 1 minute. Add broccoli or other vegetable and stir-fry 2 minutes or until crisp tender; add water if necessary to prevent scorching. Stir in seasoning sauce and stir-fry for another minute.

Sole with Tomatoes

MAKES 1 SERVING

This is an absolutely delicious and easy-to-make dish for one. Serve with a green vegetable along with potatoes, rice, or bread. For two servings, double the ingredients and place on one plate before microwaving for 4 to 5 minutes.

> 1 medium tomato, thickly sliced
> 1 5-ounce fillet sole
> ½ teaspoon olive oil
> ½ teaspoon lemon juice
> 2 teaspoons chopped fresh basil, dill or parsley (or ¼ teaspoon dried)
> Freshly ground pepper

On microwave-safe plate, arrange tomato slices in single layer. Arrange fish to cover tomatoes; drizzle with oil and lemon juice. Sprinkle with basil, and pepper to taste. Cover with vented plastic wrap; microwave at high (100%) power for 3 minutes or until fish is almost opaque and flakes easily when tested with fork. Remove from oven and let stand for 1 minute. If necessary, pour off excess liquid from plate.

CONVENTIONAL OVEN METHOD: In shallow baking dish arrange fish; cover with sliced tomato. Drizzle with oil and lemon juice. Sprinkle with basil and pepper to taste. Bake in 400°F oven for 12 minutes or until fish is almost opaque and flakes easily when tested with a fork.

Chicken for One

For one boneless chicken breast (4-ounce size), use about ¼ cup of crumb mixture used in Herb-Breaded Chicken (page 229) (freeze remaining for another time). Bake or microwave, uncovered, on high power for 2 minutes; let stand 1 minute.

Grocery Shopping

The grocery store is the first place to start thinking about healthy eating. It doesn't matter how well you cook if you haven't bought the right foods in the first place. Some of the new products on the shelves make it much easier to cook in a fast and healthy way than it was thirty years ago, but the opposite can also be true. Spend a few minutes reading labels, especially the first time you buy a new product or brand. As a rule, the more processed or prepared the food, the fewer the nutrients and the more salt, or sodium, and sugar it contains.

Choose	*Avoid (or choose less often)*
Milk and Milk Products	
2%, 1%, or skim milk	Whole milk
Plain yogurt (1 or 2% butter fat or milk fat)	Yogurt 4% or higher butterfat
Cottage cheese (1 or 2% butterfat)	
Low-fat cheeses, i.e., skim or part-skim milk mozzarella, ricotta cheese, farmer's cheese, feta	Use less of high-fat cheeses, such as Cheddar, Brie, blue, brick, Gruyère, Gouda, Swiss
Light sour cream (occasionally)	Cream, regular sour cream
Meat, Fish, Poultry	
Lean cuts of beef—round, flank; lean ground beef	Fatty cuts—prime rib, regular ground beef, bacon, spareribs
Fish, chicken, turkey	Duck, goose, self-basting turkeys, or those with added fat; breaded and fried frozen meats, fish
Tuna packed in water, canned salmon	Tuna packed in oil, luncheon meats, wieners, sausage
Fruits and Vegetables	
Fresh fruits and vegetables	Avocados
Frozen fruits and vegetables	Canned vegetables (containing salt or high-sodium compounds such as monosodium glutamate, disodium inosinate, and disodium guanylate)
Low-sodium canned tomato juice and vegetables	
Unsweetened juices	Sweetened juices
Tomato paste	Tomato sauce
Canned whole tomatoes	Canned stewed tomatoes
Fruits canned with juice or light syrup	Canned fruits in heavy syrup

Choose	*Avoid (or choose less often)*
Breads and Cereals	
100% whole-wheat bread	White bread
Whole-wheat flour	
Prepared cereals without sugar, with 2 grams or more fiber/serving	Sugar cereals, with less than 2 grams fiber/serving
Whole-wheat buns, pita bread, English muffins, pasta	Granola cereals made with palm or coconut oil
Fats, Seasonings, Desserts, Snacks	
High-polyunsaturated soft margarines (page 253)	Butter, lard, hard margarines
Oils: sunflower, safflower, canola, olive (page 254)	Palm or coconut oils, partially hydrogenated vegetable oils
Light mayonnaise	Mayonnaise
Light or low-fat salad dressings	Regular salad dressings
Ice milk, fruit sorbets	Ice cream
Frozen juice bar, frozen yogurt bar	Ice cream bar
Angel food cake, arrowroot cookies	Chocolates, many types of cakes, pies, peanuts, potato chips
	Cream substitutes

A GUIDE TO FOOD LABELS

Don't be deceived by misleading food labels: the words "light" or "lite" may mean light in color or light in calories, but not necessarily low in fat. Read the list of ingredients and nutrients per serving. Remember that ingredients are listed on the label in order of amounts by weight, beginning with the largest amount. Compare several different brands of the same product and choose the one that is lowest in fat and salt.

· The word "fat" may not appear on the label, but the following words all indicate fat: glycerides, glycerol, esters, shortening, hydrogenated oils.
· Foods containing large amounts of sugar should also be used sparingly. The word "sugar" may not appear, but the following words all mean sugar: fructose, sucrose, lactose, maltose, sorbitol, mannitol, dextrose, honey, syrups, molasses, sweeten-

ers. Although foods may be labeled "no sugar added" or "unsweetened," they may still have a high content of natural sugar.

- Food high in sodium should be consumed carefully. Again, the word "salt" may not appear on the label, but such terms as brine, baking powder, baking soda, and other sodium compounds such as monosodium glutamate (MSG), sodium benzoate, or disodium phosphate may be listed.

    Terms such as "salt-free" mean that no salt was added during processing, but salt or sodium could still be present naturally. Check the sodium content per serving.

- Check the list of ingredients on bread packages to be sure that whole wheat is the first ingredient listed. Labels such as "bread with whole grain" or "whole-wheat goodness" may not mean whole wheat.

- "No cholesterol" is a meaningless claim often used on margarines or shortenings: foods from vegetable sources (i.e., vegetable oils) never contain cholesterol. However, they could have a high level of saturated fat, which raises the level of cholesterol in the blood.

- Foods advertised on a healthy theme might not be healthy and often may be high in sugar and fat; for example, granola bars have as much sugar and fat as many chocolate bars, and some cereals have as much food value as eating sugar and a vitamin pill.

Tips When Using Frozen Dinners

- Choose broiled, baked, and stir-fry dishes; avoid ones with butter and cream sauces. Read the label and select ones with the lowest amount of fat, cholesterol, and salt.

- Watch your salt intake and choose low-salt foods the rest of the day.

- Frozen dinners are usually low in fiber. Add fiber by eating whole-wheat bread, split pea, lentil, or vegetable soup, and a raw or cooked vegetable, and finish off with fruit.

The Morning Meal

Some people are conditioned to eat breakfast while others aren't. The most important reasons for eating a good breakfast are:

- Studies have shown that children who have breakfast perform better than children who haven't.
- If you don't have breakfast it is more difficult to get all the nutrients you need in a day.
- People who maintain an ideal weight eat breakfast; overweight people tend to skip breakfast. If you miss breakfast and have a bran muffin and orange at coffee break, you are eating nutritiously; if you have a danish and coffee you are adding extra fat and calories without vitamins or fiber.

This doesn't mean you should be wolfing down fried eggs and bacon (too high in fat and cholesterol), but you should have some fruits or vegetables, milk, yogurt or low-fat cheese, and whole-grain toast or muffins. There's no need to limit your scope of breakfast foods. Dinner leftovers, a piece of pizza, fish, or salad can be as good in the morning as at night.

BREAKFAST CEREALS: It's important to read the labels, as some are much more nutritious than others. Read the ingredients per serving and the list of ingredients. Look for a short list of ingredients and one that begins with a whole grain, bran, or oats. I let my children pick whatever cereals they like as long as they aren't high in sugar and have at least two grams of fiber per serving.

Many commercial granolas are high in sugar and saturated fat from coconut oil. An alternative is to add dried fruits, such as raisins, chopped dates, or apricots, and nuts to bran flakes or other low-sugar cereal. If you are on a sodium-restricted diet, read the labels for salt and sodium, as many cereals are high in these.

FRUIT, FRUIT JUICES, OR FRUIT DRINKS: Choose fruit juices over drinks; fruit drinks are fortified with vitamin C but don't have the other nutrients that juices have. Choose fruit instead of juice for more fiber. Children don't need more than two drinks of juice a day; after that they are mainly getting sugar and might as well be drinking soft drinks. Instead, make sure they are drinking enough milk; after that give them water.

EGGS: Egg yolks have 274 milligrams cholesterol per egg. The dietary recommendation is that you limit your cholesterol intake to 300 milligrams or less a day. This means you can have two to three eggs per week. Many health professionals suggest you be more liberal in this respect with children and seniors because eggs are an easily digested and excellent source of protein and other nutrients. Dietary cholesterol shouldn't be limited in growing children unless warranted.

BACON: Bacon is high in saturated fat, salt, and nitrates and should be avoided or eaten only occasionally.

Packed Lunches

Brown-bag lunches allow you to control what you eat, save money, and have good-tasting foods. With all the new vacuum-packed containers and insulated lunch bags the choice is unlimited. Some of the salads in this book, such as Pasta and Fresh Vegetable Salad (page 80) or White Bean, Radish, and Red Onion Salad (page 66) are easy to pack and keep well. Also consider packing any of the soups from this book, either hot or cold.

When making sandwiches use a minimum of a high-polyunsaturated margarine (avoid butter because it is high in saturated fat) or light mayonnaise, not both. To keep sandwiches moist I add sliced cucumber or tomato. To prevent the bread from becoming soggy I pack sliced tomatoes separately and add them to the sandwich just before eating.

I used to pack lunches for my children but after I got a few complaints and didn't remember who liked what, they decided to pack their own. I do try to make sure there is a good supply of the kinds of nutritious food they like. I keep whole-wheat buns and bagels in the freezer; carrots, celery, lettuce, cucumber, alfalfa sprouts, cheese, and sliced turkey in the refrigerator; canned tuna and salmon, peanut butter, and jam on the shelf, plus a good selection of fresh fruit.

My children don't often take raisins or dried fruit because they are too sweet, but my son often likes popcorn for a treat. Dried fruit rolls are not recommended; they are high in sugar and stick to the teeth, promoting tooth decay.

Snacks

Snacks are part of our life-style and an important part of most children's daily food intake. Healthy snacking doesn't mean never having potato chips or soft drinks, but rather saving them for special occasions and more often having fruit, yogurt, a muffin, certain cereals, or a glass of milk. It's not fair never to let children taste the latest popular snack foods, but they don't need to have them every day. If you keep raw carrots, celery, cauliflower, and green peppers ready in the refrigerator, I think you'll be surprised at how often children will choose them. To prevent loss of vitamins, keep raw vegetables in a plastic bag, not in water.

Pita Pizzas (page 247) are a healthy snack that the whole family will enjoy. The topping is low-calorie; see the comparison after the recipe for how it stacks up against a more conventional topping.

Compare These Snack Foods:

	Grams Fat	*Milligrams Sodium*	*Calories*
Popcorn, plain (1 cup)	trace	0	23
Popcorn (1 cup, 1 teaspoon oil plus salt)	5	233	68
Popcorn, sugar-coated (1 cup)	1	0	142
Mixed nuts dry roasted, unsalted (¼ cup)	17	4	197
Mixed nuts, oil roasted plus salt (¼ cup)	19	222	210
Potato chips (10)	7	94	105
Pretzels, bread sticks (5)	trace	252	59
Doughnut, yeast type	11	98	174
Chocolate-chip cookies (2)	6	70	103
Milk-chocolate bar (1 ounce)	10	28	156
Ice cream, 10% butterfat (½ cup)	8	61	142
Frozen fruit yogurt, 6.3% butterfat (½ cup)	5	63	148
Fruit yogurt, 1.4% butterfat (½ cup)	2	81	131
Apple	0	0	84
Banana	0	1	105

"Birdseed" Granola Squares

MAKES ABOUT 40

PER SERVING (1 square)

104 calories
  5 g fat
  0 mg cholesterol
 15 mg sodium

  2 g protein
 15 g carbohydrate

GOOD: fiber

Great for school lunches. For an alternative to commercial granola bars try these tasty, easy-to-make squares that have a minimum of saturated fat and a maximum of fiber.

⅓ cup margarine
¾ cup honey
½ cup lightly packed brown sugar
2 cups rolled oats
1 cup natural bran
1 cup sunflower seeds
1 cup chopped dried apricots, dates, or raisins, or a combination
   (about 6 ounces)
½ cup chopped nuts (walnuts, pecans)
¼ cup sesame seeds

In small saucepan, melt margarine over low heat. Add honey and sugar; stir and bring to boil. Simmer for 5 minutes; remove from heat and let cool slightly.

In large bowl, combine rolled oats, bran, sunflower seeds, dried fruit, nuts, and sesame seeds. Gradually stir in sugar mixture. Firmly press into lightly greased 11- × 7-inch baking dish; bake in 350°F oven for 15 minutes or until golden. Let cool and cut into squares.

Pita Pizzas

MAKES 4 SERVINGS, 2 PIZZAS EACH

A quick snack, lunch, or light supper is easy to make using pita bread rounds as a base. Instead of mushrooms, you can add a topping of a combination of sweet red, yellow, or green peppers, sliced onion, sliced tomatoes, sliced artichokes, chopped fresh basil, and broccoli. Instead of pitas you can substitute English muffins, split in half, hamburger buns, tortillas, tostadas, or a zucchini, halved lengthwise.

(continued)

PER SERVING (2 pitas)

286 calories
6 g fat
15 mg cholesterol
718 mg sodium

23 g protein
41 g carbohydrate

GOOD: vitamin A, thiamin, riboflavin, calcium, fiber, iron
EXCELLENT: vitamin C, niacin

4 whole-wheat pitas (6- to 8-inch rounds)
¾ pound fresh mushrooms, thickly sliced
½ cup water
1⅓ cups low-fat cottage cheese (small curd)
½ cup grated low-fat mozzarella
1 teaspoon dried thyme
1 teaspoon dried oregano
⅓ cup tomato paste
⅔ cup water
1 teaspoon granulated sugar
½ cup chopped fresh chives or parsley

Cut around edge of each pita to separate into 2 rounds; place on baking sheet. Broil for 1 to 2 minutes on each side or until crisp.

In skillet, simmer mushrooms with water over medium heat, covered, for 5 minutes or until tender; drain and set aside.

In bowl or food processor, combine cottage cheese, mozzarella, thyme, and oregano; set aside.

Combine tomato paste, water, and sugar; mix well. Spread tomato mixture over pitas; top with cheese mixture. Spoon mushrooms over pitas and bake in 400°F oven for 10 to 15 minutes or until heated through. Sprinkle with chives or parsley.

Compare These Pizzas:

	Grams Fat	Milligrams Cholesterol	Milligrams Sodium	Calories
Pita Pizzas, 2 pita halves (page 247) (with mushrooms, mozzarella cheese, and chives)	6	15	718	286
Pita Pizzas, 2 pita halves (with tomato sauce, pepperoni, olives, and regular cheese)	37	65	2,644	556

Appendixes

Guide to Good Eating

Follow this healthy eating guide to obtain all the nutrients your body needs. For additional energy, increase the number and size of servings from the various food groups and/or add other foods.

Choose different kinds of foods from within each group to maintain your ideal weight. Select and prepare foods with limited amounts of fat, sugar, and salt.

MILK AND MILK PRODUCTS

Children up to 11 years	3 servings
Adolescents	4 servings
Pregnant and nursing women	4 servings
Adults	2 servings

Some examples of one serving:
1 cup milk
1 cup yogurt
1½ ounce Cheddar or process cheese

BREADS AND CEREALS
4 servings, whole-grain or enriched whole-grain products recommended

Some examples of one serving:
1 slice whole-wheat bread
½ cup/125 milliliters cooked cereal
1 cup ready-to-eat cereal

1 roll or muffin, ½ hamburger bun
½ cup cooked rice, macaroni, spaghetti

FRUITS AND VEGETABLES:
4 servings, choose a variety of fruits and vegetables (including at least 2 vegetables), cooked, raw or in their juices; include yellow and green vegetables

Some examples of one serving:
½ cup fruits, vegetables, or juice
1 medium-size potato, carrot, tomato, peach, orange, or banana

MEAT, FISH, POULTRY AND ALTERNATES
2 servings; pregnant women, 3 servings

Some examples of one serving:
2 ounces cooked lean meat, fish, poultry, or liver
¼ cup peanut butter*
1 cup cooked dried peas, beans, or lentils
2 ounces cheese*
½ cup cottage cheese
2 eggs*

*These should be used less often because of their higher fat or cholesterol content.

To reduce your cholesterol intake:

1. When possible substitute a food lower in or without cholesterol such as margarine for butter or skim milk for whole milk;
2. Use foods that are high in cholesterol in small amounts or less often.

Recommended Energy Intakes for Americans

Age (years)	Sex	Average Height (inches)	Average Weight (pounds)	Calories/Day
0–0.5	Both	24	13	690
0.5–1	Both	28	20	945
1–3	Both	35	29	1,300
4–6	Both	44	44	1,700
7–10	Both	52	62	2,400
11–14	M	62	99	2,700
	F	62	101	2,200
15–18	M	69	145	2,800
	F	64	120	2,100
19–22	M	70	154	2,900
	F	64	120	2,100
23–50	M	70	154	2,700
	F	64	120	2,000
51–75	M	70	154	2,400
	F	64	120	1,800
76+	M	70	154	2,050
	F	64	120	1,600
(Pregnant)				(+300)
(Lactating)				(+500)

Source: Washington, D.C., National Academy of Sciences. Recommended Dietary Allowances. Washington, D.C.: 1980.

Cholesterol Content of Some Foods (Approximate Milligrams Cholesterol)

Egg yolk (1)	272/yolk
Organ meats: heart, kidney, liver, sweetbreads (3 ounces)	300+
Shrimp (3 ounces)	135
Sardines (3 ounces)	118
Crab, mackerel (3 ounces)	88
Lobster (3 ounces)	78
Meats: lamb, pork, beef, veal, poultry with skin, wild game, cod (3 ounces)	65 to 80
Clams, oysters, scallops, sole, halibut, perch, trout, tuna (3 ounces)	45 to 55
Salmon (3 ounces)	35
Dairy: whipping cream (1 cup)	322
2% milk (1 cup)	19
whole milk (1 cup)	35
cheese (approximately 1½ ounces)	41
ice cream—16% butterfat (½ cup)	46
Fats: butter (1 tablespoon)	31
lard (1 tablespoon)	12
mayonnaise (1 tablespoon)	8

Reminder: Cholesterol is not found in plant foods; it is only from animal or fish sources.

FOODS HIGH IN POTASSIUM

Dry beans and peas—white, lima, kidney, chickpeas, lentils, soy-
beans, split peas
Cereals—bran cereals
Nuts and seeds—almonds, peanuts, pistachio nuts, pumpkin seeds,
sunflower seeds
Vegetables—asparagus, beets, beet greens, Brussels sprouts, celery,
Swiss chard, parsnips, potatoes, pumpkin, rutabaga, spinach,
winter squash, sweet potatoes, tomatoes, tomato juice, arti-
chokes, bamboo shoots
Fruits—bananas, dried apricots, avocados, dates, cantaloupe, hon-
eydew melon, orange, papaya, prunes, watermelon, raisins
Fish—scallops, sardines, mackerel, halibut
Calf's liver*
Blackstrap molasses

*Although calf's liver is high in potassium it is also very high in
cholesterol.

FOODS HIGH IN FIBER

As a general guide, choose one or two servings from the list of foods
highest in fiber and six to eight servings from the good sources of
fiber. It's important to have at least eight glasses (8 ounces each)
of liquid a day when increasing your fiber intake.

FOODS HIGHEST IN FIBER (over 4 grams fiber/serving)
Cereals (⅓ cup): bran and bran cereals, cereal with more than
4 grams of fiber per serving
Legumes (½ cup, cooked): baked beans, kidney beans, lima
beans, split peas, or lentils
Fruits: chopped dates (⅓ cup), figs (2), prunes (6), raisins (¼
cup)
Nuts* (½ cup): peanuts, almonds, or Brazil nuts

GOOD FIBER SOURCES (over 2 grams fiber/serving)
Breads and Cereals: cereals with 2 grams or more fiber per
serving, 2 slices whole-wheat, rye, or cracked-wheat bread,
whole-wheat rolls, bran muffins, bulgur, or cracked wheat

Fruits (1 whole or ½ cup): apple, avocado*, banana, blackberries, blueberries, cantaloupe, dates, orange, papaya, pear, raspberries, strawberries, or six dried apricots

Vegetables (½ cup or 1 whole): beans (green or yellow), broccoli, Brussels sprouts, carrots, corn, green peas, baked potato, parsnips, spinach, sweet potato, or turnip

*Are also high in fat, therefore choose less often or in small amounts

RECOMMENDED MARGARINES

This is only a partial list of recommended margarines because stores in each state may carry different brands. Hard margarines aren't recommended because they are too high in saturated fats.

Recommended Margarines

Brand Name	Approximate % Polyunsaturated Fats	Approximate % Saturated Fats
Diet*		
Weight Watchers	54	18
Imperial	36	18
Mazola	36	18
Mrs. Filbert's	36	18
Parkay	36	18
Regular		
Promise	40	20
Fleischmann's	36	18
Mazola Premium	36	18
Soft Tub		
Promise	45	20
Fleischmann's	45	20
Mrs. Filbert's	45	20
Land O'Lakes	36	18
Mother's	36	18
Parkay	36	18
Chiffon	36	18

*Calorie-reduced, light, or diet margarines (50% less fat and calories) are generally not recommended for frying or baking.

Source: Based on information from Eater's Choice by Dr. Ron Goor and Nancy Goor (Boston: Houghton Mifflin, 1987).

Check the label and choose margarines that have at least 40 percent polyunsaturated fatty acids and not more than 18 percent saturated fatty acids, or ones with 55 percent or more polyunsaturated fatty acids and not more than 25 percent saturated fatty acids.

Vegetable Oils

Type	Fatty Acid Content				Comment
	Polyunsaturated (%)	Monounsaturated (%)	Saturated (%)	Unsaturated/ Saturated Fat Ratio	
Canola	32	62	6	15.7:1	best fatty acid ratio
Safflower	75	12	9	9.6:1	highest in polyunsaturates
Sunflower	66	20	10	8.6:1	sometimes used in place of olive oil, but blander
Corn	59	24	13	6.4:1	heavy taste, often used for deep frying
Soybean	59	23	14	5.9:1	most commonly used oil—in baked goods, salad dressings, margarine, mayonnaise
Olive	9	72	14	5.8:1	highest in monounsaturated fat; expensive
Peanut	32	46	17	4.6:1	more pronounced flavor than most oils
Sesame seed	40	40	18	4.4:1	used in Oriental and Middle Eastern cooking; flavorful
Cottonseed	52	18	26	2.7:1	comparatively high in saturated fat; used in processed foods and salad dressings
Palm kernel	2	10	80	0.2:1	the only vegetable oils high in saturated fat.
Coconut	2	6	87	0.1:1	used in baked goods and candies; not recommended

Note: Other substances, such as water and vitamins, make up the total composition (100%).
Excerpted from an article in the *University of California, Berkeley, Wellness Letter,* Volume 3, Issue 6, March 1987.

Buying Guide for Vegetable Oils

Look for oils with a high percentage of monounsaturated or polyunsaturated fatty acids and a low amount of saturated fatty acids. Keep in mind that coconut and palm oil have a higher saturated fat content than some animal fats and that no vegetable oil contains cholesterol. Canola, safflower, and sunflower oils are the best all-purpose oils.

INDEX